The Portable
Financial Analyst

Founded in 1807, John Wiley & Sons is the oldest independent publishing company in the United States. With offices in North America, Europe, Australia and Asia, Wiley is globally committed to developing and marketing print and electronic products and services for our customers' professional and personal knowledge and understanding.

The Wiley Finance series contains books written specifically for finance and investment professionals as well as sophisticated individual investors and their financial advisors. Book topics range from portfolio management to e-commerce, risk management, financial engineering, valuation and financial instrument analysis, as well as much more.

For a list of available titles, please visit our Web site at www.WileyFinance.com.

The Portable
Financial Analyst

What Practitioners
Need to Know

Second Edition

MARK P. KRITZMAN

WILEY

John Wiley & Sons, Inc.

Published by John Wiley & Sons, Inc., Hoboken, New Jersey.
Published simultaneously in Canada.

For general information on our other products and services, or technical support,
please contact our Customer Care Department within the United States at
800-762-2974, outside the United States at 317-572-3993 or fax 317-572-4002.

Wiley also publishes its books in a variety of electronic formats. Some content that
appears in print may not be available in electronic books.

For more information about Wiley products, visit our web site at www.wiley.com.

Library of Congress Cataloging-in-Publication Data:

Kritzman, Mark P.
    The portable financial analyst: what practitioners need to know / Mark
Kritzman.—2nd ed.
        p.   cm.—(Wiley finance series)
    Includes bibliographical references and index.
    ISBN 0-471-26760-0 (cloth)
    1. Investment analysis.   2. Portfolio management.   3. Investments.
I. Title.   II. Series.
HG4529.K747 2003
332.6—dc21   2003057656

Printed in the United States of America.

10   9   8   7   6   5   4   3   2   1

Contents

Foreword
Time and Magic:
What This Book Is About

I once referred to financial markets as "dazzling creations." Mark Kritzman's superb essays in this book will show you where the dazzle is. Equally important, he will show you how to avoid being blinded by razzle-dazzle.

The book begins with a masterful summary of the contributions of the Nobel Prize winners to the theory of finance and investment. Before the 1950s, there was no theory in finance, just crude rules of thumb encrusted with fables, myths, and lore. Risk was measured in the gut; there were no rules for managing risk; expected return was what the latest tout proclaimed it to be; and the interactions among bonds, stocks, and other assets were a matter of little interest because bonds were for buy-and-hold investing and stocks were for trading; other assets were of no particular interest. In the course of about 20 years, from the early 1950s to the early 1970s, powerful advances in financial theory transformed a century or more of folklore about investing into a systematic structure for managing risk, for expanding the opportunities for higher rates of return, for calibrating performance, and for decision-making by issuers as well as buyers.

Financial theory as originally set forth by the Nobel laureates has undergone many modifications with the passage of time, not only in overcoming some of the oversimplifications that all theories exhibit, but also in broadening the applications of these ideas in ways no one ever conceived of in the early days. The art of investing will never be the same as it was before 1952.

This book demonstrates how investors can put these fundamental principles into practice. Nobody has made us so smart we can be certain of getting rich. But investors who heed the lessons here will gain a keen sense of how markets function; how to understand the essential character of different kinds of assets; how to measure, combine, and manage risks in a rational manner; and how to deal with the most puzzling and yet most dominant feature of investing: the passage of time.

Time is at the heart of every transaction in financial markets. Without financial markets, all assets would be buy-and-hold investments. Changing your mind after you have made an investment, at a moment of your own choosing, would be extremely costly or even impossible under such conditions. You would hesitate a long time before buying an asset with these constraints, and even then you would demand high compensation for taking the risk that matters could take a turn for the worse without any opportunity for you to get out. Or perhaps more attractive investments might come along after you have committed your money to this illiquid situation. Let's face it: Many individuals in the investment management profession take a lot longer to reach a decision about which house to buy for their family, and how much to pay for it, than they spend before committing millions of dollars of client money in stocks like General Electric or Microsoft.

Financial markets are a kind of magic elixir providing you with the opportunity to change your mind after you have made a commitment. You may have to pay a price for that reversibility—a price you will never know in advance—but the trade-off for that risk is in sustaining your flexibility instead of locking yourself up in what might be a much greater risk over the indefinite future. In more technical terms, whatever the present value of the expected future cash flows from your investment might be, you can realize them in the markets at your discretion without having to wait through the future to cash out.

That is the picture from the perspective of an investor who wants to sell an asset, but someone else is always at the other side of every market transaction. If, as I have just pointed out, sellers are realizing the present value of future cash flows today, buyers are doing the opposite. They are using today's cash—or instant purchasing power—to purchase a stream of cash flows expected to arrive in the future. In short, *financial markets are a time machine that allows selling investors to compress the future into the present while allowing buying investors to stretch the present into the future.*

But there are no free lunches and no sure things. Through all of this wonderful magic lurks uncertainty. We do not know what the future holds, we never have known, and we never shall know. As Frank Sinatra used to phrase it, "That's life!" Everyone reading these words will nod their heads in agreement. But few people reading these words will *behave* as though the future is unknown. Consider what "the future is unknown" really means: that surprise is endemic, an inescapable feature of daily life. There would be no such thing as surprise if we knew the future.

Yet humans have never learned how to live with surprise, which is just another way of saying they persist in believing they know what lies ahead. The most vivid proof of that assertion is in stock markets, where volatility seems to be a permanent feature—sometimes more, sometimes less, but always present. These sharp and often discontinuous price movements in either direction are clear evidence that surprise takes us by surprise. If we really accepted our ignorance of the future, the frequent arrival of the un-expected would not shake us up as much as it does. The very word "unex-pected" shows we had a view of what the future would bring even though we admit we do not know what the future will bring. The eternal conflict between what we expect and what actually does happen is encapsulated in that important little word, risk.

The many wisdoms in this book focus primarily on that conflict. Mark Kritzman's objective is to show you how you can deal with the harsh real-ity that we do not know what the outcomes of our decisions will be. Risk is an inescapable feature of investing, and risk, more than anything else, is what this fine book is all about.

PETER L. BERNSTEIN

Preface

*T*he *Portable Financial Analyst* is a practitioner's guide to the important concepts, analytical methods, and investment strategies of modern finance. I have tried to present this material in a style accessible to most practitioners with minimal technical jargon and mathematical symbolism. Moreover, the content is reasonably self-contained, which means you need not refer to other sources in order to proceed comfortably through these pages. My goal is to facilitate understanding rather than to persuade you to switch careers.

What is different about this second edition? I have expanded some of the original chapters, added four new chapters, clarified and refined material as needed, added a glossary of technical terms, unified the mathematical notation, and corrected alleged errors in the first edition. Thankfully, most of the revisions are additions rather than corrections. On the other hand, corrections might motivate more people who own the first edition to purchase this new edition.

New chapters include:

- Higher Moments
- Event Studies
- Value at Risk
- Risk Budgets

Some of the major additions to the original material include:

- *Time Diversification*—a discussion of option valuation and first passage risk as challenges to the notion that time diversifies risk.
- *Simulation*—a description of bootstrapping simulation, along with an application to determine the hierarchy of investment choice.
- *Future Value and Risk of Loss*—a discussion of within-horizon exposure to loss, including its estimation and comparison to conventional risk measures.
- *Optimization*—a description of Chow's mean-variance-tracking error optimization and an exposé of the sophistry surrounding the tiresome critique, "garbage in, garbage out."

- *Option Valuation and Replication*—an expanded discussion of option valuation as preparation for the review of option replication.
- *Currencies*—an appendix detailing the mathematics of currency hedging.

I previewed some of the new material in Peter Bernstein's publication, *Economics and Portfolio Strategy*. As a consequence, I have benefited enormously from Peter's insights and editorial acumen. Should you discover anything approaching eloquence in these pages, more likely than not Peter is responsible.

I am grateful to Sebastien Page, who unified the mathematical notation. The notation in the first edition was quite disjointed, because the chapters originally appeared as separate articles in the *Financial Analysts Journal*.

I owe a special debt to George Chow, my business partner and friend, who has patiently endured many long discussions about these topics and who has originated some of the ideas presented herein.

I have benefited from conversations and correspondence with many acquaintances and colleagues, who have helped me to refine and advance my understanding of these topics. Although the complete list escapes my memory, several people stand out: Jeremy Armitage, Stephen Brown, Roger Clarke, Ken Froot, Gary Gastineau, Eric Lobben, Chip Lowry, Alan Marcus, Harry Markowitz, Jack Meyer, Paul O'Connell, Krishna Ramaswamy, Gita Rao, Don Rich, Paul A. Samuelson, Bill Sharpe, Stan Shelton, Jack Treynor, and Anne-Sophie Vanroyen.

I wish to acknowledge the continued support of the Association for Investment Management and Research and, in particular, Katy Sherrerd.

I am grateful to Pamela van Giessen, my editor at John Wiley & Sons, who has been a determined and patient advocate of this book. Her guidance, humor, and friendship have been a constant source of encouragement.

My final thanks are to my wife, Elizabeth Gorman, who graciously chose to pursue a Ph.D. while I worked on this book, thereby affording me much needed time for this task. Moreover, on her way to a Ph.D. she developed quite a proficiency in quantitative methods, which proved to be most beneficial. But, of course, I am most thankful for her encouragement, understanding, and sound counsel.

CHAPTER 1

The Nobel Prize

On October 16, 1990, the Royal Swedish Academy of Sciences announced its selection for the Nobel Memorial Prize in Economic Science. For the first time since the prize for economics was established in 1968, the Royal Academy chose three individuals whose primary contributions were in finance and whose affiliations were not with arts and science schools, but rather with schools of business. Harry Markowitz was cited for his pioneering research in portfolio selection, while William Sharpe shared the award for developing an equilibrium theory of asset pricing. Merton Miller was a co-winner for his contributions in corporate finance, in which he showed, along with Franco Modigliani, that the value of a firm should be invariant to its capital structure and dividend policy.

The pioneering research of these individuals revolutionized finance and accelerated the application of quantitative methods to financial analysis.

PORTFOLIO SELECTION

In his classic article, "Portfolio Selection," Markowitz submitted that investors should not choose portfolios that maximize expected return, because this criterion by itself ignores the principle of diversification.[1] He proposed that investors should instead consider variances of return, along with expected returns, and choose portfolios that offer the highest expected return for a given level of variance. He called this rule the E-V maxim.

Markowitz showed that a portfolio's expected return is simply the weighted average of the expected returns of its component securities. A portfolio's variance is a more complicated concept, however. It depends on more than just the variances of the component securities.

The variance of an individual security is a measure of the dispersion of its returns. It is calculated by squaring the difference between each return in a series and the mean return for the series, then averaging these squared differences. The square root of the variance (the standard deviation) is often used in practice because it measures dispersion in the same units in which the underlying return is measured.

Variance provides a reasonable gauge of a security's risk, but the average of the variances of two securities will not necessarily give a good indication of the risk of a portfolio comprising these two securities. The portfolio's risk depends also on the extent to which the two securities move together—that is, the extent to which their prices react in like fashion to a particular event.

To quantify co-movement among security returns, Markowitz introduced the statistical concept of covariance. The covariance between two securities equals the standard deviation of the first times the standard deviation of the second times the correlation between the two.

The correlation, in this context, measures the association between the returns of two securities. It ranges in value from 1 to –1. If one security's returns are higher than its average return when another security's returns are higher than its average return, for example, the correlation coefficient will be positive, somewhere between 0 and 1. Alternatively, if one security's returns are lower than its average return when another security's returns are higher than its average return, then the correlation will be negative.

The correlation, by itself, is an inadequate measure of covariance because it measures only the direction and degree of association between securities' returns. It does not account for the magnitude of variability in each security's returns. Covariance captures magnitude by multiplying the correlation by the standard deviations of the securities' returns.

Consider, for example, the covariance of a security with itself. Obviously, the correlation in this case equals 1. A security's covariance with itself thus equals the standard deviation of its returns squared, which, of course, is its variance.

Finally, portfolio variance depends also on the weightings of its constituent securities—the proportion of a portfolio's market value invested in each. The variance of a portfolio consisting of two securities equals the variance of the first security times its weighting squared plus the variance of the second security times its weighting squared plus twice the covariance between the securities times each security's weighting. The standard deviation of this portfolio equals the square root of the variance.

From this formulation of portfolio risk, Markowitz was able to offer two key insights. First, unless the securities in a portfolio are perfectly inversely correlated (that is, have a correlation of –1), it is not possible to eliminate portfolio risk entirely through diversification. If we divide a portfolio equally among its component securities, for example, as the number of securities in the portfolio increases, the portfolio's risk will tend not toward zero but, rather, toward the average covariance of the component securities.

Second, unless all the securities in a portfolio are perfectly positively correlated with each other (a correlation of 1), a portfolio's standard deviation will always be less than the weighted average standard deviation of its component securities. Consider, for example, a portfolio consisting of two securities, both of which have expected returns of 10 percent and standard deviations of 20 percent and which are uncorrelated with each other. If we allocate portfolio assets equally between these two securities, the portfolio's expected return will equal 10 percent, while its standard deviation will equal 14.14 percent. The portfolio offers a reduction in risk of nearly 30 percent relative to investment in either of the two securities separately. Moreover, this risk reduction is achieved without any sacrifice of expected return.

Markowitz also demonstrated that, for given levels of risk, we can identify particular combinations of securities that maximize expected return. He deemed these portfolios "efficient" and referred to a continuum of such portfolios in dimensions of expected return and standard deviation as the efficient frontier. According to Markowitz's E-V maxim, investors should choose portfolios located along the efficient frontier. It is almost always the case that there exists some portfolio on the efficient frontier that offers a higher expected return and less risk than the least risky of its component securities (assuming the least risky security is not completely riskless).

The financial community was slow to implement Markowitz's theory, in large part because of a practical constraint. In order to estimate the risk of a portfolio of securities, one must estimate the variances of every security, along with the covariances between every pair of securities. For a portfolio of 100 securities, this means calculating 100 variances and 4,950 covariances—5,050 risk estimates! In general, the number of required risk estimates (variances and covariances) equals $n(n + 1)/2$, where n equals the number of securities in the portfolio.[2] In 1952, when Markowitz published "Portfolio Selection," the sheer number of calculations formed an obstacle in the way of acceptance. It was in part the challenge of this obstacle that motivated William Sharpe to develop a single index measure of a security's risk.

THE CAPITAL ASSET PRICING MODEL

James Tobin, the 1981 winner of the Nobel Prize in economics, showed that the investment process can be separated into two distinct steps: (1) the construction of an efficient portfolio, as described by Markowitz, and (2) the decision to combine this efficient portfolio with a riskless investment. This two-step process is the famed separation theorem.[3]

Sharpe extended Markowitz's and Tobin's insights to develop a theory of market equilibrium under conditions of risk.[4] First, Sharpe showed that there is along the efficient frontier a unique portfolio that, when combined with lending or borrowing at the riskless interest rate, dominates all other combinations of efficient portfolios and lending or borrowing.

Figure 1.1 shows a two-dimensional graph, with risk represented by the horizontal axis and expected return represented by the vertical axis. The efficient frontier appears as the positively sloped concave curve. The straight line emanating from the vertical axis at the riskless rate illustrates the efficient frontier with borrowing and lending. The segment of the line between the vertical axis and the efficient portfolio curve represents some combination of the efficient portfolio M and lending at the riskless rate, while points along the straight line to the right represent some combination of the efficient portfolio and borrowing at the riskless rate. Combinations of portfolio M and lending or borrowing at the riskless rate will always offer the highest expected rate of return for a given level of risk.

With two assumptions, Sharpe demonstrated that in equilibrium investors will prefer points along the line emanating from the riskless rate that is tangent to M. The requisite assumptions are (1) there exists a single

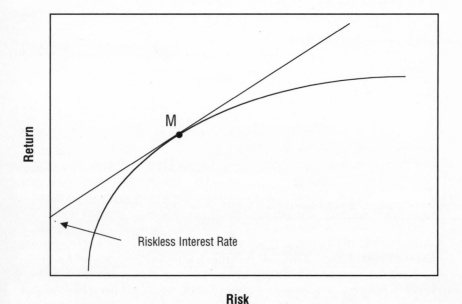

Risk

FIGURE 1.1   Efficient frontier with borrowing and lending

riskless rate at which investors can lend and borrow in unlimited amounts, and (2) investors have homogeneous expectations regarding expected returns, variances, and covariances. Under these assumptions, Sharpe showed that portfolio M is the market portfolio, which represents the maximum achievable diversification.

Within this model, Sharpe proceeded to demonstrate that risk can be partitioned into two sources—that caused by changes in the value of the market portfolio, which cannot be diversified away, and that caused by nonmarket factors, which is diversified away in the market portfolio. He labeled the nondiversifiable risk systematic risk and the diversifiable risk unsystematic risk.

Sharpe also showed that a security's systematic risk can be estimated by regressing its returns (less the riskless rate) against the market portfolio's returns (less riskless rate). The slope from this regression equation, which Sharpe called beta, quantifies the security's systematic risk when multiplied by the market risk. The unexplained variation in the security's return (the residuals from the regression equation) represents the security's unsystematic risk. He then asserted that, in an efficient market, investors are only compensated for bearing systematic risk, because it cannot be diversified away, and the expected return of a security is, through beta, linearly related to the market's expected return.

It is important to distinguish between a single index model and the Capital Asset Pricing Model (CAPM). A single index model does not require the intercept of the regression equation (alpha) to equal 0 percent. It simply posits a single source of systematic, or common, risk. Stated differently, the residuals from the regression equation are uncorrelated with each other. The important practical implication is that it is not necessary to estimate covariances between securities. Each security's contribution to portfolio risk is captured through its beta coefficient. The CAPM, by contrast, does require the intercept of the regression equation to equal 0 percent in an efficient market. The CAPM itself does not necessarily assume a single source of systematic risk. This is tantamount to allowing for some correlation among the residuals.

INVARIANCE PROPOSITIONS

Between the publication of Markowitz's theory of portfolio selection and Sharpe's equilibrium theory of asset pricing, Franco Modigliani (the 1985 Nobel Prize winner in economics) and Merton Miller published two related articles in which they expounded their now famous invariance propositions. The first, "The Cost of Capital, Corporation Finance, and the Theory of Investment," appeared in 1958.[5] It challenged the then conventional wisdom that a firm's value depends on its capital structure (i.e., its debt/equity mix).

In challenging this traditional view, Modigliani and Miller invoked the notion of arbitrage. They argued that if a leveraged firm is undervalued, investors can purchase its debt and its shares. The interest paid by the firm is offset by the interest received by the investors, so the investors end up holding a pure equity stream. Alternatively, if an unleveraged firm is undervalued, investors can borrow funds to purchase its shares. The substitutability of individual debt for corporate debt guarantees that firms in the same risk class will be valued the same, regardless of their respective capital structures. In essence, Modigliani and Miller argued in favor of the law of one price.

In a subsequent article, "Dividend Policy, Growth, and the Valuation of Shares," Modigliani and Miller proposed that a firm's value is invariant, not only to its capital structure, but also to its dividend policy (assuming the firm's investment decision is set independently).[6] Again, they invoked the notion of substitutability, arguing that repurchasing shares has the same effect as paying dividends; thus issuing shares and paying dividends is a wash. Although the cash component of an investor's return may differ as a function of dividend policy, the investor's total return, including price change, should not change with dividend policy.

Modigliani and Miller's invariance propositions provoked an enormous amount of debate and research. Much of the sometimes spirited debate centered on the assumption of perfect capital markets. In the real world, where investors cannot borrow and lend at the riskless rate of interest, where both corporations and individuals pay taxes, and where investors do not share equal access with management to relevant information, there is only spotty evidence to support Modigliani and Miller's invariance propositions.

But the value of the contributions of these Nobel laureates does not depend on the degree to which their theories hold in an imperfect market environment. It depends, rather, on the degree to which they changed the financial community's understanding of the capital markets. Markowitz taught us how to evaluate investment opportunities probabilistically, while Sharpe provided us with an equilibrium theory of asset pricing, enabling us to distinguish between risk that is rewarded and risk that is not rewarded. Miller, in collaboration with Modigliani, demonstrated how the simple notion of arbitrage can be applied to determine value, which subsequently was extended to option valuation—yet another innovation that proved worthy of the Nobel Prize.

CHAPTER 2

Uncertainty

The primary challenge to financial analysts is to determine how to proceed in the face of uncertainty. Uncertainty arises from imperfect knowledge and from incomplete data. Methods for interpreting limited information may thus help analysts measure and control uncertainty.

Long ago, natural scientists noticed the widespread presence of random variation in nature. This led to the development of laws of probability, which help predict outcomes. As it turns out, many of the laws that seem to explain the behavior of random variables in nature apply as well to the behavior of financial variables such as corporate earnings, interest rates, and asset prices and returns.

RELATIVE FREQUENCY

A random variable can be thought of as an event whose outcomes in a given situation depend on chance factors. For example, the toss of a coin is an event whose outcome is governed by chance, as is next year's closing price for the stock market. Because an outcome is influenced by chance does not mean we are completely ignorant about its possible values. We may, for example, be able to garner some insights from prior experiences.

Suppose we are interested in predicting the return of the stock market over the next 12 months. Should we be more confident in predicting that it will be between 0 and 10 percent than between 10 and 20 percent? The past history of stock market returns can tell us how often returns within specified ranges have occurred. Table 2.1 shows annual stock market returns over a 40-year period.

We simply count the number of returns between 0 and 10 percent and the number of returns between 10 and 20 percent. Dividing each figure by 40 gives us the relative frequency of returns within each range. Six returns fall within the range of 0 to 10 percent, while 10 returns fall within the

TABLE 2.1 Annual Stock Market Returns

Year	Return	Year	Return	Year	Return	Year	Return
1	24.00%	11	26.90%	21	14.30%	31	–4.90%
2	18.40%	12	–8.70%	22	19.00%	32	21.40%
3	–1.00%	13	22.80%	23	·–14.70%	33	22.50%
4	52.60%	14	16.50%	24	–26.50%	34	6.30%
5	31.60%	15	12.50%	25	37.20%	35	32.20%
6	6.60%	16	–10.10%	26	23.80%	36	18.80%
7	–10.80%	17	24.00%	27	–7.20%	37	5.30%
8	43.40%	18	11.10%	28	6.60%	38	16.60%
9	12.00%	19	–8.50%	29	18.40%	39	31.80%
10	0.50%	20	4.00%	30	32.40%	40	–3.10%

range of 10 to 20 percent. The relative frequencies of these observations are 15 and 25 percent, respectively, as Table 2.2 shows.

Figure 2.1 depicts this information graphically in what is called a discrete probability distribution. (It is discrete because it covers a finite number of observations rather than an infinite number of continuously distributed observations.) The values along the vertical axis represent the probability (equal here to the relative frequency) of observing a return within the ranges indicated along the horizontal axis.

The information we have is limited. For one thing, the return ranges (which we set) are fairly wide. For another, the sample is confined to annual returns and covers only a particular 40-year period, which may exclude important events such as wars or perhaps the Great Depression.

We can nonetheless draw some tentative inferences from this limited information. For example, we may assume we are about two-thirds more

TABLE 2.2 Frequency Distribution

Range of Return	Frequency	Relative Frequency
–30% to –20%	1	2.5%
–20% to –10%	3	7.5%
–10% to 0%	6	15.0%
0% to 10%	6	15.0%
10% to 20%	10	25.0%
20% to 30%	7	17.5%
30% to 40%	5	12.5%
40% to 50%	1	2.5%
50% to 60%	1	2.5%

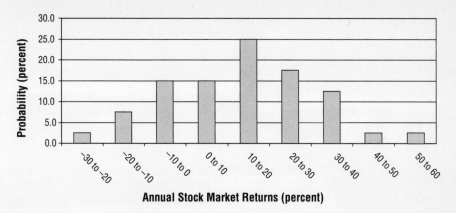

FIGURE 2.1 Discrete probability distribution

likely to observe a return within the range of 10 to 20 percent than a return within the range of 0 to 10 percent. Furthermore, by summing the relative frequencies for the three ranges below 0 percent, we may also assume there is a 25 percent chance of experiencing a negative return.

If we want to draw more precise inferences, we should increase the sample size and partition the data into narrower ranges. If we proceed along these lines, the distribution of returns should eventually resemble the familiar pattern known as the bell-shaped curve, or normal distribution.

NORMAL DISTRIBUTION

The normal distribution is a continuous probability distribution; it assumes there are an infinite number of observations covering all possible values along a continuous scale. Time, for example, can be thought of as being distributed along a continuous scale. Stocks, however, trade in discrete units, so technically stock returns cannot be distributed continuously. Nonetheless, for purposes of financial analysis, the normal distribution is usually a reasonable approximation of the distribution of stock returns, as well as the returns of other financial assets.

The formula that gives rise to the normal distribution was first published by Abraham de Moivre in 1733. Its properties were investigated by Carl Gauss in the 18th and 19th centuries. In recognition of Gauss's contributions, the normal distribution is often referred to as the Gaussian distribution.

The normal distribution has special appeal to natural scientists for two reasons. First, it is an excellent approximation of the random variation of many natural phenomena.[1] Second, it can be described fully by only two values: (1) the mean of the observations, which measures location or central tendency, and (2) the variance of the observations, which measures dispersion.

For our sample of annual stock market returns, the mean return (which is also the expected return) equals the sum of the observed returns times their probabilities of occurrence:

$$\mu = \text{Pr}_1 \times R_1 + \text{Pr}_2 \times R_2 + \ldots + \text{Pr}_n \times R_n \quad (2.1)$$

where $\quad \mu =$ the mean return
$R_1, R_2 \ldots R_n =$ observed returns in years 1 through n
$\text{Pr}_1, \text{Pr}_2 \ldots \text{Pr}_n =$ the probabilities of occurrence (or relative frequencies) of the returns in years 1 through n

The variance of returns (σ^2) is computed as the probability-weighted squared difference from the mean. To compute the variance, we subtract the mean return from each annual return, square these values, sum these squared values, and then weight them by their probability of occurrence.

$$\sigma^2 = \text{Pr}_1(R_1 - \mu)^2 + \text{Pr}_2(R_2 - \mu)^2 + \ldots + \text{Pr}_n(R_n - \mu)^2 \quad (2.2)$$

$\text{Pr}_1, \text{Pr}_2 \ldots \text{Pr}_n =$ the probabilities of occurrence (or relative frequencies) of the returns in years 1 through n

The square root of the variance, which is called the standard deviation, is commonly used as a measure of dispersion.

If we apply these formulas to the annual returns in Table 2.1, we find that the mean return for the sample equals 12.9 percent, the variance of returns equals 2.9 percent, and the standard deviation of returns equals 16.9 percent. These values, together with the assumption that the returns of the stock market are normally distributed, enable us to infer a normal probability distribution of stock market returns. This probability distribution is shown in Figure 2.2.

The normal distribution has several important characteristics. First, it is symmetric around its mean; 50 percent of the returns are below the mean return, and 50 percent of the returns are above the mean return. Also, because of this symmetry, the mode of the sample (the most common observation) and the median (the middle value of the observations) are equal to each other and to the mean.

Note that the area enclosed within one standard deviation on either side of the mean encompasses 68 percent of the total area under the curve. The area enclosed within two standard deviations on either side of the

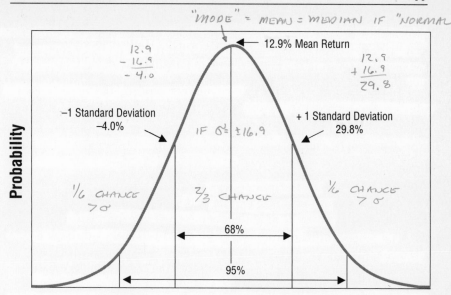

FIGURE 2.2   Normal probability distribution

mean encompasses 95 percent of the total area under the curve, and more than 99 percent of the area under the curve falls within plus and minus three standard deviations of the mean.

From this information we are able to draw several conclusions. For example, we know that 68, 95, and more than 99 percent of returns, respectively, will fall within one, two, and three standard deviations (plus and minus) of the mean return. It is thus straightforward to measure the probability of experiencing returns that are one, two, or three standard deviations away from the mean.

There is, for example, about a 32 percent chance (100 percent minus 68 percent) of experiencing returns at least one standard deviation above or below the mean return. Thus there is only a 16 percent chance of experiencing a return below –4.0 percent (mean of 12.9 percent minus standard deviation of 16.9 percent) and an equal chance of experiencing a return greater than 29.8 percent (mean of 12.9 percent plus standard deviation of 16.9 percent).

STANDARDIZED VARIABLES

We may, however, be interested in the likelihood of experiencing a return less than 0 percent or a return greater than 15 percent. In order to determine the probabilities of these returns (or the probability of achieving any return, for that matter), we can standardize the target return. We do so by subtracting the mean return from the target return and dividing by the standard deviation. (By standardizing returns we, in effect, rescale the distribution to have a mean of 0 and a standard deviation of 1.) Thus, to find the area under the curve to the left of 0 percent (which is the same as the probability of experiencing a return of less than 0 percent), we subtract 12.9 percent (the mean) from 0 percent (the target) and divide this quantity by 16.9 percent (the standard deviation):

$$\text{ODDS OF } R < 0 \qquad \frac{0.0 - 0.129}{0.169} = -0.7633$$

This value tells us that 0 percent is 0.7633 standard deviations below the mean. This is much less than a full standard deviation, so we know that the chance of experiencing a return of less than 0 percent must be greater than 16 percent.

In order to calculate a precise probability directly, we need to evaluate the integral of the standardized normal density function. Fortunately, most statistics books and spreadsheet software show the area under a standardized normal distribution curve that corresponds to a particular standardized variable. Table 2.3 is one example.

To find the area under the curve to the left of the standardized variable, we read down the left column to the value –0.7 and across this row to the column under the value –0.06. The value at this location, 0.2236, equals the probability of experiencing a return of less than 0 percent. This, of course, implies that the chance of experiencing a return greater than 0 percent equals 0.7764 (i.e., 1 – 0.2236). By comparison, the probability of experiencing a negative return as estimated from the discrete probability distribution in Table 2.2 equals 25 percent.

Suppose we are interested in the likelihood of experiencing an annualized return of less than 0 percent on average over a five-year horizon? First, we'll assume the year-to-year returns are mutually independent (that is, this year's return has no effect on next year's return). We convert the standard deviation back to the variance (by squaring it), divide the variance by 5 (the number of years in the horizon), and use the square root of this value to standardize the difference between 0 percent and the mean return. Alternatively, we can simply divide the standard deviation by the square root of 5 and use this value to standardize the difference:

$$\frac{0.0 - 0.129}{0.169 \times \sqrt{5}} = -1.71$$

Again, by referring to Table 2.3, we find that the likelihood of experiencing an annualized return less than 0 percent on average over five years equals only 0.0436, or 4.36 percent. This is much less than the probability of experiencing a negative return in any one year. Intuitively, we are less likely to lose money on average over five years than in any particular year because we are diversifying across time; a loss in any particular year might be offset by a gain in one or more of the other years.

Now suppose we are interested in the likelihood that we might lose money in one or more of the five years. This probability is equivalent to one minus the probability of experiencing a positive return in every one of the five years. Again, if we assume independence in the year-to-year returns, the likelihood of experiencing five consecutive yearly returns each greater than 0 percent equals 0.7764 raised to the fifth power, which is 0.2821. Thus the probability of experiencing a negative return in at least one of the five years equals 0.7179 (i.e., 1 − 0.2821).

Over extended holding periods, the normal distribution may not be a good approximation of the distribution of returns because short holding-period returns are compounded, rather than cumulated, to derive long holding-period returns. Because we can represent the compound value of an index as a simple accumulation when expressed in terms of logarithms, it is the logarithms of 1 plus the holding-period returns that are normally distributed. The actual returns thus conform to a lognormal distribution. A lognormal distribution assigns higher probabilities to extremely high values than it does to extremely low values; the result is a skewed distribution, rather than a symmetric one. This distinction is usually not significant for holding periods of one year or less. For longer holding periods, the distinction can be important. For this reason, we should assume a lognormal distribution when estimating the probabilities associated with outcomes over long investment horizons.[2]

CAVEATS

In applying the normal probability distribution to measure uncertainty in financial analysis, we should proceed with caution. We must recognize, for example, that our probability estimates are subject to sampling error. Our example assumed implicitly that the 40-year sample characterized the mean and variance of stock market returns. This sample, in fact, represents but a small fraction of the entire universe of historical returns and may not necessarily be indicative of the central tendency and dispersion of returns going forward.

As an alternative to extrapolating historical data, we can choose to estimate the expected stock market return based on judgmental factors, and

TABLE 2.3 Normal Distribution Table

Probability That Standardized Variable Is Less Than Z

Z	0	-0.01	-0.02	-0.03	-0.04	-0.05	-0.06	-0.07	-0.08	-0.09
0.0	0.5000	0.4960	0.4920	0.4880	0.4840	0.4785	0.4761	0.4721	0.4681	0.4641
-0.1	0.4602	0.4562	0.4522	0.4483	0.4443	0.4388	0.4364	0.4325	0.4286	0.4247
-0.2	0.4207	0.4168	0.4129	0.4090	0.4052	0.3997	0.3974	0.3936	0.3897	0.3859
-0.3	0.3821	0.3783	0.3745	0.3707	0.3669	0.3617	0.3594	0.3557	0.3520	0.3483
-0.4	0.3446	0.3409	0.3372	0.3336	0.3300	0.3249	0.3228	0.3192	0.3156	0.3121
-0.5	0.3085	0.3050	0.3015	0.2981	0.2946	0.2898	0.2877	0.2843	0.2810	0.2776
-0.6	0.2743	0.2709	0.2676	0.2643	0.2611	0.2566	0.2546	0.2514	0.2483	0.2451
-0.7	0.2420	0.2389	0.2358	0.2327	0.2296	0.2254	0.2236	0.2206	0.2177	0.2148
-0.8	0.2119	0.2090	0.2061	0.2033	0.2005	0.1966	0.1949	0.1922	0.1894	0.1867
-0.9	0.1841	0.1814	0.1788	0.1762	0.1736	0.1700	0.1685	0.1660	0.1635	0.1611
-1.0	0.1587	0.1562	0.1539	0.1515	0.1492	0.1459	0.1446	0.1423	0.1401	0.1379
-1.1	0.1357	0.1335	0.1314	0.1292	0.1271	0.1243	0.1230	0.1210	0.1190	0.1170
-1.2	0.1151	0.1131	0.1112	0.1093	0.1075	0.1049	0.1038	0.1020	0.1003	0.0985
-1.3	0.0968	0.0951	0.0934	0.0918	0.0901	0.0879	0.0869	0.0853	0.0838	0.0823

-1.4	0.0808	0.0793	0.0778	0.0764	0.0749	0.0730	0.0721	0.0708	0.0694	0.0681
-1.5	0.0668	0.0655	0.0643	0.0630	0.0618	0.0601	0.0594	0.0582	0.0571	0.0559
-1.6	0.0548	0.0537	0.0526	0.0516	0.0505	0.0491	0.0485	0.0475	0.0465	0.0455
-1.7	0.0446	0.0436	0.0427	0.0418	0.0409	0.0397	0.0392	0.0384	0.0375	0.0367
-1.8	0.0359	0.0351	0.0344	0.0336	0.0329	0.0319	0.0314	0.0307	0.0301	0.0294
-1.9	0.0287	0.0281	0.0274	0.0268	0.0262	0.0254	0.0250	0.0244	0.0239	0.0233
-2.0	0.0228	0.0222	0.0217	0.0212	0.0207	0.0200	0.0197	0.0192	0.0188	0.0183
-2.1	0.0179	0.0174	0.0170	0.0166	0.0162	0.0156	0.0154	0.0150	0.0146	0.0143
-2.2	0.0139	0.0136	0.0132	0.0129	0.0125	0.0121	0.0119	0.0116	0.0113	0.0110
-2.3	0.0107	0.0104	0.0102	0.0099	0.0096	0.0093	0.0091	0.0089	0.0087	0.0084
-2.4	0.0082	0.0080	0.0078	0.0075	0.0073	0.0071	0.0069	0.0068	0.0066	0.0064
-2.5	0.0062	0.0060	0.0059	0.0057	0.0055	0.0053	0.0052	0.0051	0.0049	0.0048
-2.6	0.0047	0.0045	0.0044	0.0043	0.0041	0.0040	0.0039	0.0038	0.0037	0.0036
-2.7	0.0035	0.0034	0.0033	0.0032	0.0031	0.0029	0.0029	0.0028	0.0027	0.0026
-2.8	0.0026	0.0025	0.0024	0.0023	0.0023	0.0022	0.0021	0.0021	0.0020	0.0019
-2.9	0.0019	0.0018	0.0018	0.0017	0.0016	0.0016	0.0015	0.0015	0.0014	0.0014
-3.0	0.0013	0.0013	0.0013	0.0012	0.0012	0.0011	0.0011	0.0011	0.0010	0.0010

we can infer the investment community's consensus prediction of the standard deviation from the prices of options on stock market indexes.[3]

Finally, we must remember that the normal distribution and the lognormal distribution are not perfect models of the distribution of asset returns and other financial variables. They are, in many circumstances, reasonable approximations. But in reality, stock prices do not change continuously, as assumed by the normal distribution, or even, necessarily, by small increments. October 19, 1987, provided sobering evidence of this fact. Moreover, many investment strategies, especially those that involve options or dynamic trading rules, often generate return distributions that are significantly skewed, rather than symmetric. In these instances, the assumption of a normal or lognormal distribution might result in significant errors in probability estimates.[4]

The normal distribution can be applied in a wide variety of circumstances to help financial analysts measure and control uncertainty associated with financial variables, but remember it is an inexact model of reality.

CHAPTER 3

Utility

An important axiom of modern financial theory is that rational investors seek to maximize expected utility. Many financial analysts, however, find the concept of utility somewhat nebulous. This chapter discusses the origin of utility theory as well as its application to financial analysis.

In his classic paper, "Exposition of a New Theory on the Measurement of Risk," first published in 1738, Daniel Bernoulli proposed the following:

> . . . the determination of the value of an item must not be based on its price, but rather on the utility it yields. The price of the item is dependent only on the thing itself and is equal for everyone; the utility, however, is dependent on the particular circumstances of the person making the estimate. Thus there is no doubt that a gain of one thousand ducats is more significant to a pauper than to a rich man though both gain the same amount.[1]

Bernoulli's insight that the utility of a gain depends on one's wealth may seem rather obvious, yet it has profound implications for the theory of risk. Figure 3.1 helps us to visualize Bernoulli's notion of utility, which economists today call *diminishing marginal utility*.

The horizontal axis represents wealth, while the vertical axis represents utility. The relationship between wealth and utility is measured by the curved line. Utility clearly increases with wealth, because the curve has a positive slope. The positive slope simply indicates that we prefer more wealth to less wealth. This assumption seldom invites dispute.[2]

As wealth increases, however, the increments to utility become progressively smaller, as the concave shape of the curve reveals. This concavity indicates that we derive less and less satisfaction with each subsequent unit of incremental wealth. Technically, Bernoulli's notion of utility implies that its first derivative with respect to wealth is positive, while its second derivative is negative.

A negative second derivative implies that we would experience greater

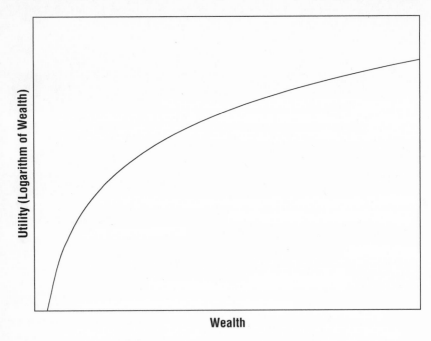

FIGURE 3.1   Diminishing marginal utility

disutility from a decline in wealth than the utility we would derive from an equal increase in wealth. This tradeoff is apparent in Figure 3.2, which shows the changes in utility associated with an equal increase and decrease in wealth.

According to Bernoulli, the precise change in utility associated with a change in wealth equals the natural logarithm of the sum of initial wealth plus the increment to wealth, divided by initial wealth.[3] For example, the increase in utility associated with an increase in wealth from \$100 to \$150 equals 0.405465, as shown.

$$0.405465 = \ln\left(\frac{100+50}{100}\right)$$

The next \$50 increment to wealth, however, yields a smaller increment to utility:

$$0.287682 = \ln\left(\frac{150+50}{100}\right)$$

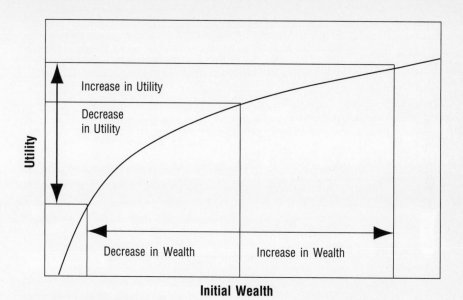

FIGURE 3.2 Changes in utility versus changes in wealth

RISK AVERSION

From Bernoulli's assumption of diminishing marginal utility, it follows that those whose utility is defined by the logarithm of wealth will reject a *fair game*—that is, a game in which the expected outcome is the same for each participant. Bernoulli offered the following example. Two participants, each of whom has $100 (Bernoulli used ducats), contribute $50 as a stake in a game in which winning is determined by the toss of a coin. Each player therefore has a 50 percent probability of ending up with $50 and a 50 percent probability of ending up with $150.

The expected value of this game is $100 (0.5 × 50 + 0.5 × 150). This is identical to the expected value of not playing, because each participant starts out with $100. The expected utility of this game, however, is found by adding the utility (logarithm) of the $50 payoff times its probability of occurrence to the utility of the $150 payoff times its probability of occurrence.

Table 3.1 shows the results. The utility of not participating in the game equals the logarithm of $100 dollars, which is 4.61. The utility of not participating is higher than the utility of participating. Thus a player whose utility with respect to wealth is defined as the logarithm of wealth will reject the game, even though it is fair.

In essence, Bernoulli's concept of utility implies that we prefer a certain

TABLE 3.1   Expected Utility of Participating in a Fair Game

Payoff	Utility of Payoff	Probability of Payoff	Probability-Weighted Utility
50	3.91	50%	1.96
150	5.01	50%	2.51
Expected Utility			4.46

prospect to an uncertain prospect of equal value. That is to say, we are risk averse. In fact, Bernoulli interpreted risk aversion as "nature's admonition to avoid the dice."[4]

CERTAINTY EQUIVALENT

With simple algebra, we can extend Bernoulli's insight a little further and determine how much value we would be willing to subtract from a certain prospect before we would select a risky prospect. The value of the certain prospect that yields the same utility as the expected utility of an uncertain prospect is called the certainty equivalent.

We have already seen that the expected utility of a risky prospect is computed as the logarithm of the favorable outcome times its probability of occurrence plus the logarithm of the unfavorable outcome times its probability of occurrence (which equals 1 minus the probability of occurrence of the favorable outcome). We can set this formula equal to the logarithm of the certain prospect and solve for the value of the certain prospect, as follows.

$$\ln(C) = \ln(W_F) \times \text{Pr} + \ln(W_U) \times (1 - \text{Pr}) \tag{3.1}$$

$$C = e^{\ln(W_F) \times \text{Pr} + \ln(W_U) \times (1 - \text{Pr})} \tag{3.2}$$

where   ln = natural logarithm
   C = certain payoff
   W_F = payoff from favorable outcome
   W_U = payoff from unfavorable outcome
   Pr = probability of occurrence for favorable outcome
   e = 2.71828

In Bernoulli's example, in which each participant has a 50 percent chance of receiving $150 and a 50 percent chance of receiving $50, the certainty equivalent is $86.60:

$$C = e^{[\ln(150) \times 0.5 + \ln(50) \times (1 - 0.5)]}$$
$$86.60 = e^{[2.5053 + 1.9560]}$$

The certainty equivalent of $86.60 implies that we would be indifferent between a certain $86.60 payoff and a risky prospect with an equal probability of paying $150 or $50. It follows that we would select the risky prospect only if it offered a higher expected value than the certain prospect. The difference in expected value that would induce us to choose the risky prospect is called the required risk premium.

We have thus far assumed initial wealth equals only $100. Assume, instead, we are starting with initial wealth of $1,000 dollars, so that we would receive $1,050 given a favorable outcome and $950 given an unfavorable outcome. The certainty equivalent would then equal $998.75. Whereas we would demand a risk premium of more than 15 percent ([100 − 86.60]/86.60) if we started out with $100, we would demand a risk premium of only one-eighth of 1 percent ([1,000 − 998.75]/998.75) if we started out with $1,000. As a wealthier person we are still risk averse, but we are not nearly as disinclined to incur the risk of losing $50, because this amount represents but a small fraction of our wealth. Of course, if the potential gain or loss from the risky prospect were $500, we would again require a 15 percent risk premium.

This framework also enables us to determine how much we should pay to insure against various risks. Suppose, for example, we have $100,000 of savings and we inherit a family heirloom valued at $10,000, which is to be mailed to us. Suppose further that we determine there is a 1 percent chance the heirloom will be lost in the mail. Based on Bernoulli's model of risk aversion, we should be willing to pay up to $104.79 to insure this heirloom.

The total payoff, should the heirloom arrive safely, equals $110,000, which yields utility of 11.6082. If the heirloom is lost in the mail, the total payoff equals $100,000, which yields utility of 11.5129. Thus the expected utility of this risky prospect equals 11.6073 (i.e., 11.6082 × 0.99 + 11.5129 × 0.01). This expected utility corresponds to a certainty equivalent of $109,895.21. Thus we should be willing to pay up to $104.79 (110,000 − 109,895.21) to insure the heirloom.

THE RHETORIC OF RISK PREFERENCE

Bernoulli's view of utility is certainly plausible, but we should not conclude that it describes everyone's attitude toward risk. Economists have generalized Bernoulli's insights into a comprehensive theory of risk preference accompanied by the usual classifications and rhetoric. For example, economists distinguish among those who are risk averse, those who are risk neutral, and those who seek risk. A risk-averse person will reject a fair game, while a risk-neutral person will be indifferent to a fair game, and a risk seeker will select a fair game. Economists also distinguish between the absolute amount of one's wealth that is exposed to risk and the proportion of one's wealth that is exposed to risk, and whether these amounts decrease, remain constant, or increase as wealth increases.

Decreasing absolute risk aversion indicates that the amount of wealth one is willing to expose to risk increases as one's wealth increases. Constant absolute risk aversion implies that the amount of wealth one is willing to expose to risk remains unchanged as wealth increases. Increasing absolute risk aversion means our tolerance for absolute risk exposure decreases as wealth increases.

Relative risk aversion refers to changes in the percentage of wealth one is willing to expose to risk as wealth increases. Decreasing relative risk aversion implies that the percentage of wealth one is willing to expose to risk increases as wealth increases. With constant relative risk aversion, the percentage of wealth one is willing to expose to risk does not change as wealth increases. Increasing relative risk aversion implies that the percentage of wealth one is willing to expose to risk decreases as wealth increases. Table 3.2 summarizes these relationships.

INDIFFERENCE CURVES

In portfolio selection, it is convenient to model expected utility as a function of expected return and risk, as measured by the variance of returns. Because most investors are indeed risk averse, expected utility is usually depicted as a positive function of expected return and a negative function of risk.

$$\text{Expected Utility} = \text{Expected Return} - \text{Risk Aversion} \times \text{Variance}$$

TABLE 3.2   Risk Aversion

	Absolute	Relative
Decreasing	Increase risky amount	Increase risky percentage
Constant	Maintain risky amount	Maintain risky percentage
Increasing	Decrease risky amount	Decrease risky percentage

The risk aversion coefficient (when risk is measured in units of variance or standard deviation squared) indicates how many units of expected return we are willing to sacrifice at the margin in order to reduce variance by one unit. Of course, if we are risk averse, the coefficient must be positive. And the higher the value of the coefficient, the more risk averse we would be.

Suppose, for example, that our risk aversion equals 5. An asset with an expected return of 8 percent and a standard deviation of 10 percent would yield expected utility of 3.0 percent. Another asset may have an expected return of 10 percent and a standard deviation of 12 percent. The expected utility from this asset, given our aversion toward risk, would equal 2.8 percent. The return of the second asset is not high enough to compensate for its higher risk, even though its expected return and risk are both 2 percent higher than those of the first asset. Given risk aversion equal to 5, we would prefer the less risky asset.

If we were less risk averse, with a coefficient of 3, say, the first asset would yield expected utility of 5.0 percent, while the second asset would yield expected utility of 5.7 percent. In this case, the incremental expected return of the second asset is sufficient to counter its higher risk. Table 3.3 summarizes these results.

It is possible to identify combinations of expected return and standard deviation (the square root of variance) that yield the same level of expected utility for a particular risk aversion coefficient. Table 3.4 shows several combinations based on risk aversion of 4. It indicates we are more inclined to incur risk in order to increase expected return at lower levels of expected return than we are at higher levels of expected return.

For example, if we are starting from an expected return of 5 percent, we are willing to accept five additional units of risk in order to increase our

TABLE 3.3   The Risk Aversion Coefficient

Coefficient = 5

	Expected Return	Standard Deviation	Expected Utility
Asset 1	8.0%	10.0%	3.0%
Asset 2	10.0%	12.0%	2.8%

Coefficient = 3

	Expected Return	Standard Deviation	Expected Utility
Asset 1	8.0%	10.0%	5.0%
Asset 2	10.0%	12.0%	5.7%

TABLE 3.4   Risk and Return Combinations with Equal Utility
(Risk Aversion Coefficient = 4)

Expected Return	Standard Deviation	Expected Utility
5.00%	0.00%	5.00%
6.00%	5.00%	5.00%
7.00%	7.07%	5.00%
8.00%	8.66%	5.00%
9.00%	10.00%	5.00%
10.00%	11.18%	5.00%
11.00%	12.25%	5.00%
12.00%	13.23%	5.00%
13.00%	14.14%	5.00%
14.00%	15.00%	5.00%
15.00%	15.81%	5.00%
16.00%	16.58%	5.00%
17.00%	17.32%	5.00%
18.00%	18.03%	5.00%
19.00%	18.71%	5.00%
20.00%	19.56%	5.00%

expected return by one unit. If, however, we are starting from an expected return of 15 percent, we are willing to accept only 0.77 units of incremental risk in order to gain one additional unit of expected return.

Tracing a curve through all the combinations of expected return and risk with equal expected utility creates an indifference curve. Figure 3.3 shows three hypothetical indifference curves. Indifference curves that are closer to the upper left corner yield more expected utility and thus are more desirable. Given a particular indifference curve, however, all the points along that curve yield the same expected utility.

If we were to combine a set of risky assets efficiently so that for any given level of expected return we minimize risk, a continuum of such combinations would form a concave curve in dimensions of expected return and risk. Figure 3.4 shows such a curve, which is called the efficient frontier, along with three indifference curves.[5]

The point of tangency between the efficient frontier and indifference curve 2 represents the precise combination of expected return and standard deviation that maximizes expected utility. It matches our preference for incurring risk in order to raise expected return with the best available trade-off of risk and return from the capital markets.

Clearly, we would prefer a combination of expected return and risk lo-

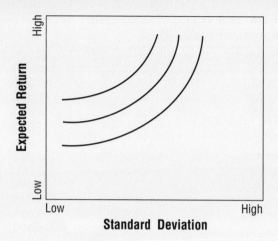

FIGURE 3.3   Indifference curves

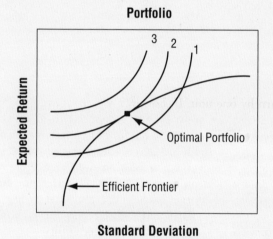

FIGURE 3.4   The optimal portfolio

cated along indifference curve 3, but indifference curve 3 is located in a region that is unobtainable. Indifference curve 1, on the other hand, is undesirable because it is dominated by many of the combinations along the efficient frontier. This illustration shows how we can employ utility theory to identify a portfolio of assets that is optimal given our particular attitude toward risk.

The concept of utility is critical to the theory of choice under uncertainty. While it is reasonable to accept the basic premises of utility theory, such as the notion that more wealth is preferred to less wealth and that investors are typically risk averse, it is important to recognize that concise mathematical models of utility do not reflect the full range of investor attitudes and idiosyncrasies. We should be sensitive to the fact that some descriptions of utility are put forth primarily for tractability or expository convenience.[6]

CHAPTER 4

Lognormality

When reading the financial literature we often see statements to the effect that a particular result depends on the assumption that returns are lognormally distributed. What exactly is a lognormal distribution, and why is it relevant to financial analysis? In order to address this question, let us start with a review of logarithms.

LOGARITHMS

A logarithm is simply the power to which a base must be raised to yield a particular value. For example, the exponent 2 is the logarithm of 16 to the base 4, because 4 squared equals 16. The logarithm of 8 to the base 4 equals 1.5, because 4 raised to the power 1.5 equals 8.

The choice of a base depends on the context in which we use logarithms. For common mathematical procedures, it is common to use the base 10, which explains why logarithms to the base 10 are called common logarithms. The base 10 is popular because the logarithms of 10, 100, 1,000 and so on equal 1, 2, 3 . . . , respectively.

Why should we care about logarithms? In the days prior to pocket calculators and computers, logarithms were useful for performing complicated computations. Financial analysts would multiply large numbers by summing their logarithms, and they would divide them by subtracting their logarithms. For example, given a base of 4, we can multiply 16 times 8 by raising the number 4 to the 3.5 power, which is the sum of the logarithms 2 and 1.5. Of course, you might argue that it is easier to multiply large numbers directly than to raise a base to a fractional power. In earlier days, however, an analyst would use a slide rule, which is a ruler with a sliding central strip marked with logarithmic scales.

e

In most financial applications, instead of logarithms to the base 10, we use logarithms to the base 2.71828, which is denoted by the letter e. These logarithms, which are called natural logarithms and are abbreviated as ln, have a special property. Suppose we invest $100 at the beginning of the year at an annual interest rate of 100 percent. At the end of the year we will receive $200—our original principal of $100 and another $100 of interest. Now suppose our interest is compounded semiannually. Our year-end payment will equal $225. By the middle of the year we will have earned $50 of interest, which is then reinvested to generate the additional $25.

In general, we use the following formula to compute the year-end value of our investment for any interest rate and for any frequency of compounding:

$$P_t = P_{t-1} \times \left(1 + \frac{R}{n} \right)^n \tag{4.1}$$

where P_t = ending value
        P_{t-1} = beginning investment
        R = annual interest rate
        n = frequency of compounding

If the 100 percent rate of interest is compounded quarterly, our $100 investment will grow to $244.14 by the end of the year. If it is compounded daily, we will receive $271.46. And if it is compounded hourly, we will receive $271.81 by year-end.

It seems as though the more frequently our interest is compounded, the more money we will end up with at the end of the year. No matter how frequently it is compounded, though, we will never receive more than $271.83. When R equals 100 percent, the limit of the function $(1 + R/n)^n$ as n approaches infinity is 2.71828, the base of the natural logarithm.

We use this result to convert discrete or periodic rates of return into continuous rates of return. A discrete rate of return is computed as the percentage change of our investment from the beginning of the period to the end of the period including reinvestment of income, assuming there are no contributions or disbursements. A continuous rate of return assumes that the income and growth are compounded instantaneously.

From our previous example we know that e, the base of the natural logarithm, raised to the power 1 (the continuous rate of return in our example) yields 1 plus 171.83 percent (the discrete rate of return in our example). The natural logarithm of the quantity 1 plus the discrete rate of return must therefore equal the corresponding continuous rate of return. For example, the natural logarithm of the quantity 1 plus 10 percent equals 9.53 percent. This means if we invest $100 at a continuously compounded rate of return of 9.53 percent, our investment will grow to $110. The value 1.10, which we compute by raising e to the power 0.0953, is called the exponential. These relationships are shown below:

$$\ln (1.10) = 0.0953$$
$$1.10 = 2.71828^{0.0953}$$

We can also compute the continuous rate of return within a period by subtracting the natural logarithm of the beginning value from the natural logarithm of the ending value. Suppose we start with $100, which is invested so that it grows to $150 after one year, $225 after two years and $337.50 after three years. The logarithms of these values equal 4.6052, 5.0106, 5.4161, and 5.8216, respectively. The difference between each logarithm and the next one equals the continuously compounded return each year, which is 40.55 percent. This continuous return corresponds to a yearly discrete return of 50 percent.

If we plot wealth as a function of time, we produce a convex curve, as shown in Figure 4.1. The logarithms of these values, however, form a straight line when plotted as a function of time, indicating a constant periodic rate of growth (See Figure 4.2). It is this relation that gives rise to the logarithmic scale, in which equal percentage changes correspond to equal vertical distances.

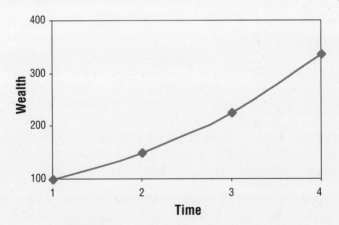

FIGURE 4.1   Wealth as a function of time

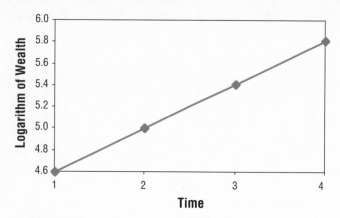

FIGURE 4.2　Logarithm of wealth as a function of time

WHY RETURNS ARE LOGNORMALLY DISTRIBUTED

Now let's see why random returns are lognormally distributed. Consider an asset that has only two possible outcomes per year. It either returns 25 percent or loses 5 percent per period with equal probability. Table 4.1 shows the four potential investment paths that could occur over two periods given these two possible returns.

After one period there is an even chance of a 25 percent return or a –5 percent return. Therefore, the average or expected return after one period equals 10.00 percent. After two periods there are four equally likely outcomes: two consecutive 25 percent returns, which results in a cumulative discrete return of 56.25 percent; a 25 percent return followed by a –5 per-

TABLE 4.1　Compounded Returns

	End of Period 1 Potential Returns	End of Period 2 Potential Returns
		56.25% (25%)
	25.00% (50%)	
		18.75% (25%)
		18.75% (25%)
	–5.00% (50%)	
		–9.75% (25%)
Expected return	10.00%	21.00%

cent return, producing a cumulative discrete return of 18.75 percent; a –5 percent return followed by a 25 percent return, also producing a cumulative discrete return of 18.75 percent; and two consecutive –5 percent returns, leading to a cumulative discrete loss of 9.75 percent.

The average of these four potential outcomes is 21.00 percent, which also equals the single period expected return of 10 percent compounded forward over two periods (1.10 × 1.10 – 1). The process of compounding causes the distribution of cumulative discrete returns to become skewed in such a way that there are fewer returns in excess of the cumulative average return, but they exceed it by a greater amount on balance than the amount by which the more plentiful below-average returns fall short of the cumulative average return. Note that the upper path produces two consecutive returns that exceed the expected return by 15.00 percent, yielding a cumulative discrete return of 56.25 percent. These two 15.00 percent above-average returns cause the cumulative discrete return to exceed the cumulative average return by 35.25 percent. Note that the lower path produces two consecutive 15.00 percent below-average returns, which result in a cumulative discrete return of –9.75 percent. However, the shortfall of this path relative to the cumulative average return is only –30.75 percent.

This example illustrates how compounding skews the distribution of cumulative returns toward the right, or further above the average return. The precise nature of this skewness after many periods conforms to a lognormal distribution. If we convert these compounded returns after two periods into logarithmic returns by taking the natural logarithms of the quantities 1 plus the cumulative discrete returns, we find that they are distributed symmetrically around the expected logarithmic return. The logarithmic return is also called the continuous return. Table 4.2 compares the distribution of cumulative discrete returns to the distribution of cumulative continuous returns after two periods.

TABLE 4.2   Discrete versus Continuous Returns

Return Sequence	Cumulative Discrete Returns	Difference from Average	Cumulative Continuous Returns	Difference from Average
25%, 25%	56.25%	35.25%	44.63%	27.44%
25%, –5%	18.75%	–2.25%	17.19%	0.00%
–5%, 25%	18.75%	–2.25%	17.19%	0.00%
–5%, –5%	–9.75%	–30.75%	–10.26%	–27.44%
Average	21.00%		17.29%	

If we were to extend this return process over many periods, the distribution of the cumulative discrete returns would become more and more skewed, while the distribution of the cumulative continuous returns would remain symmetric and conform more and more closely to a normal distribution. This simple experiment demonstrates that discrete returns are lognormally distributed, which means the logarithms of one plus the discrete returns (the continuous returns) are normally distributed.

CHAPTER 5

Return and Risk

At first glance, return and risk may seem to be straightforward concepts. Yet closer inspection reveals nuances that can have important consequences for determining the appropriate method for evaluating financial results. This chapter reviews various measures of return and risk with an emphasis on their suitability for alternative uses.

RETURN

Perhaps the most straightforward rate of return is the holding-period return (HPR). It equals the income generated by an investment plus the investment's change in price during the period the investment is held, all divided by the beginning price. For example, if we purchase a share of common stock for $50.00, receive a $2.00 dividend, and sell the stock for $55.00, we would achieve a holding-period return equal to 14 percent. In general, we use equation (5.1) to compute holding-period returns.

$$HPR = \frac{I_t + P_t - P_{t-1}}{P_{t-1}} \tag{5.1}$$

where HPR = holding period return
  I_t = income
  P_t = ending price
  P_{t-1} = beginning price

Holding-period returns are also referred to as *discrete returns* or *periodic returns*.

DOLLAR-WEIGHTED VERSUS
TIME-WEIGHTED RATES OF RETURN

Now let us consider rates of return over multiple holding periods. Suppose a mutual fund generated the following annual holding-period returns over a five-year period.

Year 1	−5.00%
Year 2	−15.20%
Year 3	3.10%
Year 4	30.75%
Year 5	17.65%

Suppose further that we had invested $75,000 in this fund by making contributions at the beginning of each year according to the following schedule.

Year 1	$ 5,000
Year 2	$10,000
Year 3	$15,000
Year 4	$20,000
Year 5	$25,000

By the end of the period, our investment would have grown in value to $103,804.56. By discounting the ending value of our investment and the interim cash flows back to our initial contribution, we determine the investment's dollar-weighted rate of return (DWR), which is also referred to as the internal rate of return.

$$5,000 = -\frac{10,000}{(1+r)} - \frac{15,000}{(1+r)^2} - \frac{20,000}{(1+r)^3} - \frac{25,000}{(1+r)^4} + \frac{103,805}{(1+r)^5}$$

$$DWR = r = 14.25\%$$

We enter the interim contributions as negative values, because they are analogous to negative dividend payments. Although we cannot solve directly for the dollar-weighted rate of return, most financial calculators and spreadsheet software have iterative algorithms that quickly converge to a solution. In our example, the solution equals 14.25 percent.

The dollar-weighted rate of return measures the annual rate at which our cumulative contributions grow over the measurement period. However, it is not a reliable measure of the performance of the mutual fund in which we invested, because it depends on the timing of the cash flows. Suppose, for example, we reversed the order of the contributions. Given this sequence of contributions, our investment would have grown to a higher value, $103,893.76. The dollar-weighted rate of return, however, would have been only 9.12 percent.

$$25,000 = -\frac{20,000}{(1+r)} - \frac{15,000}{(1+r)^2} - \frac{10,000}{(1+r)^3} - \frac{5,000}{(1+r)^4} + \frac{103,894}{(1+r)^5}$$

$$DWR = r = 9.12\%$$

In order to measure the underlying performance of the mutual fund, we calculate its time-weighted rate of return. This measure does not depend on the timing of cash flows.

We compute the time-weighted rate of return by first adding 1 to each year's holding-period return to determine the return's wealth relative. Then we multiply the wealth relatives together, raise the product to the power 1 divided by the number of years in the measurement period, and subtract 1. Equation (5.2) shows this calculation.

$$TWR = \left[\prod_{i=1}^{n} (1 + HPR_i) \right]^{1/n} - 1 \qquad (5.2)$$

where TWR = time-weighted rate of return
HPR_i = holding-period return for year i
n = number of years in measurement period

If we substitute the mutual fund's holding-period returns into equation 5.2, we discover that the fund's time-weighted rate of return equals 5.02 percent.

The time-weighted rate of return is also called the geometric return or the compound annual return. Although the geometric return and the compound annual return are often used interchangeably, technically the geometric return pertains to a population whereas the compound annual return pertains to a sample. I use the term geometric return to refer to both. It is the rate of return that, when compounded annually, determines the ending value of our initial investment, assuming there are no interim cash flows. For example, suppose we invest $10,000 in a strategy that produces a holding-period return of 50 percent in the first year and –50 percent in the second year. At the end of the second year, we will end up with $7,500. The geometric return over the two-year measurement period equals –13.40 percent.

$$[(1 + 0.5)(1 - 0.5)]^{1/2} - 1 = -0.1340$$

If we multiply $10,000 × (1 − 0.1340) and then multiply this result again by (1 − 0.1340), we arrive at the ending value of this investment, $7,500.

In order to manipulate geometric returns, we must first convert them to wealth relatives and raise the wealth relatives to a power equal to the number of years in the measurement period. Then we multiply or divide the cumulative wealth relatives, annualize the result, and subtract 1 in order to convert the result back to a geometric return.

Suppose, for example, that five years ago we invested $100,000 in a fund we thought would earn a geometric return of 8 percent over a 20-year horizon so that at the end of the horizon we would receive $466,095.71. During the past five years, however, the fund's geometric return was only 6.5 percent. What must its geometric return be for the next 15 years if we are to reach our original goal of $466,095.71? We start by raising 1.08 to the 20th power, which equals 4.6609571. This value equals the cumulative wealth relative of the anticipated geometric return. We then raise the wealth relative of the geometric return realized thus far to the 5th power, which equals 1.3700867. We then divide 4.6609571 by 1.3700867, raise this value to the power 1 over 15, and subtract 1, to arrive at 8.50 percent.

Alternatively, we can convert the wealth relatives to continuous returns by taking their natural logarithms and manipulating these logarithms. For example, the natural logarithm of 1.089 equals 0.076961, and the natural logarithm of 1.065 equals 0.062975. We multiply 0.062975 × 5 and subtract it from 0.076961 × 20, which equals 1.2243468. Then we divide this value by 15 and use the base of the natural logarithm 2.71828 to reconvert it to an annual wealth relative, which equals 1.085.[1]

GEOMETRIC RETURN VERSUS ARITHMETIC RETURN

It is easy to see why the geometric return is a better description of past performance than the arithmetic average. In the example in which we invested $10,000 at a return of 50 percent followed by a return of −50 percent, the arithmetic average overstates the return on our investment. It did not grow at a constant rate of 0 percent, but declined by 13.40 percent compounded annually for two years. The arithmetic average will exceed the geometric average except when all the holding-period returns are the same; the two return measures will be the same in that case. Furthermore, the difference between the two averages will increase as the variability of the holding-period returns increases.

If we accept the past as prologue, which average should we use to estimate a future year's expected return? The best estimate of a future year's expected return based on a random distribution of the prior years' returns is the arithmetic average. Statistically, it is our best guess for the holding-period return in a given year. If we wish to estimate the expected value of an investment over a multiyear horizon conditioned on past experience, we should also use the arithmetic average. If, however, we wish to estimate the median, we should use the geometric average.[2]

Suppose we plan to invest $100,000 in a stock market index fund, and we wish to estimate the median value of our investment five years from now. We assume there are no transaction costs or fees, and we base our estimates on the yearly results shown in Table 5.1. The arithmetic average equals 16.83 percent, while the geometric average equals 16.20 percent. Our best estimate for next year's return, or any single year's return for that matter, equals 16.83 percent, because there is a 1-in-10 chance of experiencing each of the observed returns. However, the best estimate for the median value of our fund is based on the geometric average. It equals $211,866.94, which we derive by raising 1.1620 to the 5th power and multiplying this value by $100,000.

RISK

Although the time-weighted rate of return measures the constant annual rate of growth that determines terminal wealth, it is nonetheless limited as a measure of performance because it fails to account for risk. We can adjust returns for risk in several ways. One approach is to compute a portfolio's return in excess of the riskless return and to divide this excess return by the portfolio's standard deviation. This risk-adjusted return, called the Sharpe measure, is given by equation (5.3).[3]

$$S = \frac{R_p - R_f}{\sigma_p} \tag{5.3}$$

TABLE 5.1　Annual Stock Market Returns

Year	Return	Year	Return
1	22.63%	6	16.58%
2	5.86%	7	31.63%
3	31.61%	8	−3.14%
4	18.96%	9	31.56%
5	5.23%	10	7.33%

where S = the Sharpe measure
$\quad R_p$ = portfolio return
$\quad R_f$ = riskless return
$\quad \sigma_p$ = the standard deviation of portfolio returns

Because it adjusts return based on total portfolio risk, the implicit assumption of the Sharpe measure is that the portfolio will not be combined with other risky portfolios. Thus the Sharpe measure is relevant for performance evaluation when we wish to evaluate several mutually exclusive portfolios.

The Capital Asset Pricing Model (CAPM) assumes that risk comprises a systematic component and a specific component. Risk that is specific to individual securities can be diversified away; hence an investor should not expect compensation for bearing this type of risk. Therefore, when a portfolio is evaluated in combination with other portfolios, its excess return should be adjusted by its systematic risk rather than its total risk.[4]

The Treynor measure adjusts excess return for systematic risk.[5] It is computed by dividing a portfolio's excess return, not by its standard deviation but by its *beta*, as shown in equation (5.4).

$$T = \frac{R_p - R_f}{\beta_p} \qquad (5.4)$$

where T = the Treynor measure
$\quad R_p$ = portfolio return
$\quad R_f$ = riskless return
$\quad \beta_p$ = portfolio beta

We estimate beta by regressing a portfolio's excess returns on an appropriate benchmark's excess returns. Beta is the coefficient from such a regression. The Treynor measure is a valid performance criterion when we wish to evaluate a portfolio in combination with the benchmark portfolio and other actively managed portfolios.

The intercept from a regression of the portfolio's excess returns on the benchmark's excess returns is called alpha. Alpha measures the value-added of the portfolio, given its level of systematic risk. Alpha is referred to as the Jensen measure, and is given by equation (5.5).[6]

$$\alpha = (R_p - R_f) - \beta_p (R_B - R_f) \qquad (5.5)$$

where α = the Jensen measure (alpha)
$\quad R_p$ = portfolio return
$\quad R_f$ = riskless return
$\quad \beta_p$ = portfolio beta
$\quad R_B$ = benchmark return

The Jensen measure is also suitable for evaluating a portfolio's performance in combination with other portfolios, because it is based on systematic risk rather than total risk.

If we wish to determine whether or not an observed alpha is due to skill or chance, we can compute an appraisal ratio by dividing alpha by the standard error of the regression:

$$A = \frac{\alpha}{\sigma(\varepsilon)} \qquad (5.6)$$

where A = the appraisal ratio *look up in t distribution table*
       α = alpha
      $\sigma(\varepsilon)$ = the standard error of the regression (nonsystematic risk)

The appraisal ratio compares alpha, the average unsystematic deviation from the benchmark, with the unsystematic risk incurred to generate this performance. In order to estimate the likelihood that an observed alpha is not due to chance, we can test the null hypothesis that the mean alpha does not differ significantly from 0 percent. If we reject the null hypothesis, the alpha is not due to chance.

Suppose, for example, that a portfolio's alpha equals 4 percent and that its standard error equals 3 percent, so that the appraisal ratio equals 1.33. If we look up this number in a t distribution table, we discover that, given the amount of unsystematic risk, there is a 10 percent chance of observing an alpha of this magnitude by random process. Hence, we would fail to reject the null hypothesis that alpha does not differ significantly from 0 percent if we require 95 percent confidence.[7]

DOWNSIDE RISK

In the previous example, we based the probability estimate on the assumption that alpha is normally distributed. This assumption is reasonable for evaluating returns over short measurement periods. Over multiyear measurement periods, however, it is the logarithms of the wealth relatives that are normally distributed.[8] The returns themselves are lognormally distributed, which means that they are positively skewed. Therefore, in order to estimate the likelihood of experiencing particular outcomes over multiyear horizons, we should calculate the standardized variable based on the mean and standard deviation of the logarithms of the wealth relatives.

Some investment strategies produce distributions that are skewed differently from a lognormal distribution. Dynamic trading strategies such as portfolio insurance or strategies that involve the use of options typically generate skewed distributions.[9]

A distribution that is positively (right) skewed has a long tail above the mean. Although most of the outcomes are below the mean, they are of smaller magnitude than the fewer outcomes that are above the mean. A distribution that is negatively (left) skewed has a long tail below the mean. It has more outcomes above the mean, but they are smaller in magnitude than those below the mean. Risk-averse investors prefer positive skewness, because there is less chance of large negative deviations.

When we are evaluating strategies that have skewed distributions other than lognormal, we cannot rely on only return and standard deviation to estimate the likelihood of achieving a particular result. Nor can we compare portfolios or strategies that have different degrees of skewness using only these two characteristics. One ad hoc approach would be to specify a target return and base our evaluation on the dispersion of returns below this target, rather than the dispersion of returns around the mean.[10] An alternative method for dealing with skewness is to condition utility on mean, variance, and skewness, and then to evaluate portfolios and strategies based on their expected utilities.

I have attempted to shed some light on the subtleties that distinguish various measures of return and risk. When we rely on these summary statistics to evaluate past results or to predict future consequences, it is important that we understand their precise meaning.

CHAPTER 6

Higher Moments

No, this is not about past indiscretions that may preclude appointment to the Supreme Court. Rather, it is about something much more exciting, at least to quants—the shape of return distributions and the implications for investment management. Much has been made of the observation that investment returns are not always normally distributed. How prevalent is nonnormality and what are the consequences? Does it invalidate the most common approach to portfolio construction, mean-variance optimization, as some would claim, or is it mostly hype from academics digging deeper and deeper into the surface of things? In order to answer these questions, let's start with the basics.

If returns are independent from period to period and are generated by the same distribution, then, owing to the central limit theorem, they are approximately normally distributed. I say approximately because the process of compounding leads to a lognormal distribution, which I will discuss shortly.[1] If returns indeed conform to a normal distribution, we can infer the entire distribution from just the expected return and variance of the returns.

The expected value of a distribution is the first moment of the distribution and equals the arithmetic mean of the returns. The first central moment is always zero, because central moments are measured relative to the mean. The variance, which equals the average of the squared deviations from the mean, is the second central moment and measures the dispersion of returns around the mean. Because the normal distribution is symmetric around the mean, the median (the middle value) and the mode (the most common value) are equal to each other and to the mean (see Figure 6.1). In addition to symmetry, the normal distribution has a standard degree of peakedness, which allows us to calculate the entire distribution from just the mean and the variance.

Although it is very convenient to assume returns are normally distributed, there are many different reasons why returns may depart from a normal distribution. If, therefore, we are to assess probabilities and value at

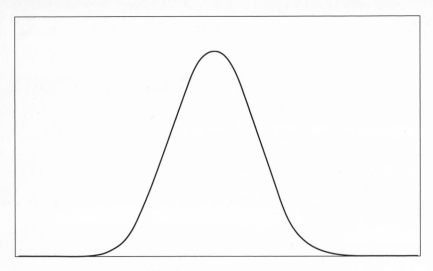

FIGURE 6.1   Normal distribution

risk[2] accurately, we must pay attention to the higher moments of a distribution, such as skewness and kurtosis.

SKEWNESS

The third central moment of a distribution is called skewness, and it measures the asymmetry of a distribution. A positively skewed distribution has a long right tail, and its mean exceeds its median, which in turn exceeds its mode. In the positively skewed distribution shown in Figure 6.2, both the mean and the median are located to the right of the peak, which represents the mode. Although there are more returns below the mean, they are of smaller magnitude than the fewer returns above the mean. The exact opposite properties hold for a negatively skewed distribution.

Skewness is measured as the average of the cubed deviations from the mean. However, we usually represent skewness as the ratio of this value to standard deviation cubed. A normal distribution has skewness equal to 0.

What gives rise to skewness? Even if we believe returns are perfectly independent and produced by the same distribution, compounding causes above-average returns to generate a greater increment to wealth than the dilution to wealth caused by below-average returns of the same magnitude. Consider an investment with an expected return of 10.00 percent. Over two periods, we would expect wealth to increase 21.00 percent ($1.10 \times 1.10 - 1 = 0.2100$). A return 15.00 percent—that is, 15 percent-

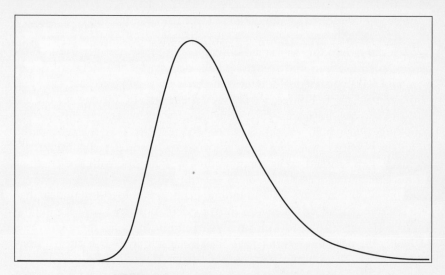

FIGURE 6.2   Positively skewed distribution

age points—above the mean for two periods increases wealth by 56.25 percent ($1.25 \times 1.25 - 1 = 0.5625$), whereas a 15.00 percent return below the mean over two consecutive periods reduces wealth by 9.75 percent ($0.95 \times 0.95 - 1 = -0.0975$). Note that the above-average sequence increases wealth 35.25 percent beyond the expected value of 21.00 percent ($0.5625 - 0.2100 = 0.3525$), while the below-average sequence reduces wealth by only 30.75 percent below the expected value ($-0.0975 - 0.2100 = -0.3075$). The distribution of compounded returns, therefore, is positively skewed.

Suppose this investment has a standard deviation equal to 15.00 percent, and its periodic returns are generated by a normal distribution rather than a lognormal distribution. Also, suppose we select 100 random returns for 10 consecutive periods from this normal distribution. Table 6.1 shows the average mean, median, standard deviation, and skewness across the 10

TABLE 6.1   Skewness from Compounding

	Average of 10 Samples	10-Year Returns
Mean	0.1066	1.7580
Median	0.1105	1.3211
Standard deviation	0.1496	1.3073
Skewness	−0.1163	1.3634

samples of 100 returns, along with the same statistics for the compounded 10-year cumulative returns.

We can ignore the very small differences in these averages from 10.00 percent for the mean and median, 15.00 percent for the standard deviation, and 0.00 percent for skewness, because they simply reflect sampling error. The substantial difference between the mean and median for the cumulative returns, however, reflects the degree of skewness caused by compounding. We would expect skewness to be close to 0 percent if the cumulative returns were normally distributed. Instead, it is substantially positive. Skewness caused by compounding will increase with the length of the horizon and also as a function of volatility.

The skewness from compounding produces a lognormal distribution.[3] We can avoid this skewness in risk calculations by transforming the lognormal distribution to a normal distribution, because the logarithms of 1 plus the periodic returns are normally distributed. This transformation allows us to employ the convenient properties of the normal distribution to calculate probabilities or value at risk measures. We simply perform our calculations based on the logarithmic counterparts of discrete returns and then convert the results back to their discrete units. The key point here is that we can deal with the skewness associated with lognormality with just the first two moments of the distribution, because we can easily convert a lognormal distribution to a normal distribution of logarithmic returns. This is true regardless of the length of the horizon and the volatility of returns, as long as skewness arises purely as a consequence of compounding.

Optionality is another source of skewness in return distributions. Consider a protective put option strategy in which the investor owns the risky asset along with a put option.[4] The investor experiences the performance of the risky asset above the strike price, including possible gains, yet is protected from losses associated with values below the strike price. The protective put option truncates the left side of the strategy's return distribution at the return associated with the strike price, thereby imparting positive skewness. Keep in mind, though, that the strategy's entire return distribution, although skewed to the right, shifts slightly to the left to reflect the dilution associated with the option premium.

Another popular option strategy is to sell covered call options. In this strategy, the investor owns a risky asset and sells an option to purchase the risky asset should its value rise above a prespecified strike price. The investor's obligation to sell the risky asset should it exceed the strike price truncates the right side of the risky asset's distribution, thereby imparting negative skewness.

In addition to these explicit options, many assets include embedded options. Convertible bonds, for example, grant the owner a call option on the equity of the firm; callable bonds grant the issuer a call option on its debt. These assets, too, have skewed return distributions.

Dynamic trading strategies also generate skewed return distributions. Strategies that shift exposure from a risky asset to a riskless asset as the risky asset's price falls, and from the riskless asset to the risky asset as its price rises, lead to positively skewed distributions.

KURTOSIS

The strategies and assets I just described affect the symmetry of a distribution. Distributions may also depart from normality, not in their symmetry but in their peakedness. This property is captured by the fourth central moment, which is called kurtosis.

Kurtosis is computed by raising the deviations from the mean to the fourth power and taking the average of these values. It is usually represented as the ratio of this value to the standard deviation raised to the fourth power.

A normal distribution has a kurtosis value equal to 3. A distribution with a narrow peak and wide tails is called leptokurtic or, more prosaically, fat tailed (see Figure 6.3). Compared to a normal distribution, a larger proportion of the returns are located near the extremes rather than the mean of the distribution. A platykurtic distribution, by contrast, has thin tails and a wider, flatter center. Relative to a normal distribution, a

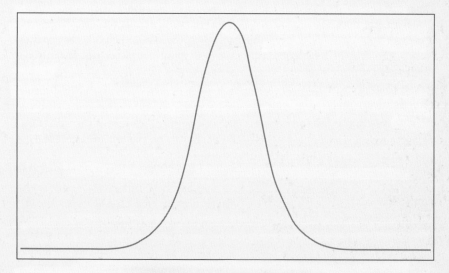

FIGURE 6.3 Leptokurtic distribution

greater fraction of its returns are clustered in the center of the distribution, and a smaller fraction lie in the extremes.

What gives rise to kurtosis? Return series that experience jumps rather than smooth changes often produce leptokurtic distributions. Suppose, for example, policy makers peg a country's currency exchange rate to a fixed level in order to curb inflation. While this policy may help to contain inflation, at the same time it impairs the competitiveness of the country's export sector by maintaining artificially high export prices. Eventually, this problem becomes more serious than inflation, at which point policy makers allow the currency to depreciate in order to promote exports. It is easy to see that such a policy of sustaining an artificial exchange rate for a period of time and then allowing it to adjust abruptly to its equilibrium value will produce a relatively high incidence of extreme returns. Witness Argentina in 2002. We should expect the same pattern of returns to emerge from other types of market intervention, such as circuit breakers on commodities and securities exchanges.

We also tend to see more leptokurtosis associated with higher frequency returns (that is, returns calculated over shorter rather than longer intervals) than with lower frequency returns. Daily asset returns, for example, may experience price jumps in response to accumulated information that is released during nontrading hours. When the markets open, prices adjust quickly to reflect the accumulated information. As we increase the return interval, we see less evidence of leptokurtosis because these price jumps cancel each other out. Table 6.2 shows the kurtosis of daily and monthly returns for U.S. stocks, U.S. bonds, the British pound, and the Japanese yen for the 10 years ending December 31, 2001.[5]

Kurtosis may also result from serial dependence in returns. If returns are positively correlated from one period to the next (which is to say they trend), then lower frequency returns will display leptokurtosis. If daily returns trend within a month, then monthly returns are likely to be more extreme than they would be were daily returns random. If, instead, daily returns mean revert, the opposite would occur. Lower frequency returns

TABLE 6.2 Kurtosis of Daily and Monthly Returns (January 1, 1992–December 31, 2001)

	Daily	Monthly
U.S. stocks	7.80	3.48
U.S. bonds	4.88	3.15
British pound	8.28	3.37
Japanese yen	11.31	5.21

(monthly, for example) would be more clustered toward the middle of the distribution, and fewer observations would lie in the tails.

IMPLICATIONS FOR RISK MANAGEMENT

Although it is convenient to assume returns are normally distributed, in many situations this assumption is not justified. If we care about long horizon results, we should recognize the impact compounding has on returns by assuming a lognormal distribution. Fortunately, there is an exact correspondence between a normal and lognormal distribution; thus, we need only to estimate the mean and variance of the distribution. We first convert our sample to logarithmic returns, then compute the mean and variance of these normally distributed returns, perform our calculations, and convert the results back to discrete units.

It is also possible to generate the return distribution of an option strategy or a dynamic trading strategy based on just the mean and variance of the risky asset. We first generate the risky asset's return distribution under the assumption of lognormality. Then we map the risky asset's returns onto the option strategy's returns according to the terms of the option contract. Consider a protective put option strategy, for example. For a risky asset return at or above the strike price, we calculate the option strategy's return as the risky asset return net of the option premium. For risky asset values below the strike price, we calculate the strategy's return as the return associated with the strike price net of the option premium.

If, instead, we believe a portfolio's returns are skewed as a feature of the data rather than deterministically, we should estimate skewness empirically or, alternatively, we should bootstrap the data in order to generate a return distribution.[6]

We should also be sensitive to the possibility of kurtosis if markets are subject to regulatory intervention, we care about high frequency returns, or we believe returns are positively autocorrelated.[7] Value at risk is especially sensitive to leptokurtosis because it is based on the tails of the return distribution.

IMPLICATIONS FOR MEAN-VARIANCE OPTIMIZATION

Perhaps the most common approach to portfolio construction is mean-variance optimization, which was introduced by Harry Markowitz in 1952.[8] This procedure identifies portfolios that offer the highest expected return for a given level of variance. Critics of mean-variance optimization argue that investors do not worry about upside volatility. They care only about downside risk. Consequently, they insist that mean-variance optimization focuses on the wrong measure of risk. Instead, they argue investors should identify portfolios that offer the highest expected return for a given level of semivariance, which is the average of the squared deviations below the mean. This line of reasoning is intuitively appealing, but in most cases wrong, to wit:

- If investors care about downside risk, but portfolio returns are not skewed,[9] mean-variance optimization will yield the same portfolios as mean-semivariance optimization.
- Probability and value-at-risk measures will not differ, whether they are estimated from variance or semivariance, unless returns are skewed.
- If investors care only about mean and variance, mean-variance optimization is the appropriate approach to portfolio construction, even if returns are skewed.
- Mean-semivariance optimization is relevant only when two conditions prevail simultaneously: Investors care about downside risk, and portfolio returns are skewed.
- Even if individual asset returns are skewed, portfolio returns are less likely to be significantly skewed owing to the central limit theorem.
- All of these statements are true even if portfolio returns are leptokurtic or platykurtic.
- However, if portfolio returns are skewed, leptokurtic, or platykurtic, we must take these features into account when we estimate probability or value-at-risk measures, even for mean-variance efficient portfolios.

The bottom line is that mean-variance optimization is appropriate for most portfolio construction problems, but we must pay attention to higher moments in order to assess the risk of these portfolios properly.

CHAPTER 7

Duration and Convexity

In 1938, Frederick Macaulay published his classic book, *Some Theoretical Problems Suggested by the Movements of Interest Rates, Bond Yields and Stock Prices in the United States Since 1865.*[1] Although Macaulay focused primarily on the theory of interest rates, as an aside he introduced the concept of duration as a more precise alternative to maturity for measuring the life of a bond. As with many of the important innovations in finance, the investment community was slow to appreciate Macaulay's discovery of duration. It was not until the 1970s that professional investors began to substitute duration for maturity in order to measure a fixed income portfolio's exposure to interest rate risk.[2] Today, duration and convexity—the extent to which duration changes as interest rates change—are indispensable tools for fixed income investors. In this chapter, I review these important concepts and show how they are applied to manage interest rate risk.

MACAULAY'S DURATION

A bond's maturity measures the time to receipt of the final principal repayment and, therefore, the length of time the bondholder is exposed to the risk that interest rates will increase and devalue the remaining cash flows. Although it is typically the case that the longer a bond's maturity, the more sensitive its price is to changes in interest rates, this relationship does not always hold. Maturity is an inadequate measure of the sensitivity of a bond's price to changes in interest rates, because it ignores the effects of coupon payments and repayment of principal.

Consider two bonds that both mature in 10 years. Suppose the first bond is a zero-coupon bond that pays $2,000 at maturity, while the second bond pays a coupon of $100 annually and $1,000 at maturity.

Although both bonds yield the same total cash flow, the bondholder must wait 10 years to receive the cash flow from the zero-coupon bond, while he receives almost half the cash flow from the coupon-bearing bond prior to its maturity. Therefore, the average time to receipt of the cash flow of the coupon-bearing bond is significantly shorter than it is for the zero-coupon bond.

The first cash flow from the coupon-bearing bond comes after one year, the second after two years, and so on. On average, the bondholder receives the cash flow in 5.5 years $(1 + 2 + 3 + \ldots + 10)/10$. In the case of the zero-coupon bond, the bondholder receives a single cash flow after 10 years.

This computation of the average time to receipt of cash flows is an inadequate measure of the effective life of a bond, because it fails to account for the relative magnitudes of the cash flows. The principal repayment of the coupon-bearing bond is 10 times the size of each of the coupon payments. It makes sense to weight the time to receipt of the principal repayment more heavily than the times to receipt of the coupon payments.

Suppose we weight it 10 times as heavily as each coupon payment and compute the weighted average of these values. This approach yields a weighted average time to receipt of 7.75 years. But this measure, too, is deficient because it ignores the time value of money. A $100 coupon payment to be received two years from today is less valuable than a $100 coupon payment to be received one year hence.

Macaulay recognized this distinction and determined that the time to receipt of each cash flow should be weighted not by the relative magnitude of the cash flow but by the relative magnitude of its present value. Macaulay's duration, therefore, equals the average time to receipt of a bond's cash flows, in which each cash flow's time to receipt is weighted by its present value as a percentage of the total present value of all the cash flows. The sum of the present values of all the cash flows, of course, equals the price of the bond.

Assume the yield to maturity of a 10-year bond equals 10 percent. The duration of the zero-coupon bond maturing in 10 years is the same as its maturity, because the time to receipt of the principal repayment is weighted 100 percent. The duration of the coupon-paying bond, though, is significantly shorter. It is not, however, as short as 5.5 years, the average time to receipt of the cash flow ignoring the relative sizes of the payments. Nor is it as long as 7.75 years, the estimate that accounts for the relative sizes of the cash flows but ignores their present values. The duration of the coupon-bearing bond equals 6.76 years, as Table 7.1 shows.

TABLE 7.1 Macaulay's Duration (Yield to Maturity = 10%)

Cash Flow	Time to Receipt (years)	Present Value of Cash Flow	Weight	Weighted Value Time to Receipt
100	1	90.91	0.0909	0.0909
100	2	82.64	0.0826	0.1653
100	3	75.13	0.0751	0.2254
100	4	68.30	0.0683	0.2732
100	5	62.09	0.0621	0.3105
100	6	56.45	0.0564	0.3387
100	7	51.32	0.0513	0.3592
100	8	46.65	0.0467	0.3732
100	9	42.41	0.0424	0.3817
1100	10	424.10	0.4241	4.2410
2000	55	1000	1.0000	6.7590

In general, we can write the formula for Macaulay's duration as follows:

$$D = \frac{\displaystyle\sum_{t=1}^{n} \frac{t \times C_t}{(1+y)^t}}{\displaystyle\sum_{t=1}^{n} \frac{C_t}{(1+y)^t}} \qquad (7.1)$$

where D = duration
n = number of cash flows
t = time to receipt of the cash flow
C = cash flow amount
y = yield to maturity

PROPERTIES OF DURATION

It is apparent from the formula for Macaulay's duration that its value depends on three factors: the final maturity of the bond, the coupon payments, and the yield to maturity.

If we hold constant the size of the coupon payments and the yield to maturity, duration in general increases with a bond's maturity. But it increases at a slower rate than the increase in maturity, because later cash flows are discounted more heavily than earlier cash flows. If we extend the maturity of the coupon-bearing bond described earlier from 10 years to 15 years, for example, its duration increases by only 1.61 years, from 6.76 years to 8.37

years. Of course, in the case of zero-coupon bonds, duration increases exactly with maturity, because these values are equal to each other.

Deep-discount bonds are another exception to the general rule. They increase in duration as maturity increases up to a distant threshold, and then decrease in duration as maturity increases beyond this threshold. This peculiar result arises because deep-discount bonds with sufficiently long maturities behave like perpetuities (bonds that pay coupons forever). Perpetuities have an infinite maturity but a finite duration, because the weight of the principal repayment is inconsequential by the time it is discounted to present value.

At a given maturity and yield to maturity, duration declines with increases in the coupon payments or principal prepayments. This is because a larger percentage of the total cash flow is received earlier; stated differently, the times to receipt of the coupon payments or principal prepayments are weighted more heavily relative to the final repayment of principal. If the coupon payments from our earlier example were $120 rather than $100, the bond's duration would equal 6.54 years instead of 6.76 years.

Finally, if we increase yield to maturity while holding the coupon payments and maturity constant, duration will fall, because the discount factors for the later cash flows increase more than the discount factors for the earlier cash flows. The duration of the coupon-bearing bond in our example, for instance, declines to 6.55 years as the yield to maturity rises to 12 percent. Table 7.2 summarizes these properties of duration.

MODIFIED DURATION

Although Macaulay conceived of duration as a measure of the effective life of a bond, it can be modified to measure the sensitivity of a bond's price to changes in the yield to maturity. The modification simply requires dividing Macaulay's duration by the quantity 1 plus the yield to maturity, as shown below.[3]

TABLE 7.2   Properties of Duration

Maturity increases	Duration increases*
Coupon payment increases	Duration decreases
Yield to maturity increases	Duration decreases

*For par and premium bonds. For deep discount bonds, duration increases up to a distant threshold and then decreases.

$$D^* = \frac{D}{1+y} \tag{7.2}$$

where D^* = modified duration
D = Macaulay's duration
y = yield to maturity

We can estimate the percentage change in the price of a bond by multiplying the basis-point change in yield to maturity by −1 times the bond's modified duration. Again, suppose that we have a 10-year bond that pays a $100 coupon annually and $1,000 at maturity; its yield to maturity is 10 percent. The Macaulay duration of this bond equals 6.76 years. Its modified duration thus equals 6.14 years, which we derive by dividing 6.76 by 1.10.

If yield to maturity increases 10 basis points to 10.1 percent, modified duration predicts that the bond's price will decline 0.614 percent, to $993.86. And if yield to maturity declines 10 basis points to 9.90 percent, modified duration predicts that the bond's price will increase 0.614 percent, to $1,006.14.

Although these predictions are close to the true answer, they are not exact. If yield to maturity does increase by 10 basis points, the price of the bond will actually decline by 0.612 percent, to $993.88, and if yield to maturity falls 10 basis points, the bond's price will increase by 0.617 percent, to $1,006.17. Modified duration apparently overestimates price declines and underestimates price increases with respect to changes in yield to maturity.

One might argue that the errors are so tiny as to be inconsequential. For larger changes in yield to maturity, however, the percentage change in price predicted by modified duration can be significantly wrong. For example, modified duration predicts a 6.14 percent change in price for a 100-basis-point change in yield to maturity, given our particular example. In fact, the bond's price would decline by only 5.89 percent if yield to maturity rose by 100 basis points, and it would rise by 6.42 percent if yield to maturity fell by 100 basis points. Figure 7.1 shows the change in price predicted by modified duration for given changes in yield to maturity compared with the change in price that would actually occur.

CONVEXITY

In Figure 7.1, the line that represents the actual price response to a given change in yield to maturity is convex. The larger the increase in yield to

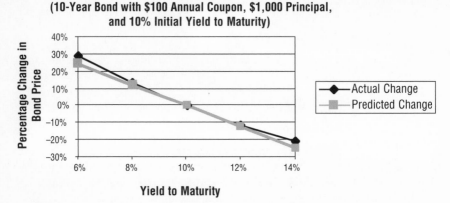

(10-Year Bond with $100 Annual Coupon, $1,000 Principal, and 10% Initial Yield to Maturity)

FIGURE 7.1   Pricing error of modified duration (10-year bond with $100 annual coupon, $1,000 principal, and 10% initial yield to maturity)

maturity, the greater the magnitude of the error by which modified dura-tion will overestimate the bond's price decline; the larger the decrease in yield to maturity, the greater the magnitude of the error by which modified duration will underestimate the bond's price rise.

This phenomenon is called convexity, and it arises for the following reason. As yield to maturity changes, a bond's duration changes as well. Modified duration is thus an accurate predictor of price change only for very small changes in yield to maturity. If yield to maturity is 10 percent, for example, modified duration equals 6.14, which implies that a 100-ba-sis-point change in yield to maturity will result in a 6.14 percent change in bond price. However, as yield to maturity increases to 10.25 percent, mod-ified duration falls to 6.02, which implies smaller price changes for subse-quent changes in yield to maturity.

The price response of a bond to changes in yield to maturity is conse-quently a function not only of the bond's modified duration but of its con-vexity as well. Whereas modified duration measures the sensitivity of bond prices to changes in yield to maturity, convexity measures the sensitivity of duration to changes in yield to maturity.

Convexity is more pronounced the farther apart the cash flows are. Imagine a bond that has 10 annual cash flows. If yield to maturity in-creases, the present value of the 10th cash flow will decrease the most, the present value of the ninth cash flow will decrease by a smaller amount, the present value of the eighth cash flow will decrease by a yet smaller amount, and so on. Duration will decrease as the more distant cash flows are as-signed less and less weight. To the extent the cash flows are not far apart from each other, however, duration will not decrease that much because the changes in the weights associated with successive cash flows will be similar to each other.

Now consider a bond that has only two cash flows, one after the first year and one after the 20th year. If yield to maturity increases, the present value of the first cash flow will change by a significantly smaller amount than the change in the present value of the second cash flow. The weight assigned to the time to receipt of the first cash flow will thus decline only slightly, whereas the weight assigned to the time to receipt of the second cash flow will decline meaningfully, resulting in a more substantial change in the bond's duration.

APPLICATIONS OF DURATION AND CONVEXITY

Duration and convexity are essential tools for fixed income portfolio management. Duration enables portfolio managers to act upon their convictions about interest rate shifts. If a manager expects interest rates to fall, she should increase the duration of her portfolio in order to leverage the price appreciation that will occur if she is correct. If she expects an increase in rates, she should of course reduce duration to protect her portfolio from price losses.

Duration and convexity are also useful for hedging a stream of liabilities. A portfolio manager can hedge a liability stream by constructing a portfolio of equal duration and convexity, as long as its present value equals the present value of the liabilities at the outset. If the present value of the liabilities exceeds the present value of the assets available for hedging, the duration of the portfolio must exceed the duration of the liabilities. The converse is true if the value of the portfolio exceeds the value of the liabilities. Moreover, modified duration relates the percentage change in price to absolute changes in yield to maturity. In order to hedge a portfolio of liabilities with a different value, we must adjust duration to relate the dollar change in price to changes in yield to maturity.

Finally, we can immunize a portfolio from interest rate shifts by setting its duration equal to our holding period. If interest rates rise, the capital loss will be offset by the gain from reinvesting the cash flows at higher yields. Conversely, if interest rates fall, the reduction in income resulting from reinvestment of cash flows at lower rates is offset by the capital gain. Of course, capital gains and losses are balanced by reinvestment gains and losses only to the extent that short-term rates and long-term rates move together. If long-term rates increase but short-term rates remain unchanged, the portfolio's income will not increase sufficiently to offset the capital loss; in this case, immunization will fail.

CONCLUSION

This chapter is intended to provide some elementary insights about duration and convexity. As such, I have ignored many of the complexities associated with these notions. For example, I have implicitly assumed throughout that a bond's cash flows are perfectly predictable. In fact, many bonds have call or put provisions that introduce an element of uncertainty to the cash flows. Moreover, the cash flows of mortgage-backed securities are uncertain because mortgage borrowers usually have the right to prepay their loans. These complexities can have a significant impact on the measurement of duration and convexity and their application to risk control.

CHAPTER 8

The Term Structure of Interest Rates

This chapter addresses the term structure of interest rates. I begin by reviewing the various ways in which the term structure is measured. Then I present the major hypotheses that purport to explain the relationship between interest rates and term to maturity. Finally, I discuss a simple technique for estimating the term structure.

WHAT IS THE TERM STRUCTURE OF INTEREST RATES?

The term structure of interest rates, sometimes referred to as the yield curve, isolates the differences in interest rates that correspond solely to differences in term to maturity. As a first approximation, we can measure the term structure by measuring the relationship between the yields to maturity on government debt instruments and their terms to maturity. By focusing on government debt instruments, we control for differences in yield that might arise from credit risk.

The yield to maturity of a bond equals the internal rate of return that discounts its cash flows, including the coupon payments and the repayment of principal, back to the bond's current price. This relationship is described by equation (8.1).

$$P = \frac{C_1}{(1+y)} + \frac{C_2}{(1+y)^2} + \ldots + \frac{C_n}{(1+y)^n} + \frac{F}{(1+y)^n} \tag{8.1}$$

where $\qquad P$ = current price
$\qquad C_1, C_2, C_n$ = coupon payments in periods 1 through n
$\qquad\qquad F$ = face value
$\qquad\qquad y$ = yield to maturity
$\qquad\qquad n$ = number of discounting periods

The yield to maturity does not provide a particularly satisfying yard-stick for measuring the term structure of interest rates, for two reasons. First of all, it is an unrealistic measure of a bond's yield because it assumes all of a bond's cash flows are reinvested at the same rate. This assumption implies that a one-year instrument nine years hence will have the same yield as a 10-year bond today. Obviously, there is no reason to expect interest rates to evolve according to this assumption.

Second, because capital gains receive favorable tax treatment relative to income, bonds with the same term to maturity might have yields to maturity that differ according to the fraction of their return that arises from income versus price change.

To control for the differential tax treatment of coupons and price change, we measure the term structure of interest rates from the yields on pure discount bonds. These bonds do not pay coupons. Instead, they are initially offered at a discount to their face value, so that their yield is equal to the annualized return resulting from their conversion to face value. The yield on a pure discount bond is referred to as the spot rate of interest.

We can think of a bond with predictable cash flows as a portfolio of pure discount bonds. In order to price coupon-bearing bonds using spot interest rates, we assign the yield of a pure discount instrument maturing in six months to the coupon payment six months from now, and the yield of a one-year, pure discount instrument to the coupon due one year from now, proceeding in this fashion until we assign yields to all the bond's cash flows. This relationship is shown in equation (8.2). For purposes of simplification, equation (8.2) assumes coupon payments occur annually.

$$P = \frac{C_1}{(1+r_1)} + \frac{C_2}{(1+r_2)^2} + \ldots + \frac{C_n}{(1+r_n)^n} + \frac{F}{(1+r_n)^n} \qquad (8.2)$$

where r_1, r_2, r_n = spot rates of interest of pure discount bonds maturing in periods 1 through n

As long as there is a reasonable supply of pure discount bonds at all relevant maturities, the spot rates of interest should reflect accurately the term structure of interest rates. It might be the case, however, that at particular maturities there is an inadequate supply of pure discount bonds, including coupons that have been stripped from coupon-bearing bonds. In this case, the yields on these bonds might misrepresent the term structure of interest rates. I will address this problem in the final section of this chapter.

We can also describe the term structure of interest rates by measuring the relationship between forward rates and term to maturity. The forward rate is the interest rate that will apply to an instrument commencing at some future date. It can be derived from the spot rates of interest.

Suppose that the spot rate of interest on a one-year instrument is 6.00 percent and the spot rate of interest on a two-year instrument is 7.50 percent. If we were to contract to purchase a one-year instrument one year from now, what rate of interest should we expect for this instrument? The forward rate on a one-year instrument one year hence is determined so that an investor is indifferent between purchasing a two-year instrument today and holding it to maturity or purchasing a one-year instrument today and entering into a forward contract to purchase a one-year instrument one year from now. This equality is shown in equation (8.3).

$$(1 + r_2)^2 = (1 + r_1) \times (1 + f_{1,1}) \tag{8.3}$$

where r_1 = spot rate for two-year instrument
r_2 = spot rate for one-year instrument
$f_{1,1}$ = one-year forward rate for one-year instrument

If we substitute the one- and two-year spot rates into equation (8.3), we find that the rate on a one-year instrument one year forward equals 9.02 percent.

Suppose the market offers a one-year forward rate on a one-year instrument equal to 8.00 percent. In this case, we would invest in the two-year instrument today because we would be sure to earn a cumulative return of 15.56 percent ($1.075 \times 1.075 - 1$), compared with a cumulative return of 14.48 percent ($1.06 \times 1.08 - 1$) were we to invest in a one-year instrument today and a forward contract to invest in a one-year instrument one year hence. By the same logic, we would choose the one-year instrument and the forward contract if the forward rate were greater than 9.02 percent. The forward rate is governed by the law of one price, which states that equivalent cash flows must sell for the same price.

In general, we can derive the forward rate for any future date and for instruments of any maturity using equation (8.4), provided we can observe instruments with the requisite maturities today.

$$f_{t,n-t} = \left[\frac{(1+r_n)^n}{(1+r_t)^t} \right]^{1/(n-t)} \tag{8.4}$$

where $f_{t,n-t}$ = t-year forward rate for $(n - t)$-year instrument
r_n = spot rate for n-year instrument
r_t = spot rate for t-year instrument

Yet another way in which we can represent the term structure of interest rates is to relate discount factors to maturity. The discount factor is equal to the reciprocal of 1 plus the spot rate raised to the maturity of the instrument, as shown in equation (8.5).

$$d(n) = \frac{1}{(1+r_n)^n} \qquad (8.5)$$

where $d(n)$ = discount factor for n periods
$\quad r_n$ = spot rate of interest for maturity n
$\quad n$ = maturity of pure discount instrument

The discount factor must fall between 0 and 1. It approaches 0 as the term to maturity approaches infinity, and it approaches 1 as the term to maturity approaches 0. Consider, for example, a situation in which the spot rates of interest are 8 percent across all maturities. Table 8.1 shows the discount factors corresponding to various maturities.

It is apparent from Table 8.1 that the discount factor is a nonlinear function of term to maturity. An increase of five years beginning with a term to maturity of one year reduces the discount factor by nearly 0.3 unit, whereas an increase of five years beginning in year 10 reduces it by less than 0.15 unit and beginning in year 15 by only 0.1 unit. As a percentage of value, however, the discount factor adjusts price proportionately with time. In all cases, an increase in term to maturity of five years reduces the value of the bond by 31.9 percent, given an 8 percent spot rate of interest.

TABLE 8.1 Discount Factors When Spot Rate of Interest = 8%

Term to Maturity	Discount Factor
1	0.9259
2	0.8573
3	0.7938
4	0.7350
5	0.6806
6	0.6302
7	0.5835
8	0.5403
9	0.5002
10	0.4632
15	0.3152
20	0.2145

WHAT DETERMINES THE TERM
STRUCTURE OF INTEREST RATES?

There are three hypotheses that are commonly cited to explain the term structure of interest rates—the expectations hypothesis; the liquidity premium hypothesis; and the segmented market hypothesis, also known as the preferred habitat hypothesis.

The expectations hypothesis holds that the current term structure of interest rates is determined by the consensus forecast of future interest rates. Suppose that the spot interest rate for a one-year instrument is 6 percent and that the spot rate of interest for a two-year instrument is 7 percent. According to the expectations hypothesis, this term structure arises from the fact that investors believe a one-year instrument one year in the future will yield 8.01 percent, because an investor could achieve the same return by investing in a one-year instrument today and a one-year instrument one year from now as she could achieve by investing in a two-year instrument today. If the investor believes that the one-year rate one year in the future will exceed 8.01 percent, she will prefer to roll over consecutive one-year instruments as opposed to investing in a two-year instrument today. But if she anticipates that the one-year rate one year ahead will be less than 8.01 percent, she will opt for the two-year instrument today.

According to the expectations hypothesis, an upward sloping yield curve indicates that investors expect interest rates to rise. A flat yield curve implies that investors expect rates to remain the same. A downward sloping yield curve indicates that investors expect rates to fall.

It is important to distinguish the future spot rates that are implied by the current term structure from the forward rates on contracts available today. Although both rates are calculated the same way and are therefore equal to each other, the interest rate on a forward contract must obtain in an arbitrage-free world, whereas the implied future spot rate is only a forecast, and not a particularly good one at that.

Based on the term structure in the previous example, the interest rate on a forward contract to purchase a one-year instrument one year from now must equal 8.01 percent. If the rate were lower, we could sell the forward contract together with a one-year instrument and use the proceeds to purchase a two-year instrument, thereby earning a riskless profit. If the rate on the forward contract were higher, we could reverse these transactions for a riskless profit.

It is not the case, however, that we would necessarily profit by combining purchases or sales today with purchases or sales in the future. Whether or not we profit would depend on the future, not forward, term structure of interest rates.

The distinction between actual forward rates and implied future rates is analogous to the difference between covered interest arbitrage and uncovered interest arbitrage. Covered interest arbitrage is an arbitrage condition that explains the relationship between the spot exchange rate on a currency and its forward exchange rate. The forward rate is set such that an arbitrageur cannot profit by borrowing in a low interest rate country, converting to the currency of a high interest rate country, lending at the higher interest rate, and selling a forward contract to hedge away the currency risk. The cost of the hedge will precisely offset the interest rate advantage.

Uncovered interest arbitrage posits that, on average, we cannot profit by borrowing in a low interest rate country, converting to the currency of a high interest rate country, and lending in that country without hedging away the currency risk. In effect, uncovered interest arbitrage is nothing more than a statement that the forward rate is an unbiased estimate of the future spot rate. "Unbiased" does not mean the forward rate is an accurate forecast of the future spot rate. It merely suggests that it does not systematically over- or underestimate the future spot rate.[1]

It is implausible that the expectations hypothesis fully accounts for the term structure of interest rates. As mentioned earlier, when the term structure of interest rates slopes upward, according to the expectations hypothesis, investors expect interest rates to rise. Historically, the term structure has had an upward slope most of the time. It seems unlikely that investors have expected interest rates to rise with that degree of frequency.

The expectations hypothesis is implausible for another reason. In order for it to be true, investors must believe that all bonds will generate about the same return. Suppose that the spot rates of interest on a one-year instrument, a four-year instrument, and a five-year instrument equal 6 percent, 7.5 percent, and 8 percent, respectively. The expectations hypothesis implies that a four-year instrument one year in the future will have a rate of 8.51 percent. Based on today's term structure, we could purchase a pure discount bond with a face value of $1,000, maturing in five years, for $680.58. If the implied future rate of 8.51 percent on a four-year discount bond is realized one year from now, we could then sell our four-year bond for $721.42, thereby earning a return of 6.0 percent, which equals the return on a one-year instrument.

Table 8.2 shows the implied term structure one year forward, given the present term structure, along with the total return one would achieve during the ensuing year by purchasing discount bonds of various maturities should the implied future term structure materialize.

The implicit forecast that all bonds will yield the same return is hard to accept. It suggests that investors are indifferent to risk. Historically, the returns of long-term bonds have been higher on average and significantly

TABLE 8.2   Total Return Implied by Forward Rates

Term to Maturity	Current Spot Rates	Implied Future Rates One Year Forward	Implied Total Return
1 year	6.00%	7.00%	6.00%
2 years	6.50%	7.50%	6.00%
3 years	7.00%	8.00%	6.00%
4 years	7.50%	8.50%	6.00%
5 years	8.00%		6.00%

more volatile than the returns on short-term instruments. This evidence suggests that investors demand and receive a premium in exchange for the higher volatility of long-term bonds.

The higher historical returns of long-term bonds relative to shorter-term instruments lend credence to an alternative explanation of the term structure—the liquidity premium hypothesis. This hypothesis holds that investors are not indifferent to risk. They recognize that a bond's price is more sensitive to changes in interest rates, the longer its maturity, and they demand compensation for bearing this interest rate risk. Thus, bonds with longer maturities typically offer a premium in their yields relative to shorter-term instruments in order to induce investors to take on additional risk. The extent of the premium increases with term to maturity but at a decreasing rate, for two reasons. Duration, a measure of a bond's price sensitivity to interest rate changes, increases at a decreasing rate with term to maturity.[2] Moreover, long-term interest rates are typically less volatile than short-term interest rates.

The notion that yields on longer-term instruments reflect a liquidity premium is consistent with the observation that the yield curve usually has an upward slope. Even when investors anticipate interest rates remaining the same or declining slightly, a liquidity premium could still cause long-term rates to exceed short-term rates.

A third explanation of the term structure of interest rates is the segmented market hypothesis, which holds that groups of investors regularly prefer bonds within particular maturity ranges in order to hedge their liabilities or to comply with regulatory requirements. Life insurance companies, for example, have historically preferred to purchase long-term bonds, whereas commercial banks have favored shorter-term instruments. To the extent the demand of one group of investors increases relative to the demand of the other group, yields within the maturity range where relative demand has risen will fall relative to the yields within the maturity range where there is slack in demand.

TERM STRUCTURE ESTIMATION

If we were to trace a line through the yields on pure discount government bonds as they relate to maturity, it is unlikely that this line would form a smooth curve. Some of the observations would likely rise abruptly and some would likely fall abruptly. These apparent jumps might reflect the fact that some of the instruments have not traded recently; thus the observations are not contemporaneous with each other. Moreover, it may be the case that we have no observations for some maturities. In an effort to overcome these limitations, financial analysts have developed methods for estimating a smooth curve to represent the term structure.

One such method is called spline smoothing. This approach assumes the discount factors corresponding to the spot interest rates are a cubic function of time to maturity, as shown in equation (8.6).

$$d(n) = a + bn + cn^2 + dn^3 \qquad (8.6)$$

where $d(n)$ = discount factor for maturity n
         a,b,c,d = coefficients
              n = term to maturity

We estimate the coefficients of equation (8.6) by regressing the observed discount factors on three independent variables—term to maturity, its value squared, and its value cubed. We then convert the estimated discount factor to its corresponding yield.

Table 8.3 shows a hypothetical observed term structure along with an

TABLE 8.3   Cubic Spline Estimated Term Structure

Maturity	Observed Spot Rate	Observed Discount Factor	Estimated Discount Factor	Estimated Spot Rate
1	5.03%	0.9521	0.9529	4.94%
2	5.89%	0.8918	0.8909	5.94%
3	6.47%	0.8285	0.8297	6.42%
4	6.57%	0.7753	0.7696	6.77%
5	7.20%	0.7064	0.7112	7.05%
6	7.35%	0.6534	0.6552	7.30%
7	7.55%	0.6008	0.6019	7.52%
8	7.60%	0.5565	0.5519	7.71%
9	7.89%	0.5049	0.5057	7.87%
10	8.00%	0.4632	0.4639	7.98%

estimated term structure based on the cubic spline method. The fitted regression equation from the observed term structure is as follows:

Discount Factor $= 1.01508 - 0.06206 \times n - 0.00017 \times n^2 + 0.000087 \times n^3$

These estimated yields allow us to price bonds for which we do not have reliable observations. Furthermore, we may believe the values along the smoothed curve represent yields toward which the observed yields will converge, thereby suggesting trading opportunities.

I have attempted to provide a broad overview of the term structure of interest rates. This topic is one of the most widely researched areas of finance; the interested reader will have no trouble pursuing more detailed analyses.[3]

CHAPTER 9

Serial Dependence

Serial dependence refers to the notion that returns evolve nonrandomly; that is, they are correlated with their prior values.

One variation of serial dependence is called mean reversion. With mean reversion, returns revert to an average value or asset prices revert to an equilibrium value. If an asset is priced above its equilibrium value, its price will not change randomly; it will be more inclined to decrease than to increase. Conversely, if an asset is priced below its equilibrium value, it will be more likely to increase than to depreciate further.

Another variation of serial dependence is known as trending. In a trending pattern, a positive return is more likely to be followed by another positive return than by a reversal, and a negative return is more likely to be succeeded by another negative return than by a positive return.

Of course, some returns may conform to nonrandom patterns that are more complex than simple mean reversion or trending. For example, the returns in a series may be correlated not with their immediately prior returns, but with more distant prior returns. Alternatively, returns may be linearly independent of prior values but display serial dependence after transformation to a nonlinear function.

The extent to which asset returns evolve nonrandomly has important consequences for financial analysis. First of all, if asset returns are nonrandom, then their variance will depend on the interval used to measure them. Instead of varying proportionately with the time interval, the variance of returns will vary at a varying rate. I will discuss some of the implications of this nonlinearity later.

Second, if investment returns are serially dependent, they are at least partly predictable. This result is of obvious interest because it raises the possibility that we can devise trading rules to generate abnormal profits.

HOW TO DETECT SERIAL DEPENDENCE

There are several ways to detect serial dependence. One of the simplest and most intuitive ways is to perform a runs test. In order to perform a runs test, we first compute the average value of the series. Then we designate every value that is above the mean as positive and every value that is below the mean as negative. Next we compute the number of runs in the series.

A run is an uninterrupted sequence of positive or negative values. For example, a sequence of four positive values (+ + + +) would constitute a single run, whereas a sequence of four alternating values (+ − + −) would constitute four runs. The expected number of runs in a random sequence is given by the following formula:

$$E(Runs) = \frac{2(n1)(n2)}{n1 + n2} + 1 \qquad (9.1)$$

where $E(Runs)$ = expected number of runs
  $n1$ = number of positive observations
  $n2$ = number of negative observations

A random series of 60 positive observations and 40 negative observations should have 49 runs. Significantly more than 49 runs would indicate that the duration of the series' typical run is shorter than we should expect from a random series. We would conclude, therefore, that the series is characterized by mean reversion. Significantly fewer than 49 runs would indicate that the duration of the series' typical run is longer than we should expect from a random series; the series is characterized by trends.

In order to determine whether or not the actual number of runs differs significantly from the expected number of runs, we must compute the standard deviation of runs. This value is given by equation (9.2):

$$\sigma(Runs) = \sqrt{\frac{2(n1)(n2)\big[2(n1)(n2) - n1 - n2\big]}{(n1 + n2)^2 (n1 + n2 - 1)}} \qquad (9.2)$$

Once we know the standard deviation of the runs, we compute a test statistic by dividing the difference between the observed number of runs and the expected number of runs by the standard deviation. Based on 60 positive values and 40 negative values, the standard deviation of runs equals 4.77. If we observe only 39 runs, we should be about 96 percent confident that the series is nonrandom; because there are fewer runs than we would expect from a random sequence, we would conclude the series trends. If we observe 59 runs, we would be equally confident that the series is nonrandom, but this time we would conclude the series is mean reverting.

A runs test is limited because it deals only with direction. It depends only on whether an observation is above or below average and not on the extent to which the observation differs from the average. Statistical procedures that deal only with rank are referred to as nonparametric procedures.

We can also measure serial dependence with procedures that rely on the magnitude of the observations instead of just their rank. One obvious procedure is to test for autocorrelation by regressing the returns in a series on their prior values. If we regress a series on the immediately prior values, we test for first-degree autocorrelation. If we regress a series on the values preceding the immediately prior values, we test for second-degree autocorrelation.

A significantly positive correlation coefficient suggests a series is prone to trends. A significantly negative correlation coefficient suggests a series is characterized by mean reversion.

Another parametric procedure for measuring serial dependence is called a variance ratio test. If a sequence of returns is random and we compute several estimates of the variance based on different return intervals, the estimates should be linearly related to one another. Specifically, the variance estimated from two-day returns should be twice as large as the variance estimated from daily returns, and the variance estimated from quarterly returns should be three times as large as the variance estimated from monthly returns. If you prefer to think in terms of standard deviations, the standard deviation of quarterly returns should exceed the standard deviation of monthly returns by a factor equal to the square root of three.

The variance ratio is computed by dividing the variance of returns estimated from the longer interval by the variance of returns estimated from the shorter interval and then normalizing this value to 1 by dividing it by the ratio of the longer interval to the shorter interval:

$$VR = \frac{\sigma_L^2 / \sigma_S^2}{n_L / n_S} \tag{9.3}$$

where VR = variance ratio

σ_L^2 = variance estimated from longer interval returns

σ_S^2 = variance estimated from shorter interval returns

n_L = number of periods in longer interval

n_s = number of periods in shorter interval

Suppose, for example, we estimate the variance of annual returns as 4.0 percent and the variance of monthly returns, using the same measurement period, as 0.4 percent. Based on these estimates, the variance ratio equals 0.8333 [(4.0%/0.4%)/12].

A variance ratio of less than 1 suggests that the shorter-interval returns tend toward mean reversion within the duration of the longer interval. By contrast, a variance ratio that exceeds one suggests that the shorter-interval returns are inclined to trend within the duration of the longer interval.

Consider an extreme and obviously unrealistic example. Suppose we observe, each year for many years, the pattern of returns given in Table 9.1. Just by inspection, it is apparent that the monthly returns trend within a quarter and that the quarterly returns mean revert within a year. This result is confirmed by the variance ratio test. The variance of the monthly returns equals 0.01 percent, and the variance of the quarterly returns equals 0.09 percent, which corresponds to a variance ratio of 3.00.

Because the annual return is the same every year, the variance of the annual returns equals 0.0 percent. The variance ratio of annual returns to quarterly returns or to monthly returns thus also equals 0, demonstrating that mean reversion produces a variance ratio that is less than 1.

Of course, whether a series is significantly nonrandom depends on the magnitude of the variance ratio and the number of observations from which it is estimated. Equation (9.4) shows how to calculate the test statistic of a variance ratio that is estimated from overlapping observations.[1]

$$z(q) = \sqrt{n}(VR-1)\left[\frac{2(2q-1)(q-1)}{3q}\right]^{-1/2} \tag{9.4}$$

where $z(q)$ = test statistic
n = number of shorter interval observations
VR = variance ratio
q = number of periods in interval used to estimate variance in numerator

The use of overlapping observations helps to preserve a sufficient number of observations for estimating the variance in the numerator as we extend the interval.

The variance in the numerator of the variance ratio in equation (9.4) is computed slightly differently from the normal method. Because the variance in the numerator is estimated from overlapping returns, it is computed by squaring the differences, not from the average return of the longer-interval returns but rather from a quantity equal to the average of the shorter-interval returns multiplied by the number of periods in the longer interval. For example, if monthly returns are used to estimate the variance in the denominator and quarterly returns are used to estimate

TABLE 9.1   Hypothetical Return Series

	Monthly	Quarterly	Annually
January	1.00%		
February	1.00%		
March	1.00%	3.03%	
April	−1.00%		
May	−1.00%		
June	−1.00%	−2.97%	
July	1.00%		
August	1.00%		
September	1.00%	3.03%	
October	−1.00%		
November	−1.00%		
December	−1.00%	−2.97%	−0.60%

the variance in the numerator, then the numerator's variance is estimated as the average of the squared differences from the average monthly return times three.

It is also important to note that equation (9.4) depends on the assumption that the nonrandomness is not caused by heteroskedasticity, which is to say it does not arise because the variance changes through time. If heteroskedasticity is present, additional adjustments are required to determine whether or not the series is serially dependent.[2]

INVESTMENT IMPLICATIONS

As noted, if returns are serially dependent, variances estimated from longer-interval returns may not be proportional to variances estimated from shorter-interval returns. If returns are positively serially correlated (that is, trending), then variance should grow at an increasing rate as the return interval increases. If returns are negatively serially correlated (that is, mean reverting), then variance should grow at a declining rate as the return interval increases.

This result has important consequences for asset allocation. Suppose we choose an asset mix by maximizing expected utility, which we define as expected return minus risk aversion times variance. If variance is proportional to time, our investment horizon does not affect our choice of asset mix. But if variance increases at an increasing rate with time, we would choose a more conservative asset mix, the longer our horizon. The opposite would hold if variance increased at a decreasing rate with time. We would be inclined to select a more aggressive asset mix over a longer horizon than we would select for a shorter horizon.[3]

Suppose, for example, that a particular asset mix has an expected annual return of 10 percent and a variance of 4 percent, estimated from annual returns. If, at the margin, we are willing to sacrifice two units of expected return to reduce variance by one unit (that is, our risk aversion equals 2), this asset mix is expected to yield 0.02 units of utility, given a one-year horizon ($0.10 - 2 \times 0.04$).

Now suppose the variance ratio of five-year returns to one-year returns equals 1.1. This variance ratio implies that the annualized variance estimated from five-year returns equals 4.4 percent. The same asset mix is expected to yield only 0.012 annualized units of utility, given a five-year horizon. We must choose a more conservative asset mix to generate the same level of expected utility that we expect from the asset mix given a one-year horizon.

If the variance ratio of five-year returns to one-year returns equals 0.9 percent, the annualized variance estimated from five-year returns would equal 3.6 percent; the same asset mix would yield 0.028 units of expected utility. We would thus have to lower the risk of the asset mix in order to generate the same level of expected utility in one year that we could achieve given a five-year horizon. Table 9.2 summarizes these results.

Now consider the implications of serial dependence on option pricing. The value of an option is conditioned on five factors: the price of the underlying asset, the strike price, the riskless rate of interest, the time remaining to expiration, and the volatility of the underlying asset. If we hold constant all the other factors, the value of an option increases with the volatility of the underlying asset because uncertainty raises the likelihood that the option will end up in the money.

If the returns of the underlying asset are positively serially correlated within a quarter, then the variance of quarterly returns will exceed three times the variance of monthly returns. Therefore, if we estimate the volatility of the underlying asset from monthly or higher frequency returns, and then extrapolate this estimate according to the Black-Scholes

TABLE 9.2 Expected Utility as a Function of Horizon When Returns Are Nonrandom

Investment Horizon	Annualized Expected Return	Risk Aversion	Annualized Variance	Expected Utility
1 year	10.00%	2.00	4.00%	2.00%
5 years ($VR = 1.1$)	10.00%	2.00	4.40%	1.20%
5 years ($VR = 0.9$)	10.00%	2.00	3.60%	2.80%

assumption that variance changes linearly with time, we will underestimate the value of the three-month option. If the returns of the underlying asset mean revert, and we extrapolate the variance in accordance with the assumptions of Black-Scholes, we will overestimate the value of the longer-dated option.

We can extrapolate the annualized variance estimated from shorter intervals simply by multiplying it by the appropriate variance ratio. Similarly, we can extrapolate an annualized standard deviation by multiplying it by the square root of the appropriate variance ratio. For example, suppose our estimate of standard deviation is based on daily returns, and we wish to estimate the value of an option that expires in three months. If the variance ratio of three-month returns to daily returns equals 1.21, we simply multiply the annualized standard deviation of daily returns by 1.10, the square root of the variance ratio, in order to value the three-month option.

If we believe that the returns of the underlying asset are serially dependent but that the market prices the option according to the Black-Scholes assumption that variance changes linearly with time, we might be able to profit by trading options on the same underlying asset but with different expiration dates. If the asset's returns trend within the horizon of a long-dated option, the long-dated option will be undervalued, on balance, relative to a short-dated option. We should, therefore, purchase the long-dated option and sell the short-dated option. By contrast, if the asset's returns mean revert within the horizon of the long-dated option, it will be overvalued relative to the short-dated option. We should thus sell the long-dated option and purchase the short-dated option.

If returns are serially dependent, it follows that they are partly predictable. We might therefore be able to devise profitable trading strategies. We might be able to exploit mean reversion with a simple linear investment rule. If the allocations of the assets in our portfolio change according to changes in their relative returns, for example, we might decide to change an asset's allocation by less than the return-induced change, anticipating that the asset return will revert toward its average level.

Suppose we allocate 50 percent of our portfolio to a risky asset that we believe mean reverts, and the balance to a riskless asset that returns 0.5 percent per month. With changes in the risky asset's return, we will change the asset's allocation by an amount equal to −5 times the percentage change that would occur in a simple buy-and-hold portfolio. Table 9.3 shows how $100 invested according to this linear investment rule grows over one year compared with a 50/50 buy-and-hold strategy, assuming the risky asset's returns revert back and forth between +6.0 percent and −4.0 percent.

TABLE 9.3 A Linear Investment Rule to Exploit Mean Reversion

Risky Asset Return	Linear Investment Rule		Buy/Hold Strategy	
	Risky Percent	Portfolio Value	Risky Percent	Portfolio Value
	50.00%	100.00	50.00%	100.00
6.00%	43.34%	103.25	51.33%	103.25
−4.00%	48.95%	101.75	50.19%	101.38
6.00%	42.29%	105.00	51.52%	104.69
−4.00%	47.86%	103.53	50.37%	102.78
6.00%	41.20%	106.77	51.70%	106.14
−4.00%	46.73%	105.32	50.56%	104.21
6.00%	40.09%	108.56	51.89%	107.62
−4.00%	45.56%	107.14	50.75%	105.65
6.00%	38.94%	110.36	52.08%	109.13
−4.00%	44.36%	108.98	50.93%	107.11
6.00%	37.77%	112.18	52.26%	110.65
−4.00%	43.12%	110.84	51.12%	108.60

The linear investment rule generates a 2.24 percent incremental return relative to the buy-and-hold strategy. Its standard deviation is also less—7.67 percent compared with 8.85 percent for the buy-and-hold strategy. Of course, it is highly improbable that any return series would follow such a reliable mean-reverting pattern.

EVIDENCE OF SERIAL DEPENDENCE

The preceding discussion invites the obvious question: Are returns serially dependent? Table 9.4 shows the variance ratios and their significance for stocks, bonds, and several currencies. The variance in the denominator is estimated from monthly returns. The significance is the value estimated by using equation (9.4).

According to the variance ratios in Table 9.4, all of the series exhibit positive serial correlation, and some of the trending is statistically significant. These results suggest that we should at least be mindful of how we estimate volatility. It might not always be prudent to assume variances change linearly with time. They also suggest we might be able to profit from trading rules designed to exploit serial dependence, but we should be mindful of transaction costs. Patterns that appear statistically significant may not be economically significant after accounting for the cost of implementation.

TABLE 9.4   Variance Ratios (July 1976–December 2002)

Numerator Denominator	1 Year 1 Month	2 Years 1 Month	3 Years 1 Month
S&P 500			
Variance ratio	1.17	1.42	1.98
Significance	0.80	1.36	2.59
Government Bonds			
Variance ratio	1.44	1.63	1.69
Significance	2.11	2.05	1.82
British Pound			
Variance ratio	1.07	1.07	1.14
Significance	0.34	0.24	0.36
Euro*			
Variance ratio	1.38	1.75	1.78
Significance	1.79	2.45	2.06
Japanese Yen			
Variance ratio	1.40	1.63	1.63
Significance	1.93	2.04	1.66

*Based on Deutschemark returns prior to 1999

CHAPTER 10

Time Diversification

Investors typically assume it is safer to invest in risky assets such as stocks over long horizons than over short horizons. They believe that over long horizons favorable stock returns are likely to offset poor stock returns; thus it is likely that stocks will realize a return close to their expected return. Over short horizons, they recognize there is less opportunity to recoup possible losses from the stock market.

THE ARGUMENT FOR TIME DIVERSIFICATION

The notion that above-average returns tend to offset below-average returns over long horizons is called time diversification. Specifically, if returns are independent from one year to the next, the standard deviation of annualized returns diminishes with time. The distribution of annualized returns consequently converges as the investment horizon increases.

Figure 10.1 shows a 95 percent confidence interval of annualized stock market returns as a function of investment horizon, assuming that the stock market's expected return is 10 percent and the standard deviation of its returns equals 15 percent.[1] It is apparent from Figure 10.1 that the distribution of annualized returns converges as the investment horizon lengthens.

It might also be of interest to focus on the notion of time diversification from the perspective of losing money. We determine the likelihood of a negative return by measuring the difference in standard deviation units between a 0.0 percent return and the expected return. Again, if we assume the stock market's expected return equals 10 percent and its standard deviation equals 15 percent, the expected return is 0.63 standard deviation above a 0 percent return, given a one-year horizon. This value corresponds to a 26 percent probability that the stock market will generate a negative return in any one year.

Given a 10-year horizon, however, the annualized expected return is 2.01 standard deviations above an annualized return of 0.0 percent.

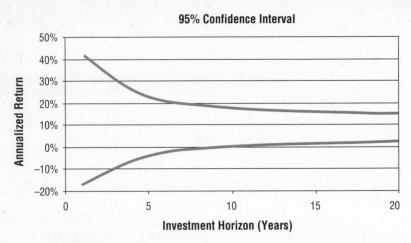

FIGURE 10.1   Annualized returns (95% confidence interval)

There is only a 2.2 percent chance that the stock market will produce a negative return, on average, over 10 years.[2] This does not imply that it is just as improbable to lose money in any one of these 10 years; it merely reflects the tendency of above-average returns to cancel out below-average returns.

TIME DIVERSIFICATION REFUTED

Several prominent financial economists, most notably Paul Samuelson, have argued that the notion of time diversification is specious for the following reason.[3] Although it is true that the annualized dispersion of returns converges toward the expected return with the passage of time, the dispersion of terminal wealth also diverges from the expected terminal wealth as the investment horizon expands.

This result implies that, although you are less likely to lose money over a long horizon than over a short horizon, the magnitude of your potential loss increases with the duration of your investment horizon. According to the critics of time diversification, if you elect the riskless alternative when you are faced with a three-month horizon, you should also elect the riskless investment when your horizon equals 10 years, 20 years, or, indeed, any duration.

This criticism is relevant to cross-sectional diversification as well as to temporal diversification. Suppose you have an opportunity to invest

$10,000 in a risky venture, and you decline this opportunity because you think it is too risky. Would you be less averse to investing in 10 independent ventures, each of which has the same risk as the venture you declined and each of which requires a $10,000 investment?

You are clearly less likely to lose money by investing in 10 equally risky but independent ventures than by investing in just one of these ventures. The amount you could conceivably lose, however, is 10 times as great as your exposure in a single venture.

Now consider a third choice. Suppose you are offered a chance to invest a total of $10,000 in 10 independent but equally risky ventures. In this case you would invest only $1,000 in each of the 10 risky ventures. This investment opportunity diversifies your risk across the 10 ventures without increasing your total exposure. You might still choose not to invest, but your opposition to it should be less intense than it was to the first two alternatives.

Perhaps you are unpersuaded by these arguments. You reason as follows. Although it is true that the dispersion of terminal wealth increases with the passage of time or with the number of risky opportunities, the expected wealth of the risky venture also increases. The dispersion of wealth thus expands around a growing mean as the horizon lengthens or as the number of independent risky ventures increases.

Consider again the choice of investing in the stock market versus a riskless asset. Suppose the riskless asset has a certain 2.5 percent annual return compared with the stock market's 10 percent expected return and 15 percent standard deviation. Table 10.1 compares the dispersion of terminal wealth of the stock market with the certain terminal wealth of the riskless investment.

After one year, the terminal wealth of an initial $100,000 investment in the stock market ranges from $83,532 to $142,211, given a confidence interval of 95 percent, while the riskless investment grows with certainty to $102,500. After 10 years, the spread in the stock market investment's terminal wealth expands from $58,679 (142,211 – 83,532) to $446,658 (548,645 – 101,987), but it surrounds a higher expected wealth. Thus the lower boundary of the 95 percent confidence interval is greater than the initial investment. If the investment horizon is extended to 20 years, the lower boundary of the 95 percent confidence interval actually exceeds the terminal wealth of the riskless investment (170,264 versus 163,862).

Although this line of reasoning might strike you as a credible challenge to the critics of time diversification, in the limit it fails to resurrect the validity of time diversification. Even though it is true that the lower boundary of a 95 percent confidence interval of the stock market investment exceeds

TABLE 10.1 Risky versus Riskless Terminal Wealth

| | Stock Market 95% Confidence Interval | | Riskless Asset |
	Lower Boundary ($)	Upper Boundary ($)	Terminal Wealth ($)
1 year	83,532	142,211	102,500
5 years	84,840	278,815	113,141
10 years	101,987	548,645	128,008
15 years	129,835	1,019,451	144,830
20 years	170,264	1,838,876	163,862

the terminal wealth of the riskless investment after 20 years, the lower boundary of a 99 percent confidence interval falls below the riskless investment, and the lower boundary of a 99.9 percent confidence interval is even worse. The growing improbability of a loss is offset by the increasing magnitude of potential losses.

It is an indisputable mathematical fact that if you prefer a riskless asset to a risky asset given a three-month horizon, you should also prefer a riskless asset to a risky asset given a 10-year horizon, assuming the following three conditions are satisfied:

1. You have constant relative risk aversion, which means you prefer to maintain the same percentage exposure to risky assets regardless of changes in your wealth.
2. You believe that risky asset returns are random.
3. Your future wealth depends only on investment results and not on your human capital or consumption habits.

Risk aversion implies that the satisfaction you derive from increments to your wealth is not linearly related to increases in your wealth. Rather, your satisfaction increases at a decreasing rate as your wealth increases. You thus derive more satisfaction when your wealth grows from $100,000 to $150,000 than you do when it grows from $150,000 to $200,000. It also follows that a decrease in your wealth conveys more disutility than the utility that comes from an equal increase in your wealth.[4]

The finance literature commonly assumes the typical investor has a utility function equal to the logarithm of wealth. This is one of several utility functions that imply constant relative risk aversion. Based on this assumption, I will demonstrate numerically why your investment horizon is irrelevant to your choice of a riskless versus a risky asset.

Suppose you have $100.00. This $100.00 conveys 4.60517 units of utility [ln(100.00) = 4.60517]. Now consider an investment opportunity that has a 50 percent chance of a $\frac{1}{3}$ gain and a 50 percent chance of a $\frac{1}{4}$ loss. A $100.00 investment in this risky venture has an expected terminal wealth equal to $104.17, but it too conveys 4.60517 units of utility [50% × ln(133.33) + 50% × ln(75.00) = 4.60517]. Therefore, if your utility function is defined by the logarithm of wealth, you should be indifferent between holding on to your $100.00 or investing it in this risky venture, because it conveys the same utility as the riskless venture.

Now suppose you are offered an opportunity to invest in this risky venture over two periods, and the same odds prevail. Your initial $100.00 investment can either increase by $\frac{1}{3}$ with a 50 percent probability in each of the two periods, or it can decrease by $\frac{1}{4}$ with a 50 percent probability in each of the two periods. Over two periods, the expected terminal wealth increases to $108.51, but the utility of the investment opportunity remains the same. You should thus remain indifferent between keeping your $100.00 and investing it over two independent periods.

The same mathematical truth prevails irrespective of the investment horizon. The expected utility of the risky venture will always equal 4.60517, implying that you derive no additional satisfaction by diversify-

TABLE 10.2 Utility = ln(Wealth)

	Starting Wealth	Distribution of Wealth After: 1 Period	2 Periods	3 Periods
				$\frac{1}{8} \times 237.04$
			$\frac{1}{4} \times 177.78$	
				$\frac{1}{8} \times 133.33$
		$\frac{1}{2} \times 133.33$		
				$\frac{1}{8} \times 133.33$
			$\frac{1}{4} \times 100.00$	
	100			$\frac{1}{8} \times 75.00$
				$\frac{1}{8} \times 133.33$
			$\frac{1}{4} \times 100.00$	
		$\frac{1}{2} \times 75.00$		$\frac{1}{8} \times 75.00$
				$\frac{1}{8} \times 75.00$
			$\frac{1}{4} \times 56.25$	
				$\frac{1}{8} \times 42.19$
Expected wealth	100.00	104.17	108.51	113.03
Expected utility	4.60517	4.60517	4.60517	4.60517

ing your risk across time. This result holds even though the standard deviation of returns increases approximately with the square root of time, while the expected terminal wealth increases almost linearly with time.

Table 10.2 shows the possible outcomes of this investment opportunity after one, two, and three periods, along with the expected wealth and expected utility after each period. The possible wealth values are computed by linking all possible sequences of return. Expected wealth equals the probability-weighted sum of each possible outcome, while expected utility equals the probability-weighted sum of the logarithm of each possible wealth outcome.

This result does not require utility to equal the logarithm of wealth. Suppose, instead, your utility function is defined by minus the reciprocal of wealth. This utility function implies greater risk aversion than a log wealth utility function. You would thus prefer to hold on to your $100.00, given the opportunity to invest in a risky venture that has an equal chance of increasing by $1/3$ or decreasing $1/4$. You would, however, be indifferent between a certain $100.00 and a risky venture that offers an equal chance of increasing by $1/3$ or decreasing by $1/5$.

Table 10.3 shows that the expected utility of this risky venture re-

TABLE 10.3   Utility = $-1/$Wealth

	Starting Wealth	Distribution of Wealth After:		
		1 Period	2 Periods	3 Periods
				$1/8 \times 237.04$
			$1/4 \times 177.78$	
				$1/8 \times 142.22$
		$1/2 \times 133.33$		
				$1/8 \times 142.22$
			$1/4 \times 106.67$	
				$1/8 \times 85.33$
	100			
				$1/8 \times 142.22$
			$1/4 \times 106.67$	
				$1/8 \times 85.33$
		$1/2 \times 80.00$		
				$1/8 \times 85.33$
			$1/4 \times 64.00$	
				$1/8 \times 51.20$
Expected wealth	100.00	106.67	113.78	121.36
Expected utility	−0.01000	−0.01000	−0.01000	−0.01000

mains constant as a function of investment horizon, even though the expected terminal wealth grows at a faster pace than it does in the previous example. Again, time diversification would not induce you to favor the risky venture over a multiperiod horizon if you did not prefer it for a single-period horizon.

THE OPTION ANGLE

Zvi Bodie argues that option pricing theory offers evidence that risky assets grow riskier with time.[5] He asserts that because the cost of insurance (a protective put option) increases with time, risk must also increase with time. Otherwise, investors would not be willing to pay a higher premium for longer-dated options. Bodie's argument relies on the same property of dispersion of wealth that underlies Samuelson's result, but it does not depend on any assumptions about investor preferences. Time enters the option valuation formula in two ways.[6] It is used to discount the strike price, which causes a put option's value to fall with time, and it operates on the dispersion of the risky asset's value in such a way that causes the option's value to increase with time. This latter effect is the same effect that explains Samuelson's result. Samuelson refuted the argument of time diversification by showing the effect of increasing cumulative volatility on investor preferences. Bodie refuted the time diversification argument by showing the effect of increasing cumulative volatility on the value of a put option. Samuelson's result is preference dependent, whereas Bodie's result is preference free.

WITHIN-HORIZON EXPOSURE TO LOSS

There is yet another way to refute the time diversification argument without invoking Samuelson's utility theory argument, which depends on the growing magnitude of loss to offset the diminishing probability of loss. If investors care about exposure to loss throughout their investment horizon and not just at its conclusion, then time diversification fails based only on the probability of loss. The likelihood of a within-horizon loss rises with time even as the likelihood of a terminal loss diminishes.[7]

By using a statistic called first passage time probability, we measure the probability of loss within an investment horizon.[8] Specifically, first passage time probability measures the probability (Pr_W) of a first occurrence of an event within a finite horizon. It is expressed as follows:

$$\mathrm{Pr}_W = N\left[\frac{\ln(1+L)-\mu T}{\sigma\sqrt{T}}\right] + N\left[\frac{\ln(1+L)+\mu T}{\sigma\sqrt{T}}\right](1+L)^{2\mu/\sigma^2} \qquad (10.1)$$

where $N[\ ]$ = cumulative normal distribution function
   $\ln$ = natural logarithm
   L = cumulative percentage loss in periodic units
   μ = annualized expected return in continuous units
   T = number of years in horizon
   σ = annualized standard deviation of continuous returns

This formula gives the probability that an investment will depreciate at least once to a particular value or below that value over some horizon if it is monitored continuously. The cumulative normal distribution function applied to the first bracketed term gives the probability of a loss at the end of the horizon. It shrinks with time because expected return, which appears as a negative value in the numerator, grows faster than standard deviation, which appears as a positive value in the denominator. However, the remainder of the equation gives the probability of a loss at any time prior to the end of the horizon, and expected return appears as a positive value in the numerator. You can prove to yourself that the probability of a within-horizon loss rises with time by substituting different values for time while holding all other variables constant. The probability increases sharply as you begin to lengthen the horizon until it eventually levels off, but it never diminishes with time.

TIME DIVERSIFICATION RESURRECTED

Now that you have been exposed to the incontrovertible truth that time does not diversify risk, would you truly invest the same in your youth as you would in your retirement? There are several valid reasons why you might still condition your risk posture on your investment horizon, even though you accept the mathematical truth about time diversification.

First, you may not believe risky asset returns are random. Perhaps investment returns follow a mean-reverting pattern. If returns revert to their mean, then the dispersion of terminal wealth increases at a slower rate than implied by a lognormal distribution (the distribution that results from random returns). If you are more averse to risk than the degree of risk aversion implicit in a log wealth utility function, then a mean-reverting process will lead you to favor risky assets over a long horizon, even if you are indifferent between a riskless and risky asset over a short horizon.[9]

Suppose, for example, returns are not random. Instead, the risky venture in Table 10.3 has a 60 percent chance of reversing direction and, therefore, only a 40 percent chance of repeating its prior return. Table 10.4 reveals that expected utility rises from −0.010 over a single period to −0.00988 over two periods and to −0.00978 over three periods. Thus, if you believe in mean reversion and you are more risk averse than a log wealth investor, you should increase your exposure to risk as your investment horizon expands.

This result does not apply, however, to investors who have a log wealth utility function. These investors would not be induced to accept more risk over longer horizons, even if they believed in mean reversion.

Second, even if you believe returns are random, you might still choose to accept more risk over longer horizons than over shorter horizons because you have more discretion to adjust your consumption and work habits.[10] If a risky investment performs poorly at the beginning of a short horizon, there is not much you can do to compensate for this loss in wealth. If a risky investment performs poorly at the beginning of a long horizon, however, you can postpone or reduce consumption or work harder to achieve your financial goals. Samuelson's argument against time diversification assumes implicitly that your terminal wealth depends only on investment performance.

TABLE 10.4   Utility = −1/Wealth with Mean Reversion

		Distribution of Wealth After:		
	Starting Wealth	1 Period	2 Periods	3 Periods
				0.08 × 237.04
			0.20 × 177.78	
				0.12 × 142.22
		½ × 133.33		
				0.18 × 142.22
			0.30 × 106.67	
				0.12 × 85.33
	100			
				0.12 × 142.22
			0.30 × 106.67	
				0.18 × 85.33
		½ × 80.00		
				0.12 × 85.33
			0.20 × 64.00	
				0.08 × 51.20
Expected wealth	100.00	106.67	112.36	118.63
Expected utility	−0.01000	−0.01000	−0.00988	−0.00978

Third, you may have a utility function that changes abruptly at a particular threshold. Consider, for example, a situation in which you require a minimum level of wealth to maintain a certain standard of living. Your lifestyle might change drastically if you penetrate this threshold, but further reductions in wealth are less meaningful. Given the same risky investment, you would be more likely to penetrate the threshold at the end of a short horizon than you would be at the end of a long horizon.

Fourth, you are irrational. This does not mean you are a bad person. It simply implies that you behave inconsistently.

CHAPTER 11

Regressions

How can we predict uncertain outcomes? We could study the relationship between the uncertain variable to be predicted and some known variable. Suppose, for example, we wished to predict the change in profits for the airline industry. We might expect to find a relationship between gross domestic product (GDP) growth in the current period and airline profits in the subsequent period, because economic growth usually foreshadows business travel as well as personal travel. We can quantify this relationship through a technique known as regression analysis.

Regression analysis can be traced to Sir Francis Galton (1822–1911), an English scientist and anthropologist who was interested in determining whether a son's height corresponded to his father's height. To answer this question, Galton measured a sample of fathers and computed their average height. He then measured their sons and computed their average height. He found that fathers of above-average height had sons whose heights were still above average but by a smaller amount. Galton termed this phenomenon regression toward the mean.

SIMPLE LINEAR REGRESSION

To measure the relationship between a single independent variable (GDP growth, in our earlier example) and a dependent variable (subsequent change in airline profits), we begin by gathering some data on each variable—for example, actual GDP growth in each quarter of a given sample period, and the change in the airline industry's profit over each subsequent quarter. We then plot the intersects of these observations. The result is a scatter diagram such as the one shown in Figure 11.1.

The horizontal axis represents a quarter's GDP growth and the vertical axis represents the percentage change in profits for the airline industry in the subsequent quarter. The plotted points in the figure indicate the actual percentage change in airline profits associated with a given level of GDP

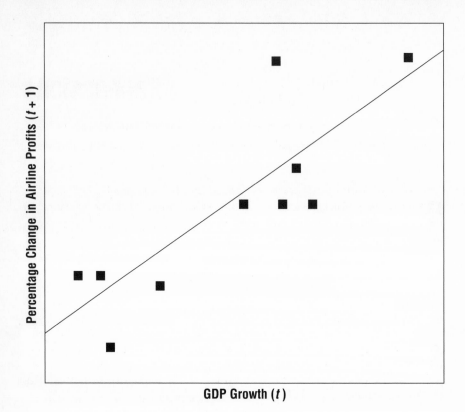

FIGURE 11.1   Scatter diagram

growth. They suggest a positive relationship; that is, as GDP growth increases so do airline profits. The straight line sloping upward from left to right measures this relationship.

That straight line is called the regression line. It is fitted to the data in such a way that the sum of the squared differences of the observed values from the values along the line is minimized. The values along the regression line corresponding to the vertical axis represent the predicted change in airline profits given the corresponding prior quarter's GDP growth along the horizontal axis. The difference between a value predicted by the regression line and the actual change in airline profits is the error, or the residual.

Given a particular value for GDP growth, we can predict airline profits in the subsequent quarter by multiplying the GDP growth value by the slope of the regression line and adding to this value the intercept of the line with the vertical axis, as shown by equation (11.1).

$$\hat{Y}_{t+1} = \hat{\alpha} + \hat{\beta} \times X_t \tag{11.1}$$

where $\hat{Y}_{t+1}$ = predicted percentage change in airline profits
$\hat{\alpha}$ = intercept of the regression line with the vertical axis
$\hat{\beta}$ = slope of the regression line
X_t = prior quarter's growth in GDP

We can write the equation for the actual percentage change in airline profits, given our observation of the prior quarter's GDP growth, by adding the error to the prediction equation:

$$Y_{t+1} = \hat{\alpha} + \hat{\beta} \times X_t + \varepsilon_{t+1} \tag{11.2}$$

where Y_{t+1} = actual percentage change in airline profits
ε_{t+1} = error associated with the predicted value

Positive errors indicate that the regression equation underestimated the dependent variable (airline profits) for a particular value of the independent variable (GDP growth), while negative errors indicate that the regression equation overestimated the dependent variable. Figure 11.2 illustrates these notions.

ANALYSIS OF VARIANCE

To determine whether the regression equation is a good predictor of the dependent variable, we start by performing an analysis of variance. This involves dividing the variation in the dependent variable (change in airline profits) into two parts—that explained by variation in the independent variable (prior quarter's GDP growth), and that attributable to error.

In order to proceed, we must first calculate three values: the total sum of the squares, the sum of the squares due to regression, and the sum of the squares due to error. The total sum of the squares is calculated as the sum of the squared differences between the observed values for the dependent variable and the average of those observations. The sum of the squares due to regression is calculated as the sum of the squared differences between the predicted values for the dependent variable and the average of the observed values for the dependent variable. Finally, the sum of the squares due to error is calculated as the sum of the squared differences between the

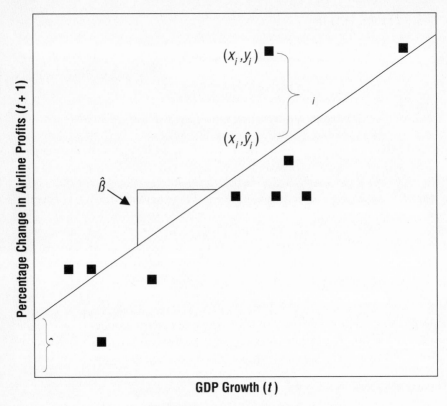

FIGURE 11.2   Regression model

observed values for the dependent variable and the predicted values for the
dependent variable.

The ratio of the sum of the squares due to regression to the total sum
of the squares equals the fraction of variation in the dependent variable
that is explained by variation in the independent variable. It is referred to
as R-squared (R^2), or the coefficient of determination. It ranges in value
from 0 to 1. A high value for R-squared indicates a strong relationship between the dependent and independent variables, whereas a low value for
R-squared indicates a weak relationship.[1]

The square root of R-squared is called the correlation coefficient. It
measures the strength of the association between the dependent and independent variables. In the case of an inverse relationship—that is, where the
slope of the regression line is negative—we adjust the sign of the correlation coefficient to accord with the slope of the regression line. The correlation coefficient ranges in value from –1 to +1.

RESIDUAL ANALYSIS

R-squared is only a first approximation of the validity of the relationship between the dependent and independent variables. Its validity rests on several assumptions: (1) The independent variable (GDP growth in the example) must be measured without error; (2) the relationship between the dependent and independent variables must be linear (as indicated by the regression line); (3) the errors, or residuals, must have constant variance (that is, they must not increase or decrease with the level of the independent variable); (4) the residuals must be independent of each other; and (5) the residuals must be normally distributed. Unless these assumptions are true, the measured relationship between the dependent and independent variables, even if it has a high R-squared, may be spurious.

The importance of the first assumption is self-evident. The importance of some of the remaining assumptions may require elaboration. In order to analyze the residuals, it is convenient to standardize each residual by dividing it by the standard error.[2] We then plot the residuals to determine whether or not the above assumptions are satisfied.

Figure 11.3 shows a plot of standardized residuals. These seem to trace a convex curve. The errors associated with low values of the independent variable are positive; but they become increasingly negative with higher levels of the independent variable and then become positive again as the independent

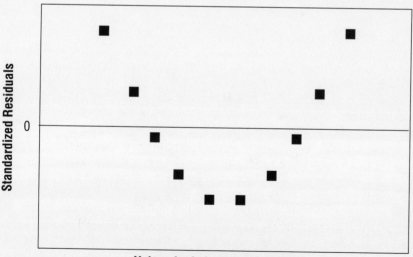

Values for Independent Variable

FIGURE 11.3 Nonlinearity

variable increases still more. In this case, it is apparent that the relationship between the dependent and independent variables violates the assumption of linearity. The dependent variable increases with the independent variable but at a decreasing rate. That is to say, the independent variable has less and less effect on the dependent variable.

This pattern is characteristic of the relationship between the level of advertising expenditures and sales, for example. Suppose a company distributes a product in several regions, and it varies the level of advertising expenditures across these regions to measure advertising's effect. The company will likely observe higher sales in a region where it advertises a little than in a region where it does not advertise at all. And as advertising increases from region to region, corresponding sales should also increase. At some level of sales, however, a region will start to become saturated with the product; additional advertising expenditures will have less and less impact on sales.

The obvious problem with using a linear model when the independent variable has a diminishing effect on the dependent variable is that it will overestimate the dependent variable at high levels of the independent variable. In many instances, we can correct this problem by transforming the values of the independent variable into their reciprocals and then performing a linear regression of the dependent variable on these reciprocals.

Figure 11.4 illustrates a case in which the absolute values of the stan-

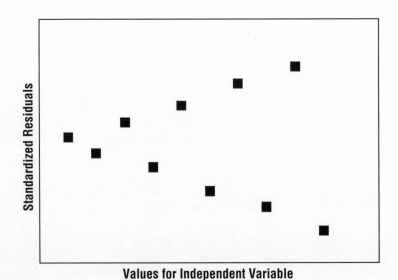

FIGURE 11.4   Heteroskedasticity

dardized residuals increase as the values for the independent variable increase. In this case, the errors involved in predicting the dependent variable will grow larger and larger, the higher the value of the independent variable. Our predictions are subject to larger and larger errors. This problem is known as heteroskedasticity. It can often be ameliorated by transforming the independent variables into their logarithmic values.

Figure 11.5 shows a plot in which all the standardized residuals are positive with the exception of a single, very large negative residual. This large negative residual is called an outlier, and it usually indicates a specious observation or an event that is not likely to recur. If we had included GDP growth in the second quarter of 2001 as one of the observations used to predict airline profitability, for example, we would have grossly overestimated airline profits in the following quarter; both business and personal air travel dropped precipitously in the wake of the September 11 terrorist attack. In this case, we might eliminate the outlying observation and rerun the regression with the remaining data, if we believe that normal travel patterns will resume.

In all these examples, the residuals form patterns rather than random distributions.

In some cases the residuals might be correlated with one another, or autocorrelated. Without examining the residuals explicitly, we test for first-order autocorrelation (correlation between successive residuals) by calcu-

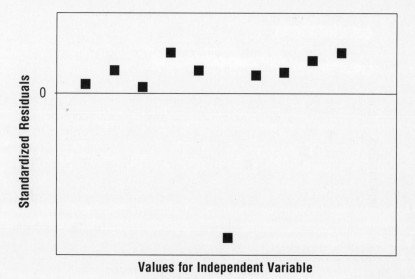

Values for Independent Variable

FIGURE 11.5   Outlier

lating a Durbin-Watson statistic. The Durbin-Watson statistic is approximately equal to $2(1 - R)$, where R equals the correlation coefficient measuring the association between successive residuals. As the Durbin-Watson statistic approaches 2, we should become more confident that the residuals are independent of each other (at least successively). Depending on the number of variables and number of observations, we can determine our level of confidence specifically.

With economic and financial data, it is often useful to transform the data into percentage changes, or first differences. This transformation often reduces autocorrelation.

MULTIPLE LINEAR REGRESSION

We have so far focused on simple linear regressions—that is, regressions between a dependent variable and a single independent variable. In many instances, variation in a dependent variable is explained by variation in several independent variables. Returning to our example of airline profits, we may wish to include percentage changes in energy prices as a second independent variable, given the relatively high operating leverage associated with the airline industry.

We express this multiple regression equation as follows:

$$\hat{Y}_{t+1} = \hat{\alpha} + \hat{\beta}_1 X_{1t} + \hat{\beta}_2 X_{2t} \tag{11.3}$$

where $\hat{\beta}_1$ = GDP growth coefficient
X_{1t} = GDP growth
$\hat{\beta}_2$ = percentage change in energy prices coefficient
X_{2t} = percentage change in energy prices

Here X_{1t} and X_{2t} equal the two independent variables (GDP growth and percentage changes in energy prices), and $\hat{\beta}_1$ and $\hat{\beta}_2$ equal their coefficients.

It seems reasonable to expect that as fuel prices rise, profit margins in the airline industry will fall, and vice versa. This would mean a negative relationship between airline profits and percentage changes in energy prices. Thus $\hat{\beta}_2$ would be a negative value. But an increase in economic activity could increase demand for energy and contribute to a rise in energy prices. Thus the two independent variables, GDP growth and percentage changes in energy prices, may not be independent of each other. This problem is known as multicolinearity.

Suppose we run two simple linear regressions using two independent variables. If the variables are independent of each other, then the sum of the R-squares from the two regressions will equal the R-squared from a multiple linear regression combining the two variables. To the extent the independent variables are correlated with each other, however, the R-squared from the multiple regression will be less than the sum from the two simple regressions.

When the independent variables in a multiple regression are colinear, we must take care in interpreting their coefficients. The coefficients $\hat{\beta}_1$ and $\hat{\beta}_2$ in equation (11.3) represent the marginal sensitivity of a change in airline profits to a one-unit increase in GDP growth and to a one-unit increase in the percentage change in energy prices in the prior quarter. If $\hat{\beta}_1$ equals 0.7 percent and $\hat{\beta}_2$ equals -0.15 percent, for example, we would expect airline profits to increase by 0.7 percent if GDP growth rose 1 percent in the prior quarter and energy prices remained constant. If the percentage change in energy prices increased by 1 percent in the prior quarter and GDP remained constant, we would expect airline profits to decrease by 0.15 percent. To the extent there is multicolinearity between the independent variables, these responses would not equal the sensitivity of airline profits to the same independent variables as measured by simple linear regressions.

Regression analysis is a powerful tool for the financial analyst. But, as I have attempted to demonstrate, the summary statistics from regression analysis can be misleading.

CHAPTER 12

Factor Methods

Financial analysts are concerned with factors, or common sources of risk that contribute to changes in security prices. By identifying such factors, analysts may be able to control a portfolio's risk more efficiently and perhaps even improve its return.

I will describe in general terms two approaches often used to identify factors. The first approach, called factor analysis, allows analysts to isolate factors by observing common variations in the returns of different securities. These factors are merely statistical constructs that represent some underlying source of risk; that source may or may not be observable. The second approach, called cross-sectional regression analysis, requires that we define a set of security attributes that measure exposure to an underlying factor, and determine whether differences across security returns correspond to differences in these security attributes.

FACTOR ANALYSIS

I begin with a nonfinancial, hopefully intuitive, example. I will apply the insights gained by this example to show how we might go about identifying the factors that underlie the stock market.

Suppose we wish to determine whether there are common sources of scholastic aptitude, based upon the grades of 1,000 students in the following nine courses: algebra, biology, calculus, chemistry, composition, French, geometry, literature, and physics. We proceed by first computing the correlation between the algebra grades of students and their grades in each of the other eight courses. Then we compute the correlations between their biology grades and their grades in each of the seven other courses. We continue until we have computed the correlations between the grades of every pair of courses—36 correlations in all. Table 12.1 displays these hypothetical correlations.

That all these correlations are positive suggests the presence of a

TABLE 12.1 Correlations of Student Grades

	Biology	Calculus	Chemistry	Composition	French	Geometry	Literature	Physics
Algebra	0.3546	0.8043	0.4497	0.2681	0.2062	0.6440	0.1979	0.3881
Biology		0.3900	0.9400	0.4900	0.2998	0.4231	0.2446	0.6845
Calculus			0.4200	0.2900	0.2249	0.8039	0.2998	0.4563
Chemistry				0.3700	0.2794	0.3977	0.3156	0.6921
Composition					0.5928	0.2369	0.7416	0.2662
French						0.1845	0.4785	0.2384
Geometry							0.2537	0.3540
Literature								0.2580

pervasive factor which is probably related to cognitive ability or study habits. In addition to this pervasive factor, there appear to be three other factors, or commonalities, in performance.

First, the variation in algebra grades is highly correlated with the variation in calculus and geometry grades. Moreover, performance in calculus is highly correlated with performance in geometry. The grades in these three courses, however, are not nearly as highly correlated with the grades in any of the other six courses. We might thus conclude there is a common aptitude that underlies performance in these three courses.

Second, performance in biology is highly correlated with performance in chemistry and physics, and performance in chemistry is highly correlated with performance in physics. Again, performance in these courses does not correspond as closely with performance in any of the other courses. We might conclude there is a common source of aptitude associated with biology, chemistry, and physics.

Finally, the grades in composition, French, and literature are all more highly correlated with each other than with the grades in any of the other courses. This leads us to deduce the presence of a third factor.

Our next task is to identify these factors. Here we must rely on our intuition. We might reasonably conclude that one of the common sources of scholastic aptitude is skill in mathematics or quantitative methods, because we observe high correlations among performances in the three math courses. Aptitude in science appears to be another common factor, given the high correlations in the three science courses. The remaining source of common variation in course grades pertains to composition, French, and literature; we might label this factor verbal aptitude.

We do not actually observe the underlying factors. We merely observe that a student who performs well in algebra is more likely to perform well in geometry and calculus than in French. From this observation, we infer that there is a particular aptitude that helps to explain performance in algebra, calculus, and geometry but not in French. This aptitude is the factor.

We should note that these results do not imply that performance in a given course is explained by a single factor. If such were the case, we would observe only correlations of 1 and 0. This point is underscored by the fact that the variation in physics grades is more highly correlated with grades in algebra, calculus, and geometry than it is with grades in composition, French, and literature. This result is intuitively pleasing, in that physics depends more on mathematics than do composition, French, and literature. We might therefore conclude that performance in physics is primarily explained by aptitude in science, but that it is also somewhat dependent on math skills.

Now we will substitute stock performance for scholastic performance.

FACTORS IN STOCK RETURNS

Suppose we wish to determine the factors that underlie performance in the stock market. We begin by calculating the daily returns of a representative sample of stocks during some period. In this study, the stocks are analogous to courses, the days in the period are analogous to students, and the returns are analogous to grades.

To isolate the factors that underlie stock market performance, we begin by computing the correlations between the daily returns of each stock and the returns on every other stock. Then we seek out groups consisting of stocks that are highly correlated with each other but not with the stocks outside the group.

For example, we might observe that stock 1's returns are highly correlated with the returns of stocks 12, 21, 39, 47, 55, 70, and 92, and that the returns of the other stocks in this group are all highly correlated with each other. From this observation, we might conclude that the returns of these stocks are explained at least in part by a common factor. We proceed to isolate other groups of stocks whose returns are highly correlated with each other, until we isolate all the groups that seem to respond to a common source of risk.

Our next task is to identify the underlying sources of risk for each group. Suppose a particular group consists of utility companies, financial companies, and a few other companies that come from miscellaneous industries but that all have especially high debt-to-equity ratios. We might reasonably conclude that interest rate risk is a common source of variation in the returns of this group of stocks. Another group might be dominated by stocks whose earnings depend on the level of energy prices; we might thus hypothesize that the price of energy is another source of risk. Yet another group might include companies across many different industries that have in common the fact that they derive a large fraction of their earnings from foreign operations; we might conclude that exchange rate risk is yet another factor.

We must first rely on our intuition to identify the factor that underlies the common variation in returns among the member stocks. Then we can test our intuition as follows. We define a variable that serves as a proxy for the *unanticipated* change in the factor value. We regress the returns of stocks that seem to depend on our hypothesized factor with the unanticipated component of the factor value. It is important that we isolate the unanticipated component of the factor value, because stock prices should not respond to an anticipated change in a factor. It is new information that causes investors to reappraise the prospects of a company.

Suppose, for example, we identify inflation as a factor. If the Consumer Price Index (CPI) is expected to rise 0.5 percent in a given month and it rises by precisely that amount, then the prices on inflation-sensitive stocks should not change in response. If the CPI rises 1.5 percent, however, then the prices of these stocks should change in response. In order to test whether a particular time series represents a factor, we must therefore model the unanticipated component of its changes.

A reasonable approach for modeling the unanticipated component of inflation is to regress inflation on its prior values under the assumption that the market's outlook is conditioned by past experience. The errors, or residuals, from this regression represent the unanticipated component of inflation. We thus regress the stock returns we believe are sensitive to inflation on these residuals to determine if inflation is indeed a factor.

The approach I have just described is heuristic. It is designed to expose factors by identifying groups of stocks with common price variations. Its intuitive appeal is offset by the fact that it produces factors that explain only part of the variation in returns. Moreover, these factors are not necessarily independent of each other.

With a more advanced mathematical technique—called maximum likelihood factor analysis—we identify several linear combinations of securities, comprising both long and short positions, which explain virtually all the covariation in the returns of a sample of securities.[1] These linear functions are called eigenvectors, and the sensitivity of a particular security to an eigenvector is called an eigenvalue.[2]

Instead of groups of highly correlated stocks, this approach yields precise linear combinations of stocks that represent independent sources of common variation in returns. In effect, the eigenvectors are the factors. Not only are the factors derived in this fashion independent of each other, but we can derive as many factors as necessary to explain as much of the covariation in a portfolio as we would like.

In order to label these factors, we proceed as described earlier. We determine whether the returns of these linear combinations of stocks correlate with the unanticipated changes in the variables that proxy for the factors. Within this context, we represent a security's return as follows.

$$R_i = \alpha_i + b_{i1}F_1 + b_{i2}F_2 + \ldots + b_{in}F_n + \varepsilon_i \qquad (12.1)$$

where R_i = the return of security i
       α_i = a constant
       b_{i1} = the sensitivity of security i to factor 1
       b_{i2} = the sensitivity of security i to factor 2
       b_{in} = the sensitivity of security i to factor n

F_1 = the first factor representing common variation in security returns

F_2 = the second factor representing common variation in security returns

F_n = the nth factor representing common variation in security returns

ε_i = variation in return that is specific to the ith security

ISSUES OF INTERPRETATION

Factors derived through factor analysis, whether we employ the heuristic approach described earlier or the more formal approach, are not always amenable to interpretation. It may be that a particular factor cannot be proxied by a measurable economic or financial variable. Instead, the factor may reflect a combination of several influences, some perhaps offsetting, that came together in a particular way unique to the selected measurement period and the chosen sample of securities. In short, factors may not be definable. Moreover, factors derived through factor analysis may not persist through time, or factor 1 in one test may be factor 5 in another test.

We thus face the following tradeoff with factor analysis. Although we can account for nearly all a sample's common variation in return with independent factors, we may not be able to assign meaning to these factors, or even know if they represent the same sources of risk from period to period or sample to sample. In the next section we consider an alternative procedure called cross-sectional regression analysis.

CROSS-SECTIONAL REGRESSION ANALYSIS

Whereas factor analysis reveals covariation in returns and challenges us to identify the sources of this covariation, cross-sectional regression analysis requires us to specify the sources of return covariation and challenges us to affirm that these sources do indeed correspond to differences in return.

Here is how we proceed. Based upon our intuition and prior knowledge, we hypothesize attributes that we believe correspond to differences in stock returns. For example, we might believe that highly leveraged companies perform differently from companies with low debt, or that performance varies according to industry affiliation. In either case, we define an attribute—not a factor. The factor that causes low-debt companies to perform differently from high-debt companies most likely has something to do with interest rates. Industry affiliation, of course, measures sensitivity to factors that affect industry performance, such as defense spending or competition.

Once we specify a set of attributes that we feel measure sensitivity to the common sources of risk, we perform the following regression. We regress the returns across a large sample of stocks during a given period—say, a month—on the attribute values for each of the stocks as of the beginning of that month. Then we repeat this regression over many different periods. If the coefficients of the attribute values are not 0 and are significant in a sufficiently high number of the regressions, we conclude that differences in return across the stocks relate to differences in their attribute values.

According to this approach, a security's return in a particular period can be expressed as follows:

$$R_i = \alpha + \lambda_1 b_{i1} + \lambda_2 b_{i2} + \ldots + \lambda_n b_{in} + \varepsilon_i \qquad (12.2)$$

where R_i = the return of security i
  α = a constant
  λ_1 = the marginal return to attribute 1
  λ_2 = the marginal return to attribute 2
  λ_n = the marginal return to attribute n
  b_{i1} = attribute 1 of security i
  b_{i2} = attribute 2 of security i
  b_{in} = attribute n of security i
  ε_i = the unexplained component of security i's return

It is not necessary for the coefficients in the above formula to be significantly positive or negative on average over all the regressions. In some periods there may be positive returns associated with an attribute and in some periods there may be negative returns associated with an attribute; hence, the average value for a coefficient over many regressions may be 0. Nonetheless, the attribute would still be important if the coefficient were a number other than 0 in a large number of the regressions.

We can measure the extent to which a coefficient is significant in a particular regression by its t-statistic. The t-statistic equals the value of the coefficient divided by its standard error. A t-statistic of 1.96 implies that the likelihood of observing a significant coefficient by chance is only 5 percent. In order to be confident that a particular attribute helps to explain differences across security returns, we should observe a t-statistic for its coefficient of 1.96 or greater in more than 5 percent of the regressions. Otherwise, it is possible that the attribute occasionally appears significant merely by chance.

WHICH APPROACH IS BETTER?

I have described two approaches for identifying common sources of variation in stock performance—factor analysis and cross-sectional regression analysis. There are pros and cons with both approaches. Through factor analysis, we can isolate independent sources of common variation in returns that explain nearly all of a portfolio's risk. It is not always possible, however, to attach meaning to these sources of risk. They may represent accidental and temporary confluences of myriad factors. Because we cannot precisely define these factors, it is difficult to know whether they are stable or simply an artifact of the chosen measurement period or sample.

As an alternative to factor analysis, we can define a set of security attributes we know are observable and measurable and, through cross-sectional regression analysis, test them to determine if they help to explain differences in returns across securities. With this approach we know the identity of the attributes, but we are limited in the amount of return variation we are able to explain. Moreover, because the attributes are typically codependent, it is difficult to understand the true relationship between each attribute and the return. Which approach is more appropriate depends on the importance we attach to the identity of the factors versus the amount of return variation we hope to explain with independent factors.

WHY BOTHER WITH FACTORS?

At this point you may question why we should bother to search for factors or attributes in the first place. Why not address risk by considering the entire covariance matrix, as originally prescribed by Markowitz?[3]

There are two reasons why we might prefer to address risk through a limited number of factors. A security's sensitivity to a common source of risk may be more stable than its sensitivity to the returns of all the other securities in the portfolio. If this is true, then we can control a portfolio's risk more reliably by managing its exposure to these common sources.

The second reason has to do with parsimony. If we limit the number of sources of risk, we might find it is easier to control risk and to improve return simply because we are faced with fewer parameters to estimate.

I have attempted to provide a flavor for the statistical methodology that underlies the search for common sources of return variation, without prejudice toward one method or the other. The choice of a particular approach should depend on one's specific needs, one's biases, and a thorough understanding of the merits and limitations of each approach.

CHAPTER 13

Estimating Volatility: Part I

Volatility is important to financial analysts for several reasons. Perhaps most obvious, estimates of volatility, together with information about central tendency, allow us to assess the likelihood of experiencing a particular outcome. For example, we may be interested in the likelihood of achieving a certain level of wealth by a particular date, depending on our choice of alternative investment strategies. In order to assess the likelihood of achieving such an objective, we must estimate the volatility of returns for each of the alternative investment strategies.

Financial analysts are often faced with the task of combining various risky assets to form efficient portfolios—portfolios that offer the highest expected return at a particular level of risk.[1] Again, it is necessary to estimate the volatility of the component assets. Also, the valuation of an option requires us to estimate the volatility of the underlying asset. These are but a few examples of how volatility estimates are used in financial analysis.

HISTORICAL VOLATILITY

The most commonly used measure of volatility in financial analysis is standard deviation. Standard deviation is computed by measuring the difference between the value of each observation in a sample and the sample's mean, squaring each difference, taking the average of the squares and then determining the square root of this average.

Suppose, for example, that during a particular month we observe the daily returns shown in column 1 in Table 13.1. The average of the returns in column 1 equals 0.2775 percent. Column 2 shows the difference between each observed return and this average return. Column 3 shows the squared values of these differences. The average of the squared differences, 0.0158 percent, equals the variance of the returns.[2] The square

TABLE 13.1   Standard Deviation of Return

Day	1 Return	2 Return—Average	3 Squared Difference
1	0.010000	0.007225	0.000052
2	0.015000	0.012225	0.000149
3	0.021000	0.018225	0.000332
4	−0.004000	−0.006775	0.000046
5	0.010000	0.007225	0.000052
6	−0.014000	−0.016775	0.000281
7	0.004500	0.001725	0.000003
8	−0.007500	−0.010275	0.000106
9	0.010000	0.007225	0.000052
10	0.014000	0.011225	0.000126
11	−0.020000	−0.022775	0.000519
12	0.010000	0.007225	0.000052
13	−0.015000	−0.017775	0.000316
14	0.003500	0.000725	0.000001
15	−0.003000	−0.005775	0.000033
16	0.010000	0.007225	0.000052
17	0.000000	−0.002775	0.000008
18	−0.006000	−0.008775	0.000077
19	−0.012000	−0.014775	0.000218
20	0.029000	0.026225	0.000688
Average	0.002775		0.000158
Square root			0.012577

root of the variance, 1.2577 percent, equals the standard deviation of the daily returns.

In this example, the standard deviation measures the volatility of daily returns. It is typical in financial analysis to annualize the standard deviation. Unlike rates of return, which increase proportionately with time, standard deviations increase with the square root of time.

There are two equivalent approaches for converting a daily standard deviation into an annual standard deviation. We can reconvert the standard deviation back to a variance by squaring it. Then we multiply the variance by 260 (the number of trading days in a year) and take the square root of this value to get the annualized standard deviation:

$$0.012577^2 = 0.000158$$
$$0.000158 \times 260 = 0.0411$$
$$\sqrt{0.0411} = 0.2028$$

Alternatively, we can multiply the daily standard deviation by the square root of 260 to determine the annualized value.

$$\sqrt{260} = 16.1245$$
$$0.012577 \times 16.1245 = 0.2028$$

The approach I have just described for estimating the standard deviation from historical returns yields an estimate that may lead to inexact inferences about the dispersion of returns. The inexactitude arises because the dispersion of investment returns conforms to a lognormal distribution, rather than a normal distribution, owing to the effect of compounding. We can attain more precise inferences by calculating the standard deviation of the logarithms of 1 plus the returns.[3] Table 13.2 shows those calculations.[4]

TABLE 13.2   Standard Deviation of Return

Day	1 ln(1+Return)	2 ln(1+Return) – Average	3 Squared Difference
1	0.009950	0.007258	0.000053
2	0.014889	0.012196	0.000149
3	0.020783	0.018090	0.000327
4	–0.004008	–0.006701	0.000045
5	0.009950	0.007258	0.000053
6	–0.014099	–0.016791	0.000282
7	0.004490	0.001797	0.000003
8	–0.007528	–0.010221	0.000104
9	0.009950	0.007258	0.000053
10	0.013903	0.011210	0.000126
11	–0.020203	–0.022895	0.000524
12	0.009950	0.007258	0.000053
13	–0.015114	–0.017806	0.000317
14	0.003494	0.000801	0.000001
15	–0.003005	–0.005697	0.000032
16	0.009950	0.007258	0.000053
17	0.000000	–0.002693	0.000007
18	–0.006018	–0.008711	0.000076
19	–0.012073	–0.014765	0.000218
20	0.028587	0.025895	0.000671
Average	0.002693		0.000157
Square root			0.012541
Annualized standard deviation			0.202220

Comparing the standard deviation from Table 13.1 with the standard deviation from Table 13.2, we see that it does not make much difference which approach we use given this short measurement interval. As the measurement interval lengthens, however, the distinction becomes more important.

IMPLIED VOLATILITY

As we have seen, estimating volatility from historical data is fairly straightforward. Unfortunately, the result may not be the best estimate if volatility is unstable through time. In the fall of 1979, for example, the Federal Reserve changed its operating policy with respect to its management of the money supply and interest rates. Over the 10 years ending in 1978, the annualized standard deviation for long-term corporate bonds was a little less than 8 percent. In the subsequent 10-year period, from 1979 through 1988, the annualized standard deviation for long-term corporate bonds rose to more than 13 percent. Clearly, historical precedent made a poor guide for estimating bond market volatility in the 1980s.

As an alternative to historical data, we can infer the investment community's consensus outlook for the volatilities of many assets by examining the prices at which options on these assets trade. These implied volatilities presumably reflect all current information that impinges on an asset's volatility.

The value of an option depends on five factors: the current price of the underlying asset; the strike price, or price at which the option can be exercised; the time remaining until expiration; the riskless rate of interest; and the volatility of the underlying asset. We know the strike price and the time remaining until expiration from the terms of the option contract. The price of the underlying asset and the riskless rate of interest are observable from a variety of market quote services. The only factor that we do not know with certainty is the volatility of the underlying asset. In order to determine volatility, we substitute various values into the option pricing formula until the solution to this formula equals the price at which the option is trading.

Consider a call option with 90 days to expiration and a strike price of $295, written on an underlying asset currently priced at $300. Suppose the annualized riskless rate of interest is 8 percent and the option trades for $15. In order to determine the standard deviation, or implied volatility, consistent with the price of this option, we start by assuming some value for volatility and use this value in the following Black-Scholes option-pricing formula.

$$C = S \times N(d) - Xe^{-rT} \times N\left(d - \sigma\sqrt{T}\right) \qquad (13.1)$$

where S = price of underlying asset
         X = strike price
         T = time remaining until expiration
         r = instantaneous riskless rate of interest

$$d = \left[\frac{\ln\left(\dfrac{S}{X}\right) + \left(\dfrac{r + \sigma^2}{2}\right)T}{\sigma\sqrt{T}}\right]$$

ln( ) = natural log
   σ = standard deviation (volatility) of underlying asset returns
   $N($) = cumulative normal distribution

Suppose we use the annualized historical volatility over the previous 90 days—say, 20 percent. By substituting this value and the values we assigned earlier into equation (13.1), we find that d equals 0.401. Thus C, the option value, is calculated as:

$$C = 300 \times N(0.401) - 295e^{-0.077(90/365)} \times N\left(0.401 - 0.2\sqrt{90/365}\right)$$

$$C = 17.69$$

This estimated value is greater than the price at which the option currently trades. We must therefore lower our estimate for volatility. Suppose we next try a value of 12 percent. Based on this volatility assumption, the option value equals $13.50; this is less than the actual price of $15, implying that we should raise our estimate.

If we continue substituting various volatility values into the Black-Scholes formula, we will eventually discover that a volatility estimate of 14.96 percent is consistent with an option value of $15—the price at which the option is currently trading. This 14.96 percent is the implied volatility, given the current values for the underlying asset, the option, and the riskless rate, and given the terms of the option contract.

NEWTON-RAPHSON METHOD

Of course, as we are solving for the implied volatility, the prices of the underlying asset and the option may be changing. We need a reasonably quick way to arrive at the implied volatility. The Newton-Raphson Method is one way.

According to the Newton-Raphson Method, we start with some reasonable estimate for volatility and evaluate the option using this estimate. Unless we are unusually lucky, however, we will not arrive at the correct value for implied volatility on our first try. We therefore revise our initial volatility estimate by subtracting an amount equal to the estimated option value minus the option's actual price, divided by the derivative of the option formula with respect to volatility evaluated at our estimate for volatility. This derivative is shown below:

$$\frac{\partial C}{\partial \sigma} = S\sqrt{T}\left(\frac{1}{\sqrt{2\pi}}\right)e^{-d^2/2} \tag{13.2}$$

where π = 3.1416
    e = 2.71828

Our earlier example used an assumed volatility of 20 percent. Using this assumption, the derivative for the Newton-Raphson Method is:

$$\frac{\partial C}{\partial \sigma} = 300\sqrt{90/365}\left(\frac{1}{\sqrt{2\pi}}\right)e^{-0.401^2/2}$$

$$\frac{\partial C}{\partial \sigma} = 54.64$$

The volatility of 20 percent resulted in an option value of $17.69. We compute the Newton-Raphson volatility estimate as follows:

$$N - R = 0.20 - \frac{17.69 - 15}{54.64} = 0.1507$$

A volatility estimate of 15.07 percent results in an option value of $15.06. One more iteration yields a volatility estimate of 14.96 percent, for an option price of $15.

METHOD OF BISECTION

The efficiency of the Newton-Raphson Method depends to a certain extent on the choice of the initial volatility estimate. An alternative search procedure, which tends to be less sensitive to the initial volatility estimate, is called the Method of Bisection.[5] This approach is more intuitive.

We start by choosing a low estimate for volatility corresponding to a low option value and a high estimate for volatility corresponding to a high option value.

For example, suppose we start with a low estimate of 10 percent and a high estimate of 30 percent. Given the assumptions from our previous example, the corresponding option values are $12.56 and $23.27. Our next estimate for volatility is found by interpolation, as shown below:

$$New\ Estimate = \sigma_L + (C - C_L)\left[\frac{\sigma_H - \sigma_L}{C_H - C_L}\right] \qquad (13.3)$$

$$0.1456 = 0.1 + (15 - 12.56) \times (0.3 - 0.1)/(23.27 - 12.56)$$
$$0.1494 = 0.1456 + (15 - 14.79) \times (0.3 - 0.1456)/(23.27 - 14.79)$$
$$0.1496 = 0.1494 + (15 - 14.99) \times (0.3 - 0.1494)/(23.27 - 14.99)$$

If the option value corresponding to our interpolated estimate for volatility is below the actual option price, we replace our low volatility estimate with the interpolated estimate and repeat the calculation. If the estimated option value is above the actual option price, we replace the high volatility estimate with the interpolated estimate and proceed accordingly. When the option value corresponding to our volatility estimate equals the actual price of the option, we have arrived at the implied volatility for that option.

HISTORICAL VERSUS IMPLIED VOLATILITY

Is it better to estimate volatility from historical observations or to infer it from the prices at which options trade? The answer, of course, depends on the quality of the inputs. If volatility is stationary through time, and we have reliable prices from which to estimate returns, then historical volatility is a reasonably good indicator of subsequent volatility. Unfortunately, and especially over short measurement intervals, nonrecurring events or conditions often cause volatility to shift up or down temporarily, so that historical volatility will over- or underestimate subsequent volatility. To the extent the investment community recognizes the transitory nature of these nonrecurring events, implied volatility may provide a superior estimate of subsequent volatility. In estimating implied volatility, however, we must be sure to use contemporaneous observations for the inputs to the Black-Scholes formula.

Yet another method for estimating volatility uses a technique known as ARCH, an acronym for Autoregressive Conditional Heteroskedast-icity. Essentially, ARCH and related models incorporate the time-series dynamics of past volatility to forecast volatility, which is the topic of the next chapter.

CHAPTER 14

Estimating Volatility: Part II

Choose the correct answer:
Autoregressive conditional heteroskedasticity (ARCH) is:

1. A psychological disorder characterized by reversion to early behavior patterns when confronted with unpleasant childhood memories.
2. In evolution, reversion to more primitive attributes resulting from inadequate diversity within a species.
3. A statistical procedure in which the dependent variable in a regression equation is modeled as a function of the time-varying properties of the error term.

To the uninitiated, all the above definitions might seem equally plausible. Moreover, the correct definition (3) may still not yield an intuitively satisfying description of ARCH.

This chapter is intended as a child's guide to ARCH, which is to say it contains no equations. My goal is to decipher the cryptic jargon of ARCH so that at the very least you will feel comfortable attending social events hosted by members of the American Association of Statisticians. Of course, you should not expect that familiarity with ARCH will necessarily cause you to have fun at these events.

NORMAL ASSUMPTIONS OF VOLATILITY

In the preceding chapter, I reviewed two procedures for estimating volatility—one by which we estimate volatility directly from historical observations, and an alternative procedure by which we infer volatility from the prices at which options on the underlying assets trade. One of the implicit assumptions of both these approaches is that volatility changes unpredictably, which means it is uncorrelated with previous levels of volatility.

For example, if we calculate the differences between monthly stock returns and their mean, and regress the squared values of these differences (called the errors squared) in month t against their values in month $t-1$, we would not expect to detect a significant relationship. More specifically, the intercept of the regression line should be close to the average value of the errors squared, and the slope of the regression line should not differ significantly from zero.[1] Figure 14.1 shows this relationship impressionistically.

The parameters of the linear regression model depicted in Figure 14.1 probably would fail to indicate that the errors squared are autocorrelated, because the slope of the regression line is flat and the intercept seems close to the average value of the observations. We should not necessarily assume, however, that the errors squared are serially independent (uncorrelated with their prior values) simply because the regression parameters from a linear regression are insignificant. We must look further and examine the residuals around the fitted values.

The residuals equal the differences between the actual values for the errors squared and the values predicted from the regression line. If the errors squared were serially independent, the residuals would be distributed randomly around an expected value of zero. If the residuals satisfied this condition, we would describe them as *homoskedastic*.

NONLINEARITY

Suppose high values for the errors squared occur in clusters. It might still be the case that the coefficients from the linear regression of the errors squared on their prior values are insignificant. If, however, the errors squared are related to their prior values in some nonlinear fashion, this

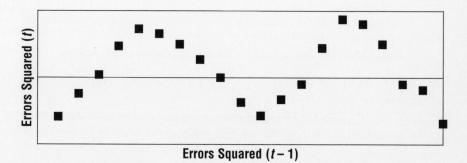

FIGURE 14.1   Variance as a function of its prior values

nonlinear relationship might be revealed by the patterns formed by the residuals around the fitted values.

Reexamining Figure 14.1, for example, we notice that positive residuals (where the regression line underestimates the actual errors squared) tend to be followed by more positive residuals and that negative residuals appear in groups as well. We refer to such patterns in the residuals as heteroskedasticity.

We can correct for this apparent nonlinearity by regressing the residuals in period t on the errors squared in period $t - 1$. We then add the intercept and slope from this regression equation to the intercept and slope from the original regression of the errors squared on their prior values. In effect, we conjecture that variance—the average value of the errors squared—is conditioned on this heteroskedasticity. This explains the term, autoregressive conditional heteroskedasticity.

The procedure is summarized as follows.

1. Subtract the observed returns from their mean and square these differences to calculate the errors squared.
2. Regress the errors squared in period t on the errors squared in period $t - 1$.
3. Subtract the fitted errors squared in period t from the observed errors squared in period $t - 1$.
4. Regress the residuals from step 3 in period t on the errors squared in period $t - 1$.
5. Add the intercept and slope from the regression equation in step 4 to the intercept and slope from the regression equation in step 2 to form a new prediction equation for variance.

The resulting equation should be a more efficient predictor of variance than the equation resulting from the original regression model of the errors squared on their prior values, to the extent that the residuals from the original model are heteroskedastic.

This sequence of linear regressions is a heuristic approach for estimating ARCH models and not the typical estimation procedure. I chose to describe this approach because most financial analysts are familiar with linear regression models. The standard methodology used to estimate ARCH models is called maximum likelihood estimation (MLE). MLE is used when the residuals from a linear regression model are not random. It identifies the coefficients of the prediction equation that give the highest probability of predicting the values that are actually observed. It is sometimes the case with maximum likelihood estimation that the coefficients are discovered through a trial and error process.

Now that you understand ARCH, I must inform you that the preferred model for estimating variance from its past values is not ARCH. Rather it is GARCH, which stands for generalized autoregressive conditional heteroskedasticity.[2] The main distinction between ARCH and GARCH is that GARCH models use lagged values for the dependent variable in addition to the residuals to estimate variance, whereas ARCH models rely only on the residuals.[3]

SUMMARY

Variance may be related to its past values. However, we may fail to detect this autoregressive relationship with a linear regression model of the errors squared if the relationship is nonlinear. If we have reason to suspect a nonlinear relationship, we should test the residuals between the actual values for the errors squared and the fitted values from an autoregressive equation for heteroskedasticity. If there is significant heteroskedasticity in the residuals, we should model the heteroskedasticity and incorporate it in our forecast equation for variance.

CHAPTER 15

Hypothesis Testing

Financial analysts work with noisy data. As a consequence, it is often difficult to determine whether observed results are due to a real effect or simply reflect noise. This chapter reviews the methodology referred to as hypothesis testing to distinguish real effects from noise.

HYPOTHESIS TEST FOR COMPARING PROPORTIONS FROM A SMALL SAMPLE

Suppose we wish to test whether or not a coin is fair. We begin by defining the null hypothesis and the alternative hypothesis. In this example, the null hypothesis, denoted by H_0, is that the coin is fair. The alternative hypothesis, denoted by H_A, is that the coin is biased.

Next we need to compute a test statistic. We do so by repeatedly tossing the coin and observing how often it comes up heads and how often it comes up tails.

Finally, we need to compute a P value, which is the probability that the test statistic would occur if the null hypothesis were true. The estimation of the P value depends on the notion of a Bernoulli trial.

A Bernoulli trial has three properties: (1) Its result must be characterized by a success or a failure; (2) the probability of a success must be the same for all of the trials; (3) the outcome of each trial must be independent of the outcomes of the other trials. The toss of a coin clearly satisfies the conditions of a Bernoulli trial.

The fraction of successes from a sequence of Bernoulli trials is called a binomial random variable and serves as the test statistic in this example. The P value, which is the probability of observing a particular test statistic from a binomial distribution, is given by equation (15.1).

$$\Pr(X) = \frac{n!}{X!\,(n-X)!}\,p^X (1-p)^{n-X} \tag{15.1}$$

where $\Pr(X)$ = probability of X heads in n tosses

    n = number of tosses in the sample

    p = expected proportion of heads resulting from tossing a fair coin

    X = number of heads observed in the sample

    ! = factorial (for example, $5! = 5 \times 4 \times 3 \times 2 \times 1$)

Suppose we toss the coin 10 times and observe 8 heads. In our example, n equals 10, p equals 0.50, and X equals 8. If we substitute these values into equation (15.1), we find that there is only a 4.39 percent probability of observing 8 heads in 10 tosses. The probability of observing 9 heads equals 0.98 percent and the probability of observing 10 heads equals 0.10 percent. Thus the probability of observing 8 or more heads equals 5.47 percent. By symmetry, the probability of observing 2 or fewer heads also equals 5.47 percent. Thus there is a 10.94 percent chance of observing 8 or more or 2 or fewer heads, given a fair coin. If we require 95 percent confidence, we would fail to reject the null hypothesis that the coin is fair.

It is important to note that we can never *accept* the null hypothesis. We can reject the null hypothesis or we can fail to reject the null hypothesis. (This is the only term I know of that constitutes a triple negative.) In the event we fail to reject the null hypothesis, we conclude the test lacks sufficient power to accept the alternative hypothesis.

HYPOTHESIS TEST FOR COMPARING PROPORTIONS FROM A LARGE SAMPLE

Now let us explore an investment example. Suppose we are evaluating an equity portfolio manager who claims she can identify companies that are likely to be takeover targets, and we arrive at a mutually acceptable definition of a takeover target. At the end of a one-year measurement period we observe that 10 percent of the companies in her portfolio were the target of takeover attempts. Should we attribute this result to her skill or to chance?

In this example the null hypothesis is that the fraction of takeover targets in her portfolio is due purely to chance. The alternative hypothesis is that she is skillful in selecting takeover targets. In order to test which hypothesis is true, we again need to develop a test statistic to weigh the evidence.

We proceed as follows. We first compute the fraction of companies that were takeover targets in the entire universe of stocks from which she selected her portfolio. Suppose there are 5,000 companies in the universe and 7 percent of them were takeover targets during the period for which she is being evaluated.

Moreover, suppose there were no commonalities among them to suggest that a particular type of company was more likely than other companies to be a takeover target. Hence we conclude that each company in the universe has the same 7 percent probability of being a takeover target.

Finally, assume that each remaining company's chance of being a takeover target is independent of the status of the companies already selected. This assumption is not literally true. When the portfolio manager selects companies for her portfolio, she slightly changes the odds that the remaining companies in the universe are takeover targets. Because the universe is so large and her sample is relatively small, however, the effect is negligible.

The process of selecting a company from a universe and determining whether or not it turns out to be a takeover target is a Bernoulli trial. Thus the fraction of takeover targets in her portfolio is a binomial random variable.

In this example, we are dealing with a relatively large sample (100 companies versus 10 coin tosses). With a large sample size, we can use the normal distribution to approximate the binomial distribution. As a rule of thumb, we can use the normal distribution to estimate the P value (probability of rejecting the null hypothesis when it is true) as long as both the sample size multiplied by the fraction of successes and the sample size multiplied by the quantity, 1 minus the fraction of successes, are greater than 5. This condition is satisfied in this example because the products of 100 times 0.10 and 100 times 0.90 both exceed 5.

Again we must compute a test statistic to measure how far the proportion of takeover targets in her portfolio differs from the proportion of takeover targets in the universe. The appropriate test statistic is given by equation (15.2).

$$z = \frac{p_p - p_u}{\sqrt{p_u(1 - p_u)/n}} \qquad (15.2)$$

where p_p = proportion of companies in her portfolio that were takeover targets

p_u = proportion of companies in the universe that were takeover targets

n = number of stocks in her portfolio

The term $p_u(1 - p_u)$ equals the variance of the proportion of takeover targets in the universe.

In our example, the test statistic z (also called the z value) equals 1.18.

If we look this value up in a normal distribution table, we find that there is a 12 percent chance that her success rate would occur even if the null hypothesis were true. Thus, if we wished to be 95 percent confident, we would fail to reject the null hypothesis and conclude instead that the hypothesis test lacks sufficient power to detect her potential skill.

For a 5 percent or lower probability of rejecting the null hypothesis when it is true, the test statistic for a normal distribution must equal or exceed 1.645, assuming the portfolio manager does not have negative skill. This type of test is called a right-handed test because we base our rejection of the null hypothesis on whether or not the area under the normal distribution curve to the right of the test statistic is greater than or equal to our prechosen threshold (5 percent in this example).

With simple algebra, we can determine how many takeover targets, expressed as a fraction of the number of stocks in her portfolio, she would have to identify before we should accept the alternative hypothesis that she is skillful. This formula is given by equation (15.3).

$$p_p = p_u + z \sqrt{\frac{p_u(1 - p_u)}{n}} \tag{15.3}$$

Based on a portfolio of 100 stocks and the fact that 7 percent of the companies in the universe from which she chose her portfolio were takeover targets, 11.2 percent of the companies in her portfolio must be takeover targets before we should characterize her as skillful.

HYPOTHESIS TEST FOR LARGE SAMPLE MEANS

In the previous example, we used the binomial distribution as approximated by the normal distribution to test the hypothesis that the proportion of takeover targets in a particular portfolio was significantly greater than the proportion of takeover targets in the universe from which the portfolio was selected. Next we test the hypothesis that the value of the yen has trended upward relative to the dollar during a three-month period.

In this example, the null hypothesis is that the slope of the yen's return relative to the dollar was flat or negative for the period. The alternative hypothesis is that the yen relative to the dollar had a positive slope during the period.

We assume the yen's returns are normally distributed. Therefore, the test statistic is computed as follows.

$$z = \frac{X - \mu}{s\sqrt{n}} \tag{15.4}$$

where X = mean of daily yen returns
$\qquad \mu$ = 0 percent daily return (corresponding to a flat slope)
$\qquad s$ = standard deviation of daily yen returns
$\qquad n$ = number of daily returns in the sample measurement period

Suppose the mean of the daily yen returns was 0.13 percent, the standard deviation of these returns was 0.66 percent, and there were 71 daily returns during the three-month period. With these assumptions the z value equals 1.66, which corresponds to slightly less than a 5 percent probability of rejecting the null hypothesis when it is true. In other words, we are a little more than 95 percent confident that the yen sloped upward during this period.

This test is also a right-handed test because we are interested in the probability that the yen's slope is greater than zero.

Suppose, instead, that we wish to test whether the yen sloped either upward or downward. We are interested in the probability that the yen's slope is different from zero—that it merely trended. Tests aimed at establishing this are called two-sided. If we require 95 percent confidence to reject the null hypothesis, the critical value is 1.96 rather than 1.645. Thus, in the above example we fail to reject the null hypotheses that the yen's slope was zero, rather than accept the alternative hypothesis that the slope was different from zero. A two-sided test in this example is more reasonable, because we have no reason to believe the yen cannot trend downward.

HYPOTHESIS TEST FOR SMALL SAMPLE MEANS

In the preceding example our sample of daily returns consisted of 71 observations. With 71 observations it is usually safe to assume that the data are approximately normally distributed, as long as the distribution of the underlying population is normally distributed. In situations where we have smaller samples, however, we should account for sampling error. Sampling error widens the distribution, which simply means that with fewer observations we are less confident in the result than we would be had we obtained the result from a larger sample. The extent to which the distribution should be widened was first estimated by William Gosset, an employee of the Guinness Brewery. Gosset published his findings under the pseudonym Student. The test statistic is called the t-statistic, and it is calculated as shown in equation (15.5).

$$t = \frac{X - \mu}{s\sqrt{n}} \qquad (15.5)$$

The t-statistic is calculated the same way as the z value except that we assume the sample standard deviation is different from the population standard deviation. In the previous example, we assumed implicitly that the sample standard deviation and the population standard deviation were the same or sufficiently close not to matter. For large samples, this assumption is harmless. For small samples, we correct for the difference between the observed sample standard deviation and the unobserved population standard deviation by using a t table instead of a normal distribution table.

A t table requires us to specify the degrees of freedom in our sample. This equals the number of observations in the sample less 1. We must subtract 1 because we use up one degree of freedom in estimating the mean. Table 15.1 shows the t-statistics required to reject the null hypothesis at the 5 percent level for various sample sizes based on a right-handed test. This means there is only a 5 percent chance of rejecting the null hypothesis when it is true. These values should be compared with a z value equal to 1.645 for a normal distribution.

It should be intuitively satisfying that for the same level of confidence, the t-statistic is greater than the z value, and that as the sample size increases, the required t-statistic approaches the required z value.

Now let us consider a small sample problem. Suppose we simulate an investment strategy over a five-year measurement period and produce quarterly returns in excess of the benchmark that average 1.5 percent, with a quarterly standard deviation in excess of the benchmark of 3.6 percent. We wish to determine whether or not this strategy adds value to the benchmark. The null hypothesis is that the strategy adds no value, while the alternative hypothesis is that the strategy adds value. (Again, I assume there is no negative skill.)

TABLE 15.1 t-Statistic Required for 5 Percent Error of Rejecting Null Hypothesis When It Is True

Degrees of Freedom	t-Statistic
1	6.31
2	2.92
3	2.35
4	2.13
5	2.01
10	1.81
20	1.72
50	1.68
100	1.66

The t-statistic in this example equals 1.86, as shown below.

$$1.86 = \frac{1.5\% - 0\%}{3.6\%/\sqrt{20}}$$

There are 19 degrees of freedom. In order to reject the null hypothesis that the strategy adds no value or, equivalently, that 1.5 percent is not positive relative to the benchmark, the t-statistic must equal or exceed 1.73, assuming our tolerance for error is 5 percent. Thus we reject the null hypothesis that the strategy does not add value.

If this result were instead obtained over 12 quarters, the t-statistic would equal 1.44, and we would fail to reject the null hypothesis. We see, therefore, that the size of the sample increases our confidence in the result, given the same sample mean and standard deviation.

TYPE I ERROR VERSUS TYPE II ERROR

The hypothesis tests I have thus far described test for a Type I error, which occurs when we reject a null hypothesis that is actually true.

A Type II error, by contrast, occurs when we fail to reject a null hypothesis that is false; that is, when the alternative hypothesis is true.

Suppose the null hypothesis is that a money manager is not skillful, and the alternative hypothesis is that the money manager is skillful.

Table 15.2 distinguishes a Type I error from a Type II error.

The probability of a Type I error is simply the probability of rejecting the null hypothesis when it is true. It is the area under the t distribution or normal distribution to the right and/or left of the test statistic.

The probability of a Type II error depends on the test statistic we choose to reject the null hypothesis and our assumption about the unobservable population mean.

Suppose, for example, we wish to evaluate a portfolio manager. The null hypothesis is that the manager will not add value, and the alternative

TABLE 15.2 Type I Error versus Type II Error
(Null Hypothesis: Manager Is Not Skillful)

	Truth	
Belief	Manager Is Not Skillful	Manager Is Skillful
Manager is not skillful	No error	Type II error
Manager is skillful	Type I error	No error

hypothesis is that he will. We intend to hire the manager if we are at least 95 percent confident he has skill. We will not hire him, however, if our doubt about his skill exceeds 5 percent. Our sample includes 10 years of monthly excess returns with a mean of 0.25 percent and a standard deviation of 2.00 percent. We thus compute the z value as follows:

$$1.37 = \frac{0.25\% - 0\%}{2.00\%/\sqrt{120}}$$

This value corresponds to a 9 percent chance of hiring a manager that has no skill. Given our 5 percent standard, therefore, we should not hire this manager.

The probability of a Type II error measures the likelihood that we do not hire a skillful manager. We compute this probability by first computing the mean return that would be necessary to reject the null hypothesis that the manager has no skill. The 5 percent cutoff that we have chosen corresponds to a z value of 1.645. Thus we require a return that is 1.645 standard deviations (adjusted for sample size) above the null hypothesis return of 0 percent. We compute this value as follows:

$$0.30\% = \frac{1.645 \times 2.00\%}{\sqrt{120}}$$

Next we compute a z value to measure the distance between this required return and our assumed unobservable future return. Suppose the unobservable future return is the same as the manager's sample return. The z value, therefore, equals

$$0.27 = \frac{0.30\% - 0.25\%}{2.00\%/\sqrt{120}}$$

This z value implies there is a 61 percent chance we will fail to hire a skillful manager. The power of this test is measured by the quantity 1 minus the probability of a Type II error. It therefore equals the probability of rejecting the null hypothesis when it is false. In this example it refers to the likelihood that the test will lead us to hire a skillful manager. Its value equals 39 percent.

Suppose that after contemplating the tradeoff between not hiring a manager with no skill and failing to hire a manager with skill, we conclude that our 5 percent standard for rejecting the null hypothesis is too strict. We decide to relax it such that we will tolerate a 10 percent chance of hiring a manager who really has no skill. (I suspect very few managers would be hired otherwise.) The new z value equals 1.28; hence, we should now hire the manager.

What is the likelihood, given our new 10 percent standard, that we will hire a manager with no skill if we still assume that the unobservable future return equals 0.25 percent?

We must compute the required return associated with a 1.28 z value. It equals 0.23 percent. Then we compute the z value for the difference between the required return and our assumption about the future unobservable return. This equals –0.09, which corresponds to a 46 percent chance of hiring a manager with no skill and a 54 percent chance of hiring a skillful manager.

The tradeoff between a Type I error and a Type II error is as follows. The stricter we are in avoiding a Type I error (in order not to hire a manager without skill), the more likely it is that we will commit a Type II error (i.e., fail to hire a skillful manager) and, by symmetry, the weaker will be the power of our test.

The choice of the appropriate threshold for rejecting the null hypothesis depends on the importance we assign to avoiding a Type I error relative to the importance we assign to avoiding a Type II error.

Future Value and the Risk of Loss

Suppose we want to estimate the future value of an investment based on its return history. This problem, at first glance, might seem pedestrian. Yet it involves subtleties that confound many financial analysts.

Some analysts argue that the best guide for estimating future value is the arithmetic average of past returns. Others claim the geometric average provides a better estimate of future value. The correct answer depends on what it is about future value we want to estimate.

AVERAGES

Let us proceed with a quick review of the geometric average. The geometric average is calculated by adding 1 to the holding-period returns,[1] multiplying these values together, raising the product to the power of 1 divided by the number of returns, and then subtracting 1. It is sometimes called the constant rate of return or the annualized return.

We also compute the geometric average by converting holding-period returns into continuous returns. A continuous return, when compounded continuously, yields the same wealth we would achieve by investing at the holding-period return. It equals the natural logarithm of the quantity 1 plus the holding-period return. If the holding-period return equals 10 percent, for example, the continuous return equals 9.53 percent. If we were to invest $1.00 at an annual rate of 9.53 percent compounded continuously throughout the year, it would grow to $1.10 by the end of the year.

We calculate the geometric average from continuous returns by raising e (2.71828), the base of the natural logarithm, to the power of the arithmetic average of the continuous returns and subtracting 1.

Table 16.1 shows how to compute the arithmetic and geometric averages. We compute the arithmetic average by summing the values in the first column and dividing by 4. It equals 8.00 percent. We compute the geometric average in two ways. We multiply the values in the second column,

TABLE 16.1 Averages

Arithmetic Holding-Period Return (HPR)	Geometric 1 + HPR		Geometric ln(1 + HPR)
0.1200		1.1200	0.1133
−0.0600		0.9400	−0.0619
0.2800		1.2800	0.2469
−0.0200		0.9800	−0.0202
Sum 0.3200	Product	1.3206	Sum 0.2781
Average 0.0800	4th root − 1	0.0720	Average 0.0695
			Exponential − 1 0.0720

which yields 1.3206, then take the fourth root of 1.3206 and subtract 1 to arrive at the geometric average, 7.20 percent. Alternatively, we can compute the arithmetic average of the third column, raise e to this value, and subtract 1 to arrive again at 7.20 percent. It follows, therefore, that the arithmetic average of the logarithms of the quantities 1 plus the holding-period returns equals the logarithm of the quantity 1 plus the geometric average.

Here is how to interpret the geometric average. If we invest $1.00 in this sequence of returns, our dollar will grow to $1.3206. We would achieve the same terminal value by investing $1.00 at a constant rate of 7.20 percent for the four periods.

EXPECTED VALUE

Now consider our earlier question: Which average should we use to estimate future value, assuming we wish to base our estimate on past returns? The question as I have posed it is too vague. We must be more precise about what we wish to know about future value. If our goal is to estimate an investment's expected value either one period forward or many periods forward, we should use the arithmetic average of holding-period returns. We estimate expected value from past returns by adding 1 to this average and compounding this quantity forward.

In order to see why the arithmetic average is used to estimate expected value, consider an investment that has a 50 percent chance of increasing by 25 percent and a 50 percent chance of decreasing by 5 percent. After one period, there is an even chance that a dollar will grow to $1.25 or decline to $0.95. The expected value after one period thus equals $1.10, which in turn equals 1 plus the arithmetic average of the two possible returns. After two periods, there are four equally likely outcomes. The investment can increase to $1.25 after the first period and then, in the second period, increase to $1.5625 or decrease to $1.1875. Or it can first decrease to $0.95 after the first period and then increase to $1.1875 or decrease further to $0.9025. Table 16.2 diagrams these four possible paths.

The expected value after two periods, which equals the probability-weighted outcome, equals 1.2100. This corresponds precisely to the quantity 1 plus the arithmetic average of 10 percent raised to the second power. The geometric average of a 25 percent increase followed by a 5 percent decrease, or a 5 percent decrease followed by a 25 percent increase, equals 8.9725 percent. If we add 1 to the geometric average and compound it forward for two periods, we arrive at a terminal value of 1.1875, which does not equal the expected value. The expected value is higher than the value we would have achieved had we invested in the returns on which the arithmetic average is based.

This result might seem paradoxical. The intuition is as follows. The expected value assumes that there is an equal chance of experiencing any of the possible paths. A path of high returns raises the expected value over multiple periods more than a path of equal-magnitude low returns lowers it. This disproportionate effect is the result of compounding. Suppose the high return is 10 percent while the low return is −10 percent. Two consecutive high returns produce a 21 percent increase in value, while two consecutive low returns produce a decrease in value of only 19 percent.

Here's how to interpret expected value. Suppose we observe 10 years of monthly returns and wish to estimate how much wealth we should expect to achieve if we were to draw randomly from these 120 monthly returns, replacing each of the returns that is drawn. If we were to invest in the 120 returns that we selected from the sample (without yet observing them), we should expect our investment to grow at a rate

TABLE 16.2 Possible Paths of $1.00 Investment

Beginning Value	End of Period 1 Values	End of Period 2 Values
		1.5625
	1.2500	
		1.1875
1.0000		
		1.1875
	0.9500	
		0.9025
Expected value:	1.1000	1.2100

equal to the quantity 1 plus the arithmetic average of the sample of monthly returns, raised to the 120th power minus 1 or, equivalently, 1 plus the arithmetic average of the yearly returns from the sample, raised to the 10th power minus 1.

If we were to repeat this experiment many times, the average of the cumulative wealth generated from the sequences of randomly selected returns would indeed converge to the wealth predicted by the compounded arithmetic average. You can verify this result with a random-number generator.

DISTRIBUTION OF FUTURE VALUE

Suppose we ask the following questions about future value. What is the likelihood or probability that an investment will grow or fall to a particular value? Or what value should we be 50 percent confident of achieving or failing to achieve?

Let's start with the assumption that the logarithms of the quantities 1 plus the holding-period returns are normally distributed.[2] This assumption implies that the returns themselves are lognormally distributed. It follows that the standardized variable used to estimate the probability of achieving a particular future value is calculated from the mean (arithmetic average) and standard deviation of these logarithms.[3]

A standardized variable measures distance from the mean in standard deviation units. It is the number that we look up in a normal distribution table to estimate the probability of achieving or falling short of a particular value, assuming the values are normally distributed.

Suppose we wish to estimate the likelihood that $1 million will grow to equal $1.5 million over five years, based on the past annual returns of a particular investment. If we believe the logarithms of the quantities 1 plus these returns are normally distributed, we proceed by computing the mean and standard deviation of these logarithms, as Table 16.3 shows.

We compute the standardized variable as follows:

$$z = \frac{\ln(1,500,000/1,000,000) - 0.064695 \times 5}{0.108744\sqrt{5}}$$

$$z = 0.3372$$

The logarithm of the quantity 1.5 million divided by 1 million (40.5465 percent) is the continuous five-year return required in order for $1 million to grow to $1.5 million. This corresponds to an annualized continuous growth rate of 8.1093 percent. The quantity 5 times 6.4695 per-

TABLE 16.3 Past Investment Returns

	Annual Return	ln(1+Return)
	−0.030200	−0.030665
	0.069500	0.067191
	0.271500	0.240197
	0.122700	0.115736
	−0.091400	−0.095850
	0.173000	0.159565
	0.021900	0.021664
	0.056500	0.054962
	−0.079100	−0.082404
	0.217200	0.196553
Arithmetic average	0.073160	0.064695
Standard deviation	0.116779	0.108744

cent is the expected five-year continuous return. The standardized variable measures how far away the required five-year continuous return is from the expected five-year continuous return. It is 0.3372 standard deviation units away. If we look up this value in a normal distribution table, we see there is a 38.6 percent chance that $1 million will grow to $1.5 million, based on the past returns of this investment.

Suppose we wish to know the likelihood our investment will generate a loss over five years. We compute the standardized variable as follows:

$$z = \frac{\ln(1,000,000/1,000,000) - 0.064695 \times 5}{0.108744\sqrt{5}}$$

$$z = -1.3303$$

There is a 9.17 percent chance that this investment will lose money, on average, over five years.

What value should we expect to equal or exceed with 50 percent confidence? This value is called the median. Half the values are expected to exceed the median and half are expected to fall short of the median. A 50 percent probability of occurrence corresponds to a standardized variable of 0.00. The standardized variable equals 0.00 only when the required continuous return equals the expected continuous return. Thus we should expect with 50 percent confidence to equal or exceed the value that corresponds to the expected five-year continuous return. We find this value by raising e, the base of the natural logarithm, to the power 5 times the expected annualized continuous return. Thus the median wealth equals $1,381,924.26. There is a 50 percent chance that the value in five years will exceed this value and a 50 percent chance that it will fall short of this value.

The geometric average is convenient for estimating probabilities, because the average of the logarithms equals the logarithm of the quantity 1 plus the geometric average.

The center of the probability distribution of terminal values is found by compounding the initial value at the geometric average. When we compound at the geometric average, we determine the future value for which there is an equal chance of exceeding or failing to exceed. Here is the logic behind this result.

1. The logarithms of the quantities 1 plus the holding-period returns are assumed to be normally distributed.
2. The mean (arithmetic average) of these logarithms equals the logarithm of the quantity 1 plus the geometric average of the holding-period returns.
3. The expected multiperiod continuous return, therefore, equals the number of periods times the logarithm of the quantity 1 plus the geometric average.
4. We convert the expected multiperiod continuous return into median wealth by raising e to the power of the multiperiod continuous return.
5. The quantity e raised to the power of the multiperiod continuous return is exactly equal to the initial wealth compounded forward at the geometric average.

The bottom line is that we should compound at the arithmetic average if we wish to estimate an investment's expected value. We should compound at the geometric average, however, if we wish to estimate the value for which there is an equal chance of exceeding or failing to exceed.

SOME FORMULAS FOR ESTIMATING FUTURE VALUE

Here are some formulas that you should carry on your person at all times in the event you are called upon to discuss future value.

Expected future value is calculated as follows:

$$P_{t+1} = P_t(1 + \mu_a)^n \qquad (16.1)$$

or

$$P_{t+1} = P_t e^{(\mu_c + \sigma_c^2/2)n} \qquad (16.2)$$

Median future value is calculated as follows:

$$\text{Median}(P_{t+1}) = P_t(1 + \mu_g)^n \tag{16.3}$$

or

$$\text{Median}(P_{t+1}) = P_t e^{\mu_c n} \tag{16.4}$$

The standardized variable for estimating the probability of achieving a target future value is:

$$z = \frac{\ln\left(P_{t+1}^T / P_t\right) - \ln\left(1 + \mu_g\right) \times n}{\sigma_c \sqrt{n}} \tag{16.5}$$

where P_t = beginning value
P_{t+1} = future value
P_{t+1}^T = target value
μ_a = arithmetic average of holding-period returns
μ_g = geometric average of holding-period returns
μ_c = arithmetic average of the logarithms of the quantities 1 plus the holding-period returns
σ_c = standard deviation of the logarithms of the quantities 1 plus the holding-period returns
e = base of the natural logarithm, 2.71828
ln = natural logarithm
n = number of periods

When deciding whether to compound at the arithmetic average to estimate expected value or the geometric average to estimate the distribution of future value, you should be aware of the following distinction. More often than not, an investment will fail to achieve or exceed its expected value (compounded arithmetic average), which in some sense implies that the expected value is not to be expected. Because of the effect of compounding, however, the fewer outcomes that exceed the expected value have a greater impact, per outcome, than the more frequent outcomes that fall below the expected value.

Half the outcomes should exceed the median value (compound geometric average) and half should fall below this value. Those values that are above the median, however, will on average exceed the median by a magnitude greater than the magnitude by which the below-median values fall short of the median. Hence the expected value will exceed the median value.

There is one subtle yet technical caveat to my assertions up to now. I have implicitly assumed the arithmetic and geometric averages are estimated without error. If these values are measured with error as they apply to a future horizon, the compounded arithmetic average will overestimate the expected value. Even if the errors are symmetric, when they are compounded they produce an asymmetric effect on the estimate of expected value. Positive errors raise the estimate of expected value more than negative errors of the same magnitude reduce the estimate. It turns out that a blend of the arithmetic and geometric averages based on the sample size and the length of the investment horizon gives a better estimate of expected value than the arithmetic average when there is measurement error.[4]

WITHIN-HORIZON EXPOSURE TO LOSS

Thus far we have focused only on end-of-horizon probability of loss. We have ignored variability in value that occurs throughout the horizon. To capture this variability, we use a statistic called first passage time probability.[5] This statistic measures the probability (P_W) of a first occurrence of an event within a finite horizon. It is equal to

$$\text{Pr}_W = N\left[\frac{\ln(1+L) - \mu T}{\sigma\sqrt{T}}\right] + N\left[\frac{\ln(1+L) + \mu T}{\sigma\sqrt{T}}\right](1+L)^{2\mu/\sigma^2} \quad (16.8)$$

where $N[\ ]$ = cumulative normal distribution function
   $\ln$ = natural logarithm
   L = cumulative percentage loss in periodic units
   μ = annualized expected return in continuous units
   T = number of years in horizon
   σ = annualized standard deviation of continuous returns

This statistic gives the probability that an investment will depreciate to a particular value over some horizon if it is monitored continuously throughout the investment horizon.[6] Figure 16.1 illustrates the difference between end-of-horizon and within-horizon probability of loss.

The lower line shows the probability of a 10 percent or greater loss at the end of the horizon for an investment with an 8 percent expected return and a 12 percent standard deviation. The top line shows the likelihood of a 10 percent or greater loss at any point throughout the horizon, including the end of the horizon. The middle line shows the likelihood of breaching the −10 percent threshold at some point during the horizon but recovering to a value above this threshold by the conclusion of the horizon.

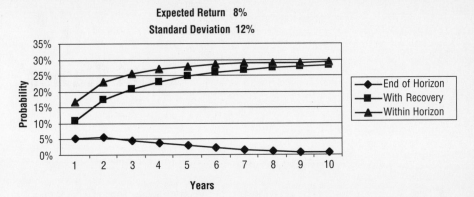

FIGURE 16.1 Probability of 10% loss

This illustration reveals two important points: (1) The likelihood of a within-horizon loss is substantially greater than the likelihood of an end-of-horizon loss; and (2) while the likelihood of an end-of-horizon loss diminishes with time beyond one year, the likelihood of a within-horizon loss never diminishes as a function of the length of the horizon. It increases at a decreasing rate and then levels off, but it never decreases.

We can use the same equation to estimate continuous value at risk.[7] Whereas value at risk measured conventionally gives the worst outcome at a chosen probability at the end of an investment horizon, continuous value at risk gives the worst outcome at a chosen probability from inception to any time during an investment horizon. It is not possible to solve for continuous value at risk analytically. We must resort to numerical methods. We set equation (16.8) equal to the chosen confidence level for the value-at-risk estimate and solve iteratively for L. Continuous value at risk equals $-L$ times initial wealth.[8]

CHAPTER 17

Event Studies

Event studies measure the relationship between an event that affects securities and the return of those securities. Some events, such as a regulatory change or an economic shock, affect many securities contemporaneously; other events, such as a change in dividend policy or a stock split, are specific to individual securities.

Event studies are often used to test the efficient market hypothesis. For example, abnormal returns that persist after an event occurs or abnormal returns that are associated with an anticipated event contradict the efficient market hypothesis. Aside from tests of market efficiency, event studies are valuable in gauging the magnitude of an event's impact.

A classic event study published in 1969 by Fama, Fisher, Jensen, and Roll examined the impact of stock splits on security prices.[1] The authors found that abnormal returns dissipated rapidly following the news of stock splits, thus lending support to the efficient market hypothesis.

HOW TO PERFORM AN EVENT STUDY IN SEVEN EASY STEPS

The following steps describe one of several approaches for conducting an event study of a firm-specific event.

1. Define the event and identify the timing of its occurrence. The timing of the event is not necessarily the period during which the event occurs. Rather, it may be the investment period immediately preceding the announcement of the event.

2. Arrange the security performance data relative to the timing of the event. If information about the event is released fully on a specific day with time remaining for traders to react, the day of the announcement period is zero. Then select measurement periods preceding and following the event. For example, if the 90 trading days preceding the event

and the 10 days following the event are designated as the pre- and post-event periods, the pre-event trading days would be labeled $t - 90$, $t - 89$, $t - 88$ ... $t - 1$; the event day, $t = 0$; and the post-event trading days, $t + 1$, $t + 2$, $t + 3$ ... $t + 10$. Because the event is specific to each security, these days will differ across securities in calendar time.

3. Separate the security-specific component of return from the security's total return during the pre-event measurement period. One approach is to use the market model to isolate security-specific returns. First, regress each security's daily returns during the pre-event measurement period from $t - 90$ through $t - 1$ on the market's returns during the same period. The security specific returns are defined as the differences between the security's daily returns and the daily returns predicted from the regression equation (the security's alpha plus its beta times the market's daily returns). This calculation is described by equation (17.1).[2]

$$\varepsilon_{i,t} = R_{i,t} - \hat{\alpha}_i + \hat{\beta}_i (R_{m,t}) \qquad (17.1)$$

where $\varepsilon_{i,t}$ = security-specific return of security i in period t
        $R_{i,t}$ = total return of security i in period t
        $\hat{\alpha}_i$ = alpha of security i estimated from pre-event measurement period
        $\hat{\beta}_i$ = beta of security i estimated from pre-event measurement period
        $R_{m,t}$ = total return of market in period t

4. Estimate the standard deviation of the daily security specific returns during the pre-event measurement period from $t - 90$ through $t - 1$. This calculation is shown in equation (17.2).

$$\sigma_{i,pre} = \sqrt{\frac{\displaystyle\sum_{t=-90}^{-1} \left(\varepsilon_{i,t} - \bar{\varepsilon}_{i,pre}\right)^2}{n-1}} \qquad (17.2)$$

where $\sigma_{i,pre}$ = standard deviation of security-specific returns of security i estimated from pre-event measurement period
        $\bar{\varepsilon}_{i,pre}$ = average of security-specific returns of security i estimated from pre-event measurement period
        n = number of days in pre-event measurement period

5. Isolate the security-specific return during the event and post-event periods. To estimate the security-specific return each day during these

periods, subtract from each security's total return each day the security's alpha and beta times the market's return on that day. The alphas and betas are the same as those estimated from the pre-event regressions. The equation for estimating these returns is the same as equation (17.1). The subscript t, however, ranges from 0 to +10 rather than from –90 to –1.

6. Aggregate the security-specific returns and standard deviations across the sample of securities on the event day and the post-event days. That is, sum the security-specific returns for each day and divide by the number of securities in the sample, as shown in equation (17.3).

$$\bar{\varepsilon}_t = \frac{\sum\limits_{i=1}^{N} \varepsilon_{i,t}}{N} \tag{17.3}$$

where $\bar{\varepsilon}_t$ = average across all securities of security-specific returns in period t

N = number of securities in sample

We aggregate the standard deviations by squaring the standard deviation of each security's specific return estimated from the pre-event period, summing these values across all securities, dividing by the number of securities, and then taking the square root of this sum. Equation (17.4) shows this calculation.

$$\sigma_{N,pre} = \sqrt{\frac{\sum\limits_{i=1}^{N} \sigma_{i,pre}^2}{N}} \tag{17.4}$$

where $\sigma_{N,pre}$ = aggregate of pre-event standard deviation of security-specific returns across all securities

7. Test the hypothesis that the security-specific returns on the event day and post-event days differ significantly from zero. The t-statistic is computed by dividing the average of the security-specific returns across all securities each day by the aggregation of the standard deviations across all securities as described in the previous step. Then, depending on the degrees of freedom, determine whether the event significantly affects returns. That is,

$$\text{t-statistic} = \frac{\bar{\varepsilon}_t}{\sigma_{N,pre}} \tag{17.5}$$

If the event is anticipated and the t-statistic is significant on the day of the event but insignificant on the days following the event, a reasonable conclusion is that the event does affect security returns but that it does not contradict the efficient market hypothesis.

If, by contrast, the t-statistics continue to be significant on the post-event days, we might conclude the market is inefficient because it does not quickly absorb new information. We might also conclude the market is inefficient if we were to observe significant t-statistics on the day of the event and we had reason to believe the event (including its magnitude) was anticipated.

ISSUES IN MEASURING EVENTS

When designing an event study, how to measure the event is not always clear. Suppose, for example, the event is an annual earnings announcement. The announcement that annual earnings are $3.00 per share is meaningless unless this number is contrasted to the market's expectation about earnings. Moreover, the market's expectation will have been conditioned by earlier information releases pertaining to earnings. Therefore, the first issue in measuring the event is to disentangle the unanticipated component of the announcement from the expected component.

The unanticipated component of the event is likely to be positive for some securities and negative for others, and the test of significance may need to be conditioned on the direction of the event. This can be accomplished by partitioning the sample into a subsample of securities for which the event was positive and a subsample for which the event was negative.

Another issue with respect to the measurement of the event is the influence of confounding factors. Suppose the event is defined as the announcement of a change in dividend policy. For many securities, this announcement may coincide with an information release about earnings. This coincident information is called a confounding event—an event that might distort or camouflage the effect of the event of interest on the security's return.

ISSUES IN MEASURING RETURN

In my description of the steps involved in an event study, I isolated the security-specific component by using the market model. The returns must be normalized so that the expected value of their unanticipated component is equal to 0 percent. It is perfectly acceptable that the expected value of the unanticipated component of return conditioned on the event not equal 0, and it is equally acceptable that the unanticipated component of return conditioned on the absence of the event be systematically nonzero. The probability-weighted sum of the unanticipated components of return must equal 0, however.

The market is but one method for adjusting returns. Some event studies adjust returns by subtracting the average return of the securities during the pre-event period. This adjustment procedure is called mean adjustment. An alternative procedure is to subtract the market's coincident return from the security's return. This adjustment procedure is called the market adjustment.

The procedure described to normalize the unanticipated component of return to 0 using the market model is called risk adjustment. We can also risk adjust the returns by using a procedure pioneered by Fama and Mac-Beth in 1973.[3] We derive the unanticipated component of return by computing an expected return in period t and then subtracting it from the security's actual return in period t.

The first step in this procedure is to estimate each security's beta by regressing its returns on the market's returns over some pre-event measurement period. Then we regress the returns across many securities in the same period t on their historical betas as of the beginning of period t. We then use the intercept and slope from this cross-sectional regression to measure the security's expected return.

Specifically, a security's expected return in period t is equal to the cross-sectional alpha in period t plus the cross-sectional beta in period t times the security's historical beta. The security's unanticipated component of return, therefore, equals its actual return in period t minus its expected return in period t (estimated from the cross-sectional coefficients and the security's historical beta).

The final approach for normalizing the unanticipated component of return to 0 uses control portfolios. We construct a control portfolio of sample securities to have a beta equal to 1. We compute the unanticipated component of return in an event-related period as the return of the control portfolio less the return of the market.

ISSUES IN EVALUATING THE RESULTS

In the earlier example, we used a t-statistic to evaluate whether the event affected security returns. The use of a t-test presupposes that the returns of the securities from which the sample is drawn are distributed normally.

If we have reason to believe the returns are not normally distributed, we can use a nonparametric test to evaluate the result. A nonparametric test, which is sometimes referred to as a distribution-free test, does not depend on the assumption of normality.

One of the simplest nonparametric tests is called a sign test. Not only is the sign test distribution-free, it is also insensitive to the magnitude of the returns. It simply tests whether there are more positive returns (or negative returns, as the case may be) than would be expected if the returns and the event are not related. This test statistic is computed as shown in equation (17.6).

$$Z = \frac{(X - 0.5) - 0.5N}{0.5\sqrt{N}} \qquad (17.6)$$

where Z = standardized variable
X = number of security-specific returns that are positive (or negative)
N = number of securities in sample

For example, if 13 returns are positive out of a sample of 20 securities, the standardized variable would equal 1.12, and we would fail to reject the null hypothesis that the event has no effect on security returns. If, instead, 65 returns are positive from a sample of 100 securities (which is the same proportion as 13 out of 20), the standardized variable would equal 2.90, and we would conclude that the event does affect security returns.

The sign test is but one of several nonparametric tests that we can use when we are doubtful about the assumption of normality or when the data are limited to ordinal values.

The t-statistic also assumes the returns across the sample of securities are independent of one another. In many cases, security returns may not be mutually independent, even after we adjust them for risk. Securities may have other common sources of risk besides their exposure to the market. Perhaps the market-adjusted returns of securities within the same industry are correlated with each other. This type of cross-correlation is particularly common in event studies of mergers when the propensity for mergers is an industry-related phenomenon. Sometimes we can remedy the problem of cross-correlation by embellishing the risk adjustment procedure to account for the portion of return that arises from industry affiliation or from exposure to other sources of common risk.

THE BROWN AND WARNER STUDY

In a classic article evaluating event study methodology, Stephen Brown and Jerold Warner simulated various risk adjustment procedures to determine their efficacy.[4] They first applied various methodologies to samples of securities that were contrived to have no abnormal returns, in order to determine whether a particular methodology would reject the null hypothesis when it was true (a Type I error). Then they artificially induced abnormal returns in samples to determine whether a particular methodology would fail to reject the null hypothesis when it was false (a Type II error). Finally, they compared the various methodologies based on their power to detect abnormal performance. The residual of a Type II error measures the power of a particular methodology.[5]

Brown and Warner concluded that none of the more elaborate procedures to isolate security-specific returns improved upon the simple market model adjustment and that some of these procedures did not even improve upon the mean adjustment procedure. Their message is that a financial analyst's time would be spent more productively by identifying and measuring the event rather than by devising elaborate procedures for controlling risk.

CHAPTER 18

Simulation

Marcel Proust spent 15 years cloistered in a cork-lined room writing his massive novel, *Remembrance of Things Past*, in which he explored the experiences of his adolescence and adulthood. By thoughtful retrospection Proust was able to appreciate his life more richly than he appreciated the actual experiences. In a parody of Proust's great novel, François Truffaut created a film character who, in order to impress a woman, introduces himself as a novelist. When she asks him the name of his novel he responds, *Remembrance of Things to Come*. Truffaut's point is that the film character has thus far led an uninteresting life. As financial analysts we should also bear in mind that the future may hold a more interesting range of possibilities than those revealed by history. This chapter describes two types of simulation that allow us to pre-experience the future: Monte Carlo simulation and bootstrapping.

MONTE CARLO SIMULATION

Monte Carlo simulation is a procedure by which we generate possible future outcomes by drawing random numbers from a theoretical distribution with predefined parameters. Stanislaw Ulam and John von Neumann introduced the term Monte Carlo simulation when they worked on the Manhattan Project at the Los Alamos National Laboratory. Ulam invented the procedure of substituting a sequence of random numbers into equations to solve problems relating to nuclear explosions. (This, in my opinion, is one of the better examples of why simulation is often preferable to the empirical alternative.) In honor of Ulam's relative, who was known to frequent the gambling casinos at Monte Carlo, Ulam and von Neumann used Monte Carlo as a code name for their secret work.[1]

Von Neumann developed one of the first algorithms for generating random numbers, which proceeds as follows. Select the middle four numbers from your phone number and square them. Then select the middle four numbers of the squared value and square them. Continue until you generate a sufficient supply of four-digit random numbers. My phone number is 617-576-7360. Therefore, I would square 5,767, which equals 33,258,289, and select 2,582 as my first random number. Then I would square this value, which equals 6,666,724. I would then select 6,667 or 6,672 as my next random number. This process will generate a sequence of four digit numbers that are relatively independent and distributed uniformly, which means they have an equal chance of occurrence.

In most financial applications the random numbers we wish to generate are rates of return, which we typically assume are normally distributed or, in many cases, lognormally distributed.[2] The central limit theorem allows us to convert uniformly distributed random numbers into normally distributed random numbers. It states that the distribution of the average of independent random variables, which are not individually normally distributed, will approach a normal distribution if the number of variables is large enough. Therefore, in order to produce a sequence of random numbers from a normal distribution, we generate many sequences of uniformly distributed random numbers and average them.

Today many software programs include a feature that allows random sampling from normally distributed distributions, thus obviating the need to create our own random number generator. We simply specify a mean and standard deviation for the distribution and instruct the program to generate as many random observations as we would like.

If we wish to simulate outcomes that are relatively far into the future, it is important to recognize the effect of compounding. Compounding leads to a lognormal distribution rather than a normal distribution. Compared to a normal distribution, which is symmetrical, a lognormal distribution has a longer right tail than left tail and an average value that exceeds the median value.[3] Even if our software only allows us to generate values from a normal distribution, we can use it to generate returns as though they come from a lognormal distribution, because the continuous counterparts of discrete returns are normally distributed. A continuous return, if compounded instantaneously, would produce the corresponding discrete return.

In order to sample from a lognormal distribution, we simply convert the mean and standard deviation of random discrete returns into their continuous counterparts, draw random continuous returns from a normal distribution, and then convert the random continuous returns to discrete returns. We need three equations to generate random returns from a lognormal distribution. Although these equations are quite messy and unintuitive, they are very handy.

Equation (18.1) converts the standard deviation of discrete returns into the standard deviation of continuous returns.

$$\sigma_C = \sqrt{\ln\left(\frac{\sigma_D^2}{(1+\mu_D)^2}+1\right)} \qquad (18.1)$$

where σ_C = the standard deviation of continuous returns
  ln = the natural logarithm
  σ_D = the standard deviation of discrete returns
  μ_D = the mean of discrete returns

Equation (18.2) converts the discrete mean into the continuous mean.

$$\mu_C = \ln(1+\mu_D) - \frac{\sigma^2}{2} \qquad (18.2)$$

where μ_C = the mean of continuous returns

Finally, equation (18.3) converts the continuous returns that are drawn randomly from the normal distribution with a continuous mean and standard deviation into their discrete counterparts, which is equivalent to drawing random discrete returns from a lognormal distribution.

$$R_P = e^{R_c} - 1 \qquad (18.3)$$

where e = the base of the natural logarithm (2.71828)
  R_P = the discrete return
  R_C = the continuous return

Let's now perform a Monte Carlo simulation of value at risk for an asset with a 10 percent mean and a 20 percent standard deviation. We first apply equation (18.1) to convert the 20.00 percent standard deviation to its continuous counterpart, which equals 18.03 percent. Then we use equation (18.2) to convert the 10.00 percent mean to its continuous counterpart, which is 7.90 percent. We then instruct the computer to select 1,000 returns (or more if we require greater accuracy) from a normal distribution with a 7.90 percent mean and an 18.03 percent standard deviation, and to rank these randomly chosen returns from highest to lowest. If we wish to estimate value at risk at a 5 percent confidence level, we take the 950th continuous return, which equals –22.82 percent, and apply equation (18.3) to convert it to its corresponding discrete return, which equals –20.40 percent. Thus, simulated value at risk equals $20.40 for every $100.00 invested in this asset.

We can check to see how close this result is to the theoretically correct result by calculating value at risk analytically.[4]

$$VaR = -\left(e^{\,R_C - 1.645\sigma_C} - 1\right) \times V \tag{18.4}$$

where 1.645 = the distance below the mean of the 5th percentile
observation measured in standard deviation units
V = the portfolio's value

If we substitute 7.90 percent and 18.03 percent into equation (18.4), we discover that value at risk based on the theoretical distribution equals $19.56 per $100.00 of portfolio value.

Why would we bother to simulate value at risk if we can calculate it analytically? We wouldn't. I simply wanted to demonstrate Monte Carlo simulation with a very simple example and to provide some measure of its accuracy. There are many problems, though, that we cannot easily solve analytically, or even with difficulty. As discussed in Chapter 19, simulation often yields a more accurate description of a portfolio's distribution than analytical methods, especially if the portfolio includes short positions. Also, it is usually more convenient to use simulation when dealing with contingent strategies. Suppose, for example, we wish to simulate value at risk at the end of a 10-year horizon for a fund that remains invested in a risky asset with a 10.00 percent mean and a 20.00 percent standard deviation as long as it remains above 80 percent of its initial value as of any calendar year-end. Otherwise it is switched to a safer asset with a 5.00 percent expected return and a 2.00 percent standard deviation.

To perform a Monte Carlo simulation of value at risk for this dynamic strategy, we proceed as follows.

1. We draw a random return from a normal distribution with a continuous mean of 7.90 percent and a continuous standard deviation of 18.03 percent.
2. We then convert this continuous return to its corresponding discrete return, add 1.00, and multiply this value by the fund's preceding value.
3. If the fund's new value is at least 80 percent of its initial value, we repeat steps 1 and 2.
4. If the fund's value is less than 80 percent of its initial value, we draw a random return from a normal distribution with a continuous mean of 4.86 percent and a continuous standard deviation of 1.90 percent.
5. We then convert this continuous return to its corresponding periodic return, add 1.00, and multiply this value by the fund's preceding value.
6. We repeat steps 1 through 5 until 10 returns are selected.
7. We repeat steps 1 through 6, 1,000 times to generate 1,000 10-year sequences.

8. Finally, we rank the 1,000 final values from highest to lowest and subtract the 950th value from the initial value to derive value at risk.

As you can imagine, once we develop the appropriate random return generator, we can introduce all types of contingent behavior to simulate a wide variety of dynamic strategies, or strategies that are subject to cash flows. Moreover, because this simulation produces distributions of 1,000 values at each year-end along the way, we can estimate value at risk at a variety of percentiles throughout the investment period. Alternatively, we can estimate the likelihood the fund will exceed or fall short of any value as of any year-end. Finally, we can generate random returns at higher frequencies such as months, weeks, or days in order to refine our estimate of the fund's risk exposure.

SIMULATION BY BOOTSTRAPPING

Monte Carlo simulation assumes the future state of the world is best captured by a theoretical distribution with assumed parameters. History is irrelevant to Monte Carlo simulation. Bootstrapping, by comparison, relies to varying degrees on historical precedent. Parametric bootstrapping is most similar to Monte Carlo simulation. Parametric bootstrapping also selects returns from a theoretical distribution, but it relies on historical data to estimate the mean and standard deviation of the distribution. Some statisticians claim that parametric bootstrapping is a misnomer because it resembles Monte Carlo simulation more than it does standard bootstrapping.

Standard bootstrapping assumes the distribution of future returns is best represented by an historical sample. This sample, however, is but one pass through history and thus an inadequate description of all possible passes. Nonetheless, we can use it over and over again to create as many passes through history as we would like, all emanating from the original data and therefore preserving history's statistical attributes.

To perform a standard bootstrapping simulation of value at risk for the strategy described earlier, we proceed as follows.

1. We draw a random return from the historical sample of annual returns for the risky asset and replace it in the sample.
2. We then add 1.00 to the randomly chosen risky return and multiply this value by the fund's preceding value.
3. If the fund's new value is at least 80 percent of its initial value, we repeat steps 1 and 2.

4. If the fund's value is less than 80 percent of its initial value, we draw a random return from the historical sample of annual returns for the safe asset and replace in the sample.
5. We then add 1.00 to the randomly chosen safe return and multiply this value by the fund's preceding value.
6. We repeat steps 1 through 5 until 10 returns are selected.
7. We repeat steps 1 through 6, 1,000 times (or more if we desire greater accuracy).
8. Finally, we rank the final values from highest to lowest and subtract the 950th value from the initial value to derive value at risk.

Notice that bootstrapping does not require us to deal with the complexity of lognormality. We ignore this complexity because bootstrapping assumes the historical distribution best characterizes the distribution of potential future returns. Lognormality is a mathematical consequence that arises from compounding independent and identically distributed returns. It is not necessarily an empirical feature of returns. The sample of historical returns may not have come from the same distribution, nor were the returns necessarily independent of each other. Bootstrapping captures the effect of multiple distributions, but it may not capture return patterns if it randomly selects individual returns. In order to capture serial dependence in the data, we perform a variation of the procedure just described, called block bootstrapping. If we believe, for example, that risky asset returns over three-year periods are serially correlated, we would randomly select blocks of three-year returns instead of individual yearly returns.

SIMULATING THE HIERARCHY OF INVESTMENT CHOICE

We can also use simulation to evaluate the relative importance of various investment activities. Some researchers have explored this issue by analyzing the historical performance of managed funds. For example, the widely held view that asset allocation is more important than security selection arises in part from a study by Brinson, Hood, and Beebower called "Determinants of Portfolio Performance."[5] In this study, the authors attributed the performance of 91 large corporate pension plans to three investment activities: policy, timing, and security selection. They defined the policy return as the return of the long-term asset mix invested in passive asset class benchmarks. They then measured the return associated with deviations from the policy mix, assuming investment in passive benchmarks, and attributed this component of return to timing. Finally, they measured the return associated with deviations from the passive benchmarks within each asset class and attributed this component of return to security selection. For each of the 91 funds, they regressed total return through time on these respective components of return. These regression analyses revealed that asset allocation policy on average across the 91 funds accounted for 93.6 percent of total return variation through time, and in no case less than 75.5 percent.

Although this study accurately measures the influences of these activities on past performance, it does not reveal the relative importance of these activities because the results depend on two separate influences: the investment opportunities available from variation in asset class and security returns, and the extent to which investors chose to exercise discretion in exploiting these opportunities. Therefore, this study confounds investment opportunity with investor behavior. Bootstrapping allows us to disentangle investment opportunity from investor behavior. The following analysis summarizes the results from an article I co-authored with Sebastien Page.[6]

We analyzed five types of global investment choices: asset allocation, country allocation, global sector allocation, country sector allocation, and security selection from a normative perspective. These investment choices are relevant to investors who regard their investment universe as the developed world markets.

Here is how we performed the simulations. For the global asset allocation simulation, we randomly selected 100 asset class returns with replacement 10,000 times from a sample that was weighted 60 percent stocks, 30 percent bonds, and 10 percent cash. We therefore generated 10,000 portfolios whose asset mixes varied randomly around an average asset mix of 60 percent stocks, 30 percent bonds, and 10 percent cash. The country weights of each asset class were fixed each year according to their relative capitalization within each asset class. Also, the sector and individual security weights of the equity component were fixed according to their relative capitalization. We repeated these procedures for each year beginning with 1987 and ending with 2001. Then we calculated the cumulative returns of the 10,000 portfolios and ranked them. Therefore, variation in cumulative return arises purely from variation in asset mix.

For the country allocation simulation, we chose 100 country index returns with replacement 10,000 times from a sample of 23 developed market countries. When we selected a return we also selected its capitalization, so that we could scale the returns according to their relative capitalization within the equity component. As a result, the returns of the random portfolios varied symmetrically around the world index return. We held constant the exposures to stocks, bonds, and cash at 60 percent, 30 percent, and 10 percent, respectively, so that this simulation was unbiased relative to the asset allocation simulation. Sector and individual security weights within each country were fixed according to their relative capitalization. Thus our simulated portfolios can be implemented with country-level index funds. This procedure generated 10,000 portfolios for each of 15 years that varied randomly by their country weights within the equity component. We then ranked them by cumulative return.

For the simulation of global sector allocation, we randomly selected 100 global sector returns with replacement 10,000 times from a sample of 23 global sectors. Again, when we selected a return we also selected its capitalization, so that we could scale the returns according to their relative capitalization within the equity component. The asset allocation remained constant at 60 percent stocks, 30 percent bonds, and 10 percent cash, and country and individual security weights within each global sector were fixed according to their relative capitalization. Therefore, we randomly generated 10,000 portfolios each year that varied by their global sector weights within the equity component. Again we ranked them by cumulative performance.

We performed the same simulation for country sectors with the exception that we choose randomly from a sample of country sectors rather than global sectors. Hence the number of sectors increased by a factor equal to the number of countries ($23 \times 23 = 529$). Again, when we selected a return we also selected its capitalization in order to scale the returns according to their relative capitalization within the equity component. The country and sector weights varied according to the random selection of country sectors. The individual security weights within each country sector were fixed according to their relative capitalization. Therefore, we randomly generated 10,000 portfolios each year that varied by their country sector weights within the equity component, and we ranked them by cumulative return.

For the security selection simulation we randomly chose 100 individual security returns with replacement 10,000 times from a global sample of 1,512 securities. Again, when we selected a return we also selected its capitalization in order to scale the returns according to their relative capitalization within the equity component. We held constant the asset class exposures. The country and sector exposures varied according to the random selection of individual securities. We did this for each of 15 years and ranked them by cumulative return.

Figure 18.1 shows the extent to which a talented investor (top 25th or 5th percentile) could have improved upon average performance by engaging in various investment choices across a global universe. It also shows how far below average performance an unlucky investor (bottom 75th or 95th percentile) could have performed depending on the choice of investment discretion. Contrary to received doctrine, dispersion around average performance arising from security selection is substantially greater than dispersion around average performance arising from all other investment choices. Moreover, asset allocation, which is widely considered the most important investment choice, produces the least dispersion; thus, from a normative perspective it is the least important investment choice.

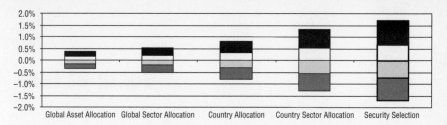

FIGURE 18.1 Global choices

SUMMARY

1. History is but one path of many paths that might have occurred. If we wish to assess our true range of opportunities and exposure to risk, we must account for paths that have not occurred.
2. Simulation allows us to pre-experience alternative paths that have not occurred but may prevail in the future.
3. Monte Carlo simulation assumes the distribution of future outcomes is best described theoretically and not empirically.
4. Parametric boostrapping combines theory with empiricism. It relies on theory to define the shape of the distribution of future returns, but relies on history to estimate the parameters of the theoretical distribution.
5. Standard bootstrapping ignores theory and relies strictly on historical returns to generate the distribution of potential returns.
6. Block bootstrapping represents the empirical extreme. Not only does it assume future returns emanate exclusively from past returns; it preserves the serial correlation of historical return sequences to generate potential return paths.
7. Simulation methods can also be used to assess the relative importance of various investment activities. Contrary to the received doctrine, a bootstrapping analysis reveals security selection to be significantly more important than asset allocation.

These are the essential simulation tools. Which you prefer depends on whether you think of yourself as a theoretician or an empiricist.

CHAPTER 19

Value at Risk

Value at risk is the maximum loss or minimum gain that could occur at a given confidence level over a specified horizon. Although it is widely perceived as a recent innovation, it is nothing more than a rearrangement of a risk measure that financial analysts have used since the beginning of modern finance, which is probability of loss. It is easy to see the connection between these two risk measures if we ignore the effect of compounding and assume returns are normally distributed.

Suppose we have a portfolio with an expected return equal to 8.10 percent and a standard deviation equal to 17.08 percent, and we wish to estimate the probability that this portfolio will suffer a loss of at least 20.00 percent in any given year. We simply calculate the area to the left of –20.00 percent under the normal distribution by dividing the distance between –20.00 percent and 8.10 percent by the standard deviation, 17.08 percent, which equals –1.645. This value is called the standardized variable and means that –20.00 percent is 1.645 standard deviation units below the expected return of 8.10 percent. If we look this value up in a normal distribution table, we find that 5.00 percent of the area under a normal distribution with an 8.10 percent mean and a 17.08 percent standard deviation is to the left of –20.00 percent; thus the likelihood of a 20 percent loss equals 5.00 percent.

Value at risk turns the question around. Instead of measuring the likelihood of a particular loss, value at risk measures how much can be lost given a particular likelihood. Because we know that a 5.00 percent probability corresponds to a standardized variable of –1.645, we estimate the percentage loss associated with a 5.00 percent probability as (8.10 percent – 1.645 × 17.08 percent), which equals –20 percent.[1] Value at risk goes one step further and converts this percentage loss to a monetary value. Thus the value at risk of a $100 million portfolio with an 8.10 percent expected return and 17.08 percent standard deviation equals $20 million. Table 19.1 summarizes the connection between probability of loss and value at risk.

TABLE 19.1 Probability of Loss and Value at Risk

Probability of Loss

1. (percentage loss – expected return)/standard deviation = standardized variable
2. standardized variable is converted to probability of loss

Value at Risk

1. expected return – (standardized variable × standard deviation) = percentage loss
2. percentage loss × portfolio value = value at risk

Why has value at risk captured so much attention in recent years when in fact the investment community has been applying a variation of it for more than a quarter of a century? Its popularity arose in response to the highly publicized financial disasters that have plagued the derivatives industry in recent years, such as Barings, Orange County, and Metallgesellschaft. In anticipation of legislative and regulatory intervention, the private sector introduced risk measurement systems that included value-at-risk calculations. And, as expected, regulators began to scrutinize risk management practices within the derivatives industry. The strongest impetus for the use of value at risk, however, came from bank regulators. The Group of 10,[2] meeting in Basle, Switzerland, in 1988, agreed to establish uniform capital adequacy requirements for commercial banks to guard against credit risk. By 1993, this initial agreement evolved into an explicit proposal to use a standard value-at-risk model for measuring exposure to fluctuations in interest rates, exchange rates, equity prices, and commodity prices. Finally, by 1995, the Basle Committee endorsed the banking industry's use of proprietary value-at-risk models.

Although financial institutions typically calculate value at risk over short horizons such as a single day or a week, investment managers use value at risk to gauge their portfolios' exposure to risk over longer horizons such as a month, a quarter, or a year, during which the effect of compounding is more significant.

VALUE AT RISK ASSUMING LOGNORMALITY

Compounding leads to a lognormal distribution rather than a normal distribution, which introduces considerable complexity.[3] Again, consider a portfolio with an 8.10 percent expected return and a 17.08 percent standard deviation. In order to estimate the probability that this asset will suffer a loss of 20.00 percent or more in a given year assuming lognormality, we must first convert the discrete expected return and standard deviation into their continuous counterparts, as shown.

$$\mu_C = \ln(1 + \mu_D) - \frac{\sigma_C^2}{2} \tag{19.1}$$

$$\sigma_C = \sqrt{\ln\left(\frac{\sigma_D^2}{(1 + \mu_D)^2} + 1\right)} \tag{19.2}$$

where μ_C = continuous expected return
μ_D = discrete expected return
σ_C = standard deviation of continuous returns
σ_D = standard deviation of discrete returns

The continuous expected return and standard deviation equal 6.56 percent and 15.70 percent, respectively. We must also convert –20.00 percent to its continuous counterpart, which equals –22.31 percent [ln (0.80)]. We proceed as we did earlier by first dividing the distance between –22.31 percent and 6.56 percent by the continuous standard deviation, 15.70 percent, which equals –1.839. If we look this value up in a normal distribution table, we find that 3.30 percent of the distribution of continuous returns is to the left of –22.31 percent. Therefore, the likelihood of a 20 percent loss equals 3.30 percent, not 5.00 percent, because –20.00 percent is the discrete counterpart of a –22.31 percent continuous return ($e^{-0.2231} - 1 = -0.20$). Lognormality, therefore, has a beneficial impact. There is a smaller probability of a given loss assuming lognormality than there is under the assumption of normality. As we will soon see, this distinction has intriguing implications.

Now let's estimate value at risk under the assumption of lognormality at a 5.00 percent confidence level. Because we know that a 5.00 percent probability corresponds to a standardized variable of –1.645, we subtract 1.645 times the continuous standard deviation from the continuous expected return to arrive at the percentage loss in continuous units (6.56 percent – 1.645 × 15.70 percent = –0.2023 percent), which corresponds to a discrete loss of 18.31 percent. We then convert this percentage loss to a monetary value. For a $100 million asset with an 8.10 percent expected return and 17.08 percent standard deviation, value at risk equals $18.31 million. The formulas for probability of loss and value at risk assuming lognormality are as follows.

Probability of loss:

$$Z = \frac{\ln(1+L) - \mu_C}{\sigma_C}$$

$$Pr = N[Z] \tag{19.3}$$

Value at risk:

$$L_C = \mu_C - Z\sigma_C$$

$$VaR = -\left(e^{L_C} - 1\right) \times V \tag{19.4}$$

where L = percentage loss in discrete units
$\quad L_C$ = percentage loss in continuous units
$\quad Z$ = standardized variable
$\quad N[\ ]$ = normal distribution function
$\quad Pr$ = probability of loss
$\quad V$ = asset value
$\quad VaR$ = value at risk

To be fair, I have described the simplest conception of value at risk. Portfolio returns are not always normally or even lognormally distributed. The inclusion of derivatives or the application of dynamic trading rules may introduce additional skewness to a portfolio's return distribution, and illiquidity and trading interruptions may increase the likelihood of extreme returns, which would cause a portfolio's return distribution to have fatter tails than a normal or lognormal distribution. Under these conditions, it is prudent to employ Monte Carlo or bootstrapping techniques to estimate value at risk. Moreover, even if we believe that individual asset returns are exactly lognormally distributed, a portfolio comprising these assets is not itself lognormally distributed. This inconsistency does not matter much for portfolios that contain only long positions. It is significant, however, for portfolios that include both long and short positions.

VALUE AT RISK FOR PORTFOLIOS WITH SHORT POSITIONS[4]

When we estimate value at risk for assets in which we own a long position, we focus on the left tail of its return distribution, as shown in Figure 19.1.

If, instead, we held a short position in this asset, we would suffer a loss

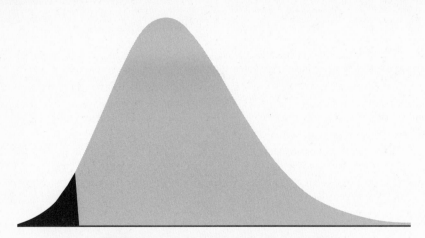

FIGURE 19.1   Value at risk for long positions

if it rose in value; hence we would be interested in the right tail of this distribution to estimate value at risk, as shown in Figure 19.2.

The 5 percent right tail is further right from the center than the 5 percent left tail is left of the center, owing to the effect of compounding.

We estimate the continuous percentage loss of a short position by adding the standardized variable times the standard deviation to the expected return and multiplying this quantity by –1, as shown by equation (19.5). Then we apply equation (19.4) to convert percentage loss in continuous units into value at risk.

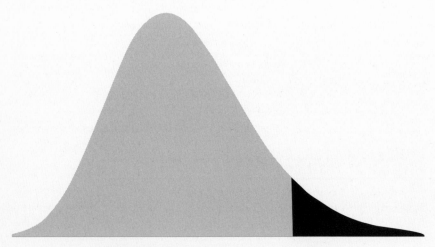

FIGURE 19.2   Value at risk for short positions

$$L_c = -(\mu_C + Z\sigma_C) \qquad\qquad (19.5)$$

The assumption of portfolio lognormality leads us to underestimate value at risk for portfolios with short positions. In order to gauge the degree of error associated with the assumption of portfolio lognormality, we can compare value at risk assuming portfolio returns are lognormally distributed, with value at risk assuming the individual assets' returns are lognormal.

Consider a portfolio that comprises two assets: a bond with an 8.00 percent expected return and a 10.00 percent standard deviation, and a stock with a 10.00 percent expected return and a 20.00 percent standard deviation. Also, assume these assets are 30.00 percent correlated with one another.

We obtain value at risk assuming the portfolio is lognormally distributed, as follows:

1. We calculate the portfolio's discrete expected return and standard deviation.
2. We convert these values to their continuous counterparts.
3. We calculate the portfolio's theoretical normal distribution in continuous units.
4. We convert the theoretical normal distribution into its lognormal counterpart by taking the exponentials of the normal observations.
5. We plot the distribution of the fitted portfolio returns.

Next we obtain value at risk assuming the assets within the portfolio are lognormally distributed:

1. We convert the discrete expected returns and standard deviations of the assets into continuous units.[5]
2. We draw 50,000 random continuous return pairs from a 30 percent correlated bivariate normal distribution.
3. We convert these 50,000 continuous return pairs into discrete returns by taking their exponentials.
4. We calculate portfolio returns from the individually simulated asset returns.
5. We plot the distribution of the simulated portfolio returns.

Figure 19.3 compares the fitted lognormal distribution (shown by the curve; portfolio returns are lognormal) with the simulated distribution (indicated by the bars; individual asset returns are lognormal) for a portfolio allocated equally to the bond and stock assets.

Figure 19.3 reveals very little difference between the fitted and simulated

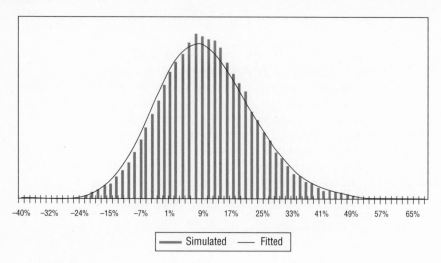

FIGURE 19.3   Fitted and simulated distributions: bonds 50%, stocks 50%

distributions. Value at risk at a 5 percent confidence level equals 10.20 percent of initial value versus 10.02 percent for the simulated distribution. At a 1 percent confidence level, fitted value at risk equals 16.90 percent compared to 17.13 percent for simulated value at risk. The closeness of these results suggests that the assumption of portfolio lognormality is not problematic for long-only portfolios.

As we introduce short positions to the portfolio, however, we see that it is no longer prudent to employ the expedient assumption of portfolio lognormality. Figure 19.4 compares fitted and simulated distributions for a portfolio that has a −50 percent exposure to bonds and a 150 percent exposure to stocks.

That the fitted distribution is slightly displaced toward the right implies that it underestimates the probability of loss and overestimates the probability of gain. Indeed, fitted value at risk at a 5 percent confidence level equals 29.51 percent of initial value compared to 31.58 percent for the simulated distribution. At a 1 percent confidence level, fitted value at risk equals 40.79 percent compared to a simulated value at risk of 45.05 percent.

The underestimation of value at risk based on a fitted lognormal distribution increases as the degree of leverage increases. Figure 19.5 illustrates this effect for a portfolio that has a −100 percent exposure to bonds and a 200 percent exposure to stocks.

Fitted value at risk at a 5 percent confidence level equals 38.58 percent

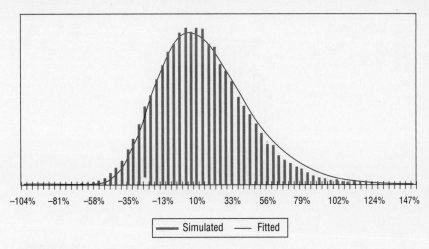

FIGURE 19.4   Fitted and simulated distributions: bonds –50%, stocks 150%

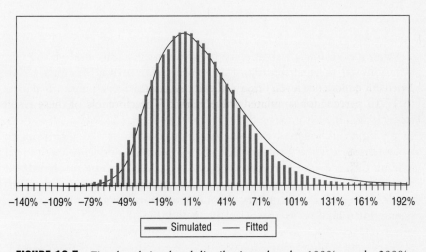

FIGURE 19.5   Fitted and simulated distributions: bonds –100%, stocks 200%

versus 44.53 percent for simulated value at risk. At a 1 percent confidence level, the comparison is 51.01 percent versus 62.79 percent.

These graphs illustrate that the lognormal approximation is a poor representation of the true distribution of returns for portfolios with short positions. This problem also arises when we compare the returns of a portfolio relative to a benchmark. Let us revisit the 50/50 stock/bond portfolio

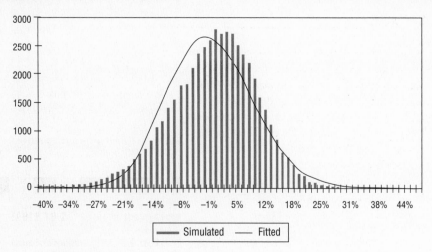

FIGURE 19.6   Deviation from benchmark: +50% bonds, −50% stocks

shown in Figure 19.3. Rather than focus on its absolute returns, though, let us consider the distribution of its returns relative to a benchmark that has a 100 percent stock allocation. Compared to this benchmark, this portfolio is 50 percent long bonds and 50 percent short stocks, as shown in Figure 19.6.

As expected, we find that the assumption of portfolio lognormality also understates relative value at risk. At a 5 percent confidence level, fitted value at risk is 16.17 percent compared to 18.28 percent for simulated value at risk. At 1 percent the comparison is 21.60 percent versus 27.10 percent. Table 19.2 summarizes the misestimation of value risk when we assume portfolio returns are lognormally distributed.

TABLE 19.2   Value at Risk per $100

Bonds/Stocks	5% Fitted	5% Simulated	1% Fitted	1% Simulated
50/50	10.20	10.02	16.90	17.13
−50/150	29.51	31.58	40.79	45.05
−100/200	38.58	44.53	51.01	62.79
50/−50*	16.17	18.28	21.60	27.10

*relative to 100% stock benchmark

SUMMARY

Value at risk is the maximum loss or minimum gain that could occur at a given confidence level over a specified horizon. If we assume asset returns are lognormally distributed, we can easily estimate value at risk analytically. However, if the individual assets that make up a portfolio are lognormally distributed, then a portfolio comprising them cannot itself be lognormal. For portfolios that hold only long positions in assets with typical return and risk profiles, the assumption of portfolio lognormality does not seriously misstate value at risk. For portfolios with short positions, however, such as leveraged portfolios and portfolios measured relative to a benchmark, the assumption of portfolio lognormality introduces a serious bias to value at risk estimation. There are many other reasons why portfolio returns may not be lognormally distributed. The inclusion of derivatives or the application of dynamic trading rules may introduce additional skewness to a portfolio's return distribution. Also, illiquidity and trading interruptions may increase the likelihood of extreme returns, which would cause a portfolio's return distribution to have fatter tails than a normal or lognormal distribution. Under these conditions, it is prudent to employ simulation techniques to estimate value at risk.

CHAPTER 20

Optimization

Optimization is a process by which we determine the most favorable tradeoff between competing interests, given the constraints we face. Within the context of portfolio management, the competing interests are risk reduction and return enhancement. Asset allocation is one form of optimization. We use an optimizer to identify the asset weights that produce the lowest level of risk for various levels of expected return. Optimization is also used to construct portfolios of securities that minimize risk in terms of tracking error relative to a benchmark portfolio. In these applications, we are usually faced with the constraint that the asset weights must sum to 1.

We can also employ optimization techniques to manage strategies that call for offsetting long and short positions. Suppose, for example, that we wish to purchase currencies expected to yield high returns and to sell currencies expected to yield low returns, with the net result that we are neither long nor short the local currency. In this case, we would impose a constraint that the currency exposures sum to 0.

This chapter is intended as a tutorial on optimization. I will demonstrate, through the use of numerical examples, how to optimize a two-asset portfolio with only a pencil and the back of an envelope. If you wish to include three assets, you may need the front of the envelope as well. Beyond three assets, a computer would come in handy.

THE OBJECTIVE FUNCTION

Suppose we wish to identify combinations of stocks and bonds that produce the lowest levels of risk for varying amounts of expected return. To begin, we must define a portfolio's expected return and risk.

The expected return of a portfolio comprised of just stocks and bonds is simply the weighted average of the assets' expected returns, as shown in equation (20.1):

$$\mu_p = w_S \mu_S + w_B \mu_B \tag{20.1}$$

where μ_p = the portfolio's expected return
μ_S = the expected return of stocks
μ_B = the expected return of bonds
w_S = the percentage of the portfolio allocated to stocks
w_B = the percentage allocated to bonds

Portfolio risk is a little trickier. It is defined as volatility, and it is measured by the standard deviation or variance (the standard deviation squared) around the portfolio's expected return. To compute a portfolio's variance, we must consider not only the variance of the component assets' returns, but also the extent to which the assets' returns co-vary.[1] The variance of a portfolio of stocks and bonds is computed as follows:

$$\sigma_p^2 = w_S^2 \sigma_S^2 + w_B^2 \sigma_B^2 + 2 w_S w_B \rho \sigma_S \sigma_B \tag{20.2}$$

where σ_p^2 = the portfolio variance
σ_S = the standard deviation of stocks
σ_B = the standard deviation of bonds
ρ = the correlation between stocks and bonds

Our objective, as stated earlier, is to minimize portfolio risk. Our first constraint is that the weighted average of the stock and bond returns must equal the expected return for the portfolio. We are also faced with a second constraint: We must allocate our entire portfolio to some combination of stocks and bonds. We would not want to leave part of it uninvested. Therefore, the fraction we allocate to stocks plus the fraction we allocate to bonds must equal 1.

We can combine our objective and constraints to form the following objective function, in which $E(U)$ equals expected utility.

$$\begin{aligned} E(U) = &\left(w_S^2 \sigma_S^2 + w_B^2 \sigma_B^2 + 2 w_S w_B \rho \sigma_S \sigma_B \right) \\ &+ \lambda_1 \left[w_S \mu_S + w_B \mu_B - \mu_p \right] + \lambda_2 \left(w_S + w_B - 1 \right) \end{aligned} \tag{20.3}$$

The first line of equation (20.3) simply equals portfolio variance, the quantity to be minimized. The second line represents the two constraints. The first constraint ensures that the weighted average of the stock and bond returns equals the portfolio's expected return. The Greek letter lambda (λ) is called a Lagrange multiplier. It is a variable introduced to facilitate optimization when we face constraints, and it does not always lend itself to economic interpretation. The second constraint guarantees that the portfolio is fully invested. Again, lambda serves to facilitate a solution.

A DIGRESSION ON CALCULUS

You may recall from elementary calculus that a function reaches its minimum or maximum value when its first derivative, or slope, equals 0. The first derivative measures the amount by which the value of the function changes given a one-unit change in the variable upon which it depends. Consider the following quadratic function:

$$y = x^2 - 4x + 10$$

If we set its derivative, $2x - 4$, equal to 0 and solve for x, we find that this function reaches its minimum value when x equals 1. Figure 20.1 illustrates this.

As Figure 20.1 shows, a function reaches its extreme value when it flattens out or has no slope, which is to say when its first derivative equals 0. With this insight, let us return to our objective function.

Unlike the quadratic function described above, which has a single unknown value, our objective function has four unknown values: (1) the percentage of the portfolio to be allocated to stocks, (2) the percentage to be

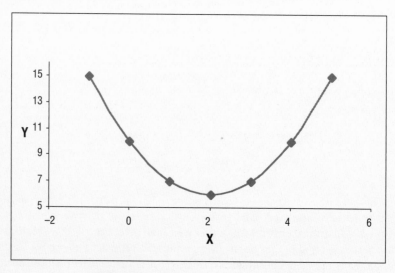

FIGURE 20.1 The function $y = x^2 - 4x + 10$

allocated to bonds, (3) the Lagrange multiplier for the first constraint, and (4) the Lagrange multiplier for the second constraint. To minimize portfolio risk given our constraints, we must take the partial derivative of the objective function with respect to each asset weight and with respect to each Lagrange multiplier and set it equal to zero, as shown below:

$$\frac{\partial E(U)}{\partial w_S} = 2w_S\sigma_S^2 + 2w_B\rho\sigma_S\sigma_B + \lambda_1\mu_S + \lambda_2 = 0 \qquad (20.4)$$

$$\frac{\partial E(U)}{\partial w_B} = 2w_B\sigma_B^2 + 2w_S\rho\sigma_S\sigma_B + \lambda_1\mu_B + \lambda_2 = 0 \qquad (20.5)$$

$$\frac{\partial E(U)}{\partial \lambda_1} = w_S\mu_S + w_B\mu_B - \mu_p = 0 \qquad (20.6)$$

$$\frac{\partial E(U)}{\partial \lambda_2} = w_S + w_B - 1 = 0 \qquad (20.7)$$

Given assumptions for expected return, standard deviation, and correlation (which I will specify later), we wish to find the values of w_S and w_B associated with different values of R_p, the portfolio's expected return. The values for λ_1 and λ_2 are merely mathematical by-products of the solution.

One approach for solving a system of linear equations is by matrix inversion. Again, let us digress for a moment and focus on a simpler example of matrix inversion.[2]

A DIGRESSION ON MATRIX ALGEBRA

In simple algebra, we would solve for x in an expression such as $y = bx$ by dividing y by b. In matrix algebra, however, we cannot divide. The analogous operation is called matrix inversion.

Suppose we have the following system of linear equations:

$$6x_1 + 3x_2 + x_3 = 22$$

$$x_1 + 4x_2 - 2x_3 = 12$$

$$4x_1 - x_2 + 5x_3 = 10$$

We can represent this system of linear equations with a coefficient matrix, a vector for the variables, and a vector for the constants, as follows:

$$\begin{bmatrix} 6 & 3 & 1 \\ 1 & 4 & -2 \\ 4 & -1 & 5 \end{bmatrix} \times \begin{bmatrix} x_1 \\ x_2 \\ x_3 \end{bmatrix} = \begin{bmatrix} 22 \\ 12 \\ 10 \end{bmatrix}$$

In order to solve for x_1, x_2, and x_3, we must find the inverse of the coefficient matrix and multiply it by the vector of constants. The inverse of the coefficient matrix is as follows:[3]

$$\begin{bmatrix} 18/52 & -16/52 & -10/52 \\ -13/52 & 26/52 & 13/52 \\ -17/52 & 18/52 & 21/52 \end{bmatrix}$$

We multiply this inverse by the vector of constants to yield a vector with the values for x_1, x_2, and x_3, as follows:

$$\begin{bmatrix} x_1 \\ x_2 \\ x_3 \end{bmatrix} = \begin{bmatrix} 18/52 & -16/52 & -10/52 \\ -13/52 & 26/52 & 13/52 \\ -17/52 & 18/52 & 21/52 \end{bmatrix} \times \begin{bmatrix} 22 \\ 12 \\ 10 \end{bmatrix} = \begin{bmatrix} 2 \\ 3 \\ 1 \end{bmatrix}$$

Now let us return to our system of linear equations, (20.4) through (20.7), and rewrite it in matrix notation.

$$\begin{bmatrix} 2\sigma_S^2 & 2\rho\sigma_S\sigma_B & \mu_S & 1 \\ 2\rho\sigma_S\sigma_B & 2\sigma_B^2 & \mu_B & 1 \\ \mu_S & \mu_B & 0 & 0 \\ 1 & 1 & 0 & 0 \end{bmatrix} \times \begin{bmatrix} w_S \\ w_B \\ \lambda_1 \\ \lambda_2 \end{bmatrix} = \begin{bmatrix} 0 \\ 0 \\ \mu_p \\ 1 \end{bmatrix}$$

We must next estimate the inputs for expected return, standard deviation, and correlation. Suppose that, after careful examination of historical data and thorough analysis of current economic and capital market conditions, we arrive at the assumptions shown in Table 20.1.

TABLE 20.1 Capital Market Assumptions

	Expected Return	Standard Deviation	Correlation
Stocks	12%	20%	
Bonds	8%	10%	50%

With these assumptions, we can rewrite the coefficient matrix as follows:

$$
\begin{bmatrix}
0.08 & 0.02 & 0.12 & 1.00 \\
0.02 & 0.02 & 0.08 & 1.00 \\
0.12 & 0.08 & 0.00 & 0.00 \\
1.00 & 1.00 & 0.00 & 0.00
\end{bmatrix}
$$

Its inverse is as follows:

$$
\begin{bmatrix}
0 & 0 & 25 & -2 \\
0 & 0 & -25 & 3 \\
25 & -25 & -37.5 & 3 \\
-2 & 3 & 3 & -0.26
\end{bmatrix}
$$

Because the constant vector includes a variable for the portfolio's expected return, we obtain a vector of formulas rather than values, when we multiply the inverse matrix by the vector of constants, as shown below.

$$
\begin{bmatrix}
w_S \\
w_B \\
\lambda_1 \\
\lambda_2
\end{bmatrix}
=
\begin{bmatrix}
25 \times \mu_p - 2 \\
-25 \times \mu_p + 3 \\
-37.5 \times \mu_p + 3 \\
3 \times \mu_p - 0.26
\end{bmatrix}
$$

We are interested only in the first two formulas. The first formula yields the percentage to be invested in stocks in order to minimize risk when we substitute a value for the portfolio's expected return. The second formula yields the percentage to be invested in bonds. Table 20.2 shows

TABLE 20.2 Optimal Portfolios

Expected Return	Standard Deviation	Stock Percent	Bond Percent
8.00%	10.00%	0%	100%
9.00%	10.90%	25%	75%
10.00%	13.23%	50%	50%
11.00%	16.39%	75%	25%
12.00%	20.00%	100%	0%
13.00%	23.85%	125%	-25%

the allocations to stocks and bonds that minimize risk for portfolio expected returns ranging from 8 percent to 13 percent.

From Table 20.2 we see that we must sell bonds short and leverage our exposure to stocks in order to achieve a portfolio expected return that is greater than the higher of the expected returns on stocks or bonds.

AN ALTERNATIVE APPROACH

In 1987, William Sharpe published an algorithm for portfolio optimization that has the dual virtues of accommodating many real-world complexities while appealing to our intuition.[4] Consider the following objective function to be maximized.

$$E(U) = \mu_p - \lambda_{RA}\sigma_p^2 \tag{20.8}$$

where μ_p = portfolio expected return
λ_{RA} = risk aversion
σ_p^2 = portfolio variance

Risk aversion measures how many units of expected return we are willing to sacrifice in order to reduce risk (variance) by one unit. By maximizing this objective function, we maximize expected return minus a quantity representing our aversion to risk times risk (as measured by variance).

Again assume we have a portfolio consisting of stocks and bonds. Substituting the equations for portfolio expected return and variance (equations [20.1] and [20.2]), we can rewrite the objective function as follows.

$$E(U) = w_S\mu_S + w_B\mu_B - \lambda_{RA}(w_S^2\sigma_S^2 + w_B^2\sigma_B^2 + 2\rho w_S w_B \sigma_S \sigma_B) \tag{20.9}$$

This objective function measures the expected utility or satisfaction we derive from a particular combination of expected return and risk, given our attitude toward risk. Its partial derivative with respect to each asset weight is expressed as follows:

$$\frac{\partial E(U)}{\partial w_S} = \mu_S - \lambda_{RA}\left(2w_S\sigma_S^2 + 2w_B\rho\sigma_S\sigma_B\right) = 0 \tag{20.10}$$

$$\frac{\partial E(U)}{\partial w_B} = \mu_B - \lambda_{RA}\left(2w_B\sigma_B^2 + 2w_S\rho\sigma_S\sigma_B\right) = 0 \tag{20.11}$$

The equation for each asset measures how much we increase or decrease our expected utility, starting from our current asset mix, by increasing our exposure to that asset. A negative partial derivative indicates that we improve expected utility by reducing exposure to that asset, while a positive partial derivative indicates that we should raise the exposure to that asset in order to improve our expected utility.

Let us retain our earlier assumptions about the expected returns and standard deviations of stocks and bonds and their correlation. Further, let's assume our portfolio is currently allocated 60 percent to stocks and 40 percent to bonds and that our aversion toward risk equals 2. Risk aversion of 2 means we are willing to reduce expected return by two units in order to lower variance by one unit.

If we substitute these values into the partial derivative equations, we find that we improve our expected utility by 0.008 units if we increase our exposure to stocks by 1 percent, and that we improve our expected utility by 0.04 units if we increase our exposure to bonds by 1 percent. Both derivatives are positive. However, we can only allocate 100 percent of the portfolio. We should therefore increase our exposure to the asset class with the higher derivative by 1 percent and reduce by the same amount our exposure to the asset class with the lower derivative. In this way, we ensure that we are always 100 percent invested.

Having switched our allocations in line with the relative magnitudes of the derivatives, we recompute the partial derivatives given our new allocation of 59 percent stocks and 41 percent bonds. Again, bonds have a higher derivative than stocks; hence we shift again from stocks to bonds. If we proceed in this fashion, we will find when our portfolio is allocated one-third to stocks and two-thirds to bonds, the derivatives are exactly equal to each other. At this point, we cannot improve our expected utility any further by changing the allocation between stocks and bonds. We have maximized our objective function.

By varying the values we assign to λ we identify mixes of stocks and bonds for many levels of risk aversion, thus enabling us to construct the entire efficient frontier of stocks and bonds.

By now you are probably wondering why you should bother with fancy computer programs to optimize portfolios, since you can optimize them on the back of an envelope. I have purposely dealt with only two assets. As we increase the number of assets under consideration, we increase by a faster rate the number of variables to be included in our objective function. The sum of the number of expected returns, standard deviations, and correlations to be included equals $(n^2 + n)/2$, where n equals the number of assets we wish to consider. Moreover, our examples are abstractions of real-world optimization problems. In the real world, we may be faced with short selling constraints and other allocation constraints, as well as with transaction costs. Although it is certainly useful to understand the intuition and mathematical techniques that underlie optimization, most practical applications require sophisticated computer programs.

ERROR MAXIMIZATION

There is a dark side to optimization. Cynics refer to it as error maximization. In search of assets that increase a portfolio's expected return and lower its risk, optimization, by its very nature, favors assets for which expected return is overestimated and risk is underestimated.

Consider, for example, two assets, both of which have expected returns of 10 percent. We do not know the true expected returns, however. We must estimate them, and in so doing we are vulnerable to errors. Suppose we estimate one asset to have an expected return of 8 percent and the other to have an expected return of 12 percent. If they both contribute the same degree of risk to the portfolio, the optimizer will favor the asset with the 12 percent return estimate.

This problem pertains as well to errors in our risk estimates. Moreover, the problem is exacerbated as we increase the number of assets. The errors do not cancel each other out. Rather, they accumulate.

This bias leads to two problems. First, the expected return of the optimized portfolio is overstated, while its risk is understated. We can redress this problem to some extent by reducing our portfolio's estimated expected return or by augmenting its estimated risk to account for estimation error.

There is a more pernicious consequence of error maximization, though. Not only do we misestimate the portfolio's expected return and risk, we do so for the wrong portfolio. Essentially, we have excluded or underweighted assets for which we have underestimated return and overestimated risk, substituting for them assets for which we have erred in the opposite direction.

A common palliative for error maximization is to blend each expected return with the cross-sectional average of returns or, if we are purists, with the expected return of the minimum variance combination of the assets. The blending weights are determined by the size of the samples used to derive the means. As an alternative, we might try to scale our estimates based on whatever information we can gather about their reliability. If we derive our estimates by extrapolating historical data, for example, we might wish to scale them as a function of the number of observations we used.

Richard Michaud has proposed an alternative approach for dealing with these issues. He claims that optimization should be viewed as a statistical procedure, in which many efficient frontiers are estimated based on distributions of the inputs rather than point estimates. He argues that investors should take action only if the mean and variance of the current portfolio fall outside of a given range associated with a statistically generated frontier.[5]

WRONG AND ALONE

Although most serious investors follow Markowitz's prescription for constructing portfolios, they frequently impose constraints to force a more palatable solution. For example, an investor might instruct the optimizer to find the combination of assets with the lowest standard deviation for a particular expected return, subject to the constraint that no more than 10 percent of the portfolio is allocated to foreign assets or nontraditional investments and that no less than 40 percent is allocated to domestic equities. Investors impose such constraints because they are reticent to depart from the crowd when there is a significant chance they will be wrong. The matrix in Table 20.3 illustrates this point.

If we believe investors care not only about how they perform in an absolute sense but also about how their performance stacks up against other investors, there are four possible outcomes. An investor achieves favorable absolute returns and at the same time outperforms his or her peers, which would be great, as represented by quadrant 1. Alternatively, an investor might beat the competition but fall short of an absolute target (quadrant 2). Or an investor might generate a high absolute return but underperform the competition (quadrant 3). These results would probably be tolerable because the investor produces superior performance along at least one dimension. However, it would likely be very unpleasant to generate an unfavorable absolute result and at the same time perform poorly relative to other investors (quadrant 4). It is the fear of this outcome that induces investors to conform to the norm.

In 1995 George Chow introduced a technique that optimally deals with absolute and relative performance simultaneously.[6] In order to describe Chow's innovation, recall Sharpe's approach to optimization, which identifies the optimal portfolio by maximizing expected return minus risk aversion times variance. It is easy to modify this objective function to deal

TABLE 20.3 Possible Joint Outcomes

	Absolute Returns	
Relative Returns	Favorable	Unfavorable
Favorable	1. Great	2. Tolerable
Unfavorable	3. Tolerable	4. Very unpleasant

with aversion to tracking error. Tracking error is a measure of relative risk. Just as the standard deviation measures dispersion around an average value, tracking error also measures dispersion, but instead around a benchmark's returns. It is literally the standard deviation of relative returns. Imagine subtracting a sequence of benchmark returns from a sequence of portfolio returns covering the same period. The standard deviation of these differences is what we call tracking error.

If we care only about relative performance, we could define our returns net of a benchmark and optimize in dimensions of expected relative return and tracking error. This approach would address our concern about deviating from the norm, assuming our benchmark represents normal investment choices. However, we would fail to address our concern about absolute results. Chow showed how to augment the objective function to include both measures of risk:

$$\text{Expected Return} - \text{Risk Aversion} \times \text{Variance}$$
$$- \text{Tracking Aversion} \times \text{Tracking Error}^2$$

This measure of investor satisfaction simultaneously addresses concern about absolute performance and relative performance. Instead of producing an efficient frontier in two dimensions, however, this optimization process, which Chow calls mean-variance–tracking error optimization, produces an efficient surface in three dimensions: expected return, standard deviation, and tracking error, as displayed in Figure 20.2.

The efficient surface is bounded on the upper left by the traditional mean-variance efficient frontier, which comprises efficient portfolios in dimensions of expected return and standard deviation. The leftmost portfolio on the mean-variance efficient frontier is the riskless asset. The right boundary of the efficient surface is the mean–tracking error efficient frontier. It comprises portfolios that offer the highest expected return for varying levels of tracking error. The leftmost portfolio on the mean–tracking error efficient frontier is the benchmark portfolio, because it has no tracking error. The efficient surface is bounded on the bottom by combinations of the riskless asset and the benchmark portfolio. All of the portfolios that lie on this surface are efficient in three dimensions. It does not necessarily follow, however, that a three-dimensional efficient portfolio is always efficient in any two dimensions. Consider, for example, the riskless asset. Although it is on both the mean-variance efficient frontier and the efficient surface, if it were plotted in dimensions of just expected return and tracking error, it would appear very inefficient if the benchmark included higher expected return assets such as stocks and bonds. This asset has a low ex-

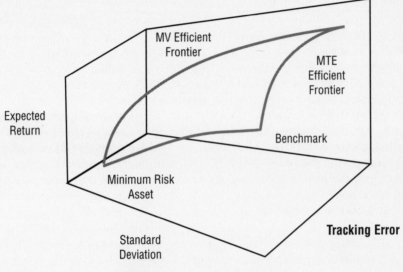

FIGURE 20.2   The efficient surface

pected return compared to the benchmark and yet a high degree of tracking error.

This approach to optimization will almost certainly yield a result that is superior to constrained mean-variance optimization in the following sense. For a given combination of expected return and standard deviation, it produces a portfolio with less tracking error. Or, for a given combination of expected return and tracking error, it identifies a portfolio with a lower standard deviation. Or, finally, for a given combination of standard deviation and tracking error, it finds a portfolio with a higher expected return than a constrained mean-variance optimization. Most of the portfolios identified by constrained mean-variance optimization would lie beneath the efficient surface. In fact, the only way in which Chow's procedure would fail to improve upon a constrained mean-variance optimization is if the investor knew in advance what constraints were optimal. But, of course, this knowledge could only come from a mean-variance–tracking error optimization.

To date, the investment community has addressed aversion to being wrong and alone in an ad hoc fashion by imposing allocation constraints on the mean-variance optimization process. A superior approach is to encompass both absolute and relative measures of risk simultaneously in an unconstrained optimization.

VALUE IN—GARBAGE OUT

During medieval times there was widespread belief in a chemical process known as alchemy, in which chemists would transmute base metals into gold. Most educated people today have since abandoned this view—most, but not all. There are still some investors who contend that financial alchemy is the only justification for optimization. They invoke the tiresome adage, "garbage in—garbage out," to criticize the use of optimization to form portfolios. Apparently these critics believe we should either require optimizers to convert valueless inputs into efficiently diversified portfolios, or we should not use them at all. If we extend this logic, it follows that we should also abandon calculators, for they, too, fail to convert mistaken inputs into correct solutions.

I suspect the optimization critics hide behind this ridiculous adage in order to conceal their ignorance about optimization. I am led to this conclusion because many of these critics believe that optimization demands historical means, variances, and correlations as inputs, whether or not these historical values are good predictors of future means, variances, and correlations. We can easily refute this belief by referring to Markowitz's classic article, "Portfolio Selection," which begins with these revealing sentences:

> *The process of selecting a portfolio may be divided into two stages. The first stage starts with observation and experience and ends with beliefs about the future performances of available securities. The second stage starts with the relevant beliefs about future performances and ends with the choice of portfolio. This paper is concerned with the second stage.*[7]

Markowitz is clear, right from the outset, that optimization is about the choice of a portfolio given a set of beliefs, and not about how to form those beliefs. Moreover, he explicitly acknowledges that beliefs are derived from observation and experience, neither of which limits the formation of beliefs to extrapolation of historical values. Because investors often refer to Markowitz's approach to portfolio selection as mean-variance optimization, it's possible some of them assume the inputs must be historical means and variances. These terms, in fact, pertain to the means and variances of future returns, and they need not be linked to the past. We are free to use whatever return and risk estimates we like when optimizing a portfolio. If we believe the past is informative we should use it, but not to the exclusion of other useful information about the future.

We would be naïve if we expected optimization to convert valueless return and risk estimates into efficient portfolios. Rather, we optimize to preserve whatever value there is in our return and risk estimates when we translate them into portfolios. The matrix in Table 20.4 illustrates this point.

If we start out with pure garbage as inputs, whether or not we optimize makes little difference. We will most likely fail to identify portfolios that are even remotely efficient. If, however, we start out with return and risk estimates that contain some information, we must optimize in order to transmit the value of this information to our portfolio. Therefore, both good inputs and optimization are necessary for success, but neither by itself is sufficient.

Let's also be clear about what we mean by success. Although optimization identifies efficient portfolios in-sample, it is unrealistic to expect these portfolios to lie on the efficient frontier out-of-sample.[8] In fact, to generate portfolios that are perfectly mean-variance efficient out-of-sample, we must optimize with perfectly precise inputs, which of course is impossible. Therefore, we should consider optimization successful if it identifies portfolios with return and risk profiles that are superior to alternative weighting schemes out-of-sample.

Table 20.5 shows the annualized total return and standard deviation of two portfolios: the capitalization-weighted MSCI world index of developed market equity indexes, and an optimized portfolio of these same indexes. Notice that the optimized portfolio produced a higher return than the capitalization-weighted portfolio. Moreover, it achieved this higher return with much less risk. Clearly, optimization succeeded in producing a superior result. But how much precision was required of the inputs?

Decide for yourself whether this outcome required unrealistic forecasting ability. I rebalanced the optimized portfolio each month based on inputs that would have been available prior to each optimization; hence the

TABLE 20.4 Possible Joint Outcomes

Inputs	Don't Optimize	Optimize
Favorable	Garbage	Garbage
Unfavorable	Garbage	Efficient portfolio

TABLE 20.5 Out-of-Sample (5/31/90–7/31/01)

	MSCI World Index	Optimized Portfolio
Return	9.65%	10.51%
Risk	15.10%	13.32%

optimization results are out-of-sample. I estimated the variances and correlations from monthly returns during the five-year period preceding each optimization. I did not try any other sample size, nor did I employ any clever weighting scheme. I simply weighted each return equally and applied the standard formulas to calculate variances and correlations. Moreover, I looked at only one measurement period, the entire history available to me up to the time I performed the back test. The MSCI index began in 1985, and I needed the first five years to calculate the variances and correlations for my first optimization in 1990. I then moved forward one month to estimate the variances and correlations for the second optimization, and proceeded accordingly month by month through 2001.

Many investors have argued that historical variances and correlations are not sufficiently informative to be of any value; that in effect these values are garbage. Perhaps they are correct. Maybe I was so skillful at forecasting returns I didn't need useful risk estimates. But this was not the case. I assumed I knew nothing about return differences across countries and set each country's return equal to 0.00 percent in all of the monthly optimizations. The mere process of optimization produced this superior out-of-sample performance without benefit of any forecasting ability; that is, garbage in—value out. Although my results effectively constitute financial alchemy, I doubt such an outcome is common. I wish simply to demonstrate that we do not always need a high degree of accuracy in our estimates of means, variances, and correlations for optimization to improve upon alternative weighting schemes.

Optimization is a process for combining assets into efficient portfolios based on a set of beliefs about expected returns, variances, and correlations.[9] It places no restrictions on how we form these beliefs, nor does it require us to extrapolate historical values. Although optimization is unlikely to transform garbage into perfectly efficient portfolios, it will often transform even marginally informative inputs into portfolios with return and risk profiles that are superior to alternative weighting schemes. At the very least, it will prevent us from squandering whatever value there may be in our inputs; thus it is a necessary condition for success.

CHAPTER 21

Risk Budgets

For many investors, risk budgets are an essential feature of their investment process, yet it seems as though not everyone agrees on the precise
meaning of the term. Intuitively, a risk budget conveys the notion that a
portfolio's risk is somehow apportioned to various components such as asset classes or investment managers, but this notion involves certain issues
that are stubbornly complex. First of all, it would not make much sense to
apportion risk without regard to the associated expected returns. Moreover, for many descriptions of risk, the quantities associated with the various components will not sum to the quantity associated with the total
portfolio. Finally, if risk is to be apportioned efficiently, the allocations
must correspond to efficient mean-variance portfolio allocations. Let's explore these issues so that we might better understand risk budgets and their
role in the investment process.

WHICH RISK?

Risk is usually construed as uncertainty around the expected return, and it
is most often measured as the standard deviation of returns or its squared
value, variance.[1] It would not make much sense, however, to say we wish to
expose our portfolio to a certain amount of risk from a particular component without also considering how much return we expect that component
to produce. For this reason investors have embraced a risk measure known
as value at risk, for budgeting purposes.[2]

Value at risk is generally understood to mean the maximum loss or
lowest gain which could occur at a given confidence level over a specified
horizon, and it is based on both expected return and standard deviation.
We can therefore define a risk budget as the assignment of value-at-risk
measures to various components of a portfolio. These components can
be defined in many ways, and measured either in absolute terms or relative to a benchmark.

EFFICIENT RISK BUDGETS

How do we determine the assignment of value-at-risk measures? One's initial response may be to divide the portfolio's total value at risk into various components, but value at risk cannot be disaggregated. It is a function of standard deviation, which is not additive, and it depends on interaction effects, which cannot be disentangled. Instead, we convert the percentage of the portfolio value allocated to a particular component into a value-at-risk measure.

Although the conversion of these percentage allocations into value-at-risk measures produces a risk budget, it may not result in a mean-variance efficient risk budget. A risk budget is mean-variance efficient only if the portfolio allocations themselves are mean-variance efficient.[3] The intuition here is that for any given expected return, a portfolio located on the efficient frontier has the lowest standard deviation. Thus, for any given expected return, the portfolio with the lowest value at risk must also lie on the efficient frontier. Therefore, any risk budget that is not mean-variance efficient has a higher portfolio value at risk for any given confidence level than a corresponding portfolio that is mean-variance efficient.

We should prefer risk budgets that are mean-variance efficient, but we should not regard risk budgeting as a process for choosing a particular portfolio along the efficient frontier. More specifically, we should not necessarily select the portfolio with the lowest value at risk. Portfolio choice based on minimizing value at risk implies an improbable attitude toward risk. It would assign infinite displeasure to any breach of a value-at-risk constraint regardless of the extent, and it would give no credit to outcomes that offer a substantial cushion with respect to a value-at-risk constraint. Very few investors have such a narrow attitude toward risk. Instead, investors should consider portfolios all along the efficient frontier and evaluate them based on their entire probability distributions. By employing this approach to portfolio selection, an investor implicitly considers a wide range of possible outcomes, not just a single threshold. We should therefore think of risk budgeting as an extension of mean-variance optimization that translates portfolio allocations into value-at-risk measures.

Suppose we wish to allocate a $100 million portfolio among three investment managers who have the expected returns, standard deviations, and correlations shown in Table 21.1. Also assume our risk aversion equals 2.5, which means we are willing to give up 2.5 units of expected return in order to lower variance by one unit. With these assumptions, the optimal percentage allocation to these managers is given in the far right column of Table 21.1.[4]

The traditional approach for implementing these portfolio allocations would be to invest $20.70 million with manager 1, $30.73 million with

TABLE 21.1 Optimal Allocation

	Expected Return	Standard Deviation	Correlations Manager 1	Manager 2	Manager 3	Efficient Allocations
Manager 1	12.00%	25.00%	100.00%	30.00%	10.00%	20.70%
Manager 2	8.00%	15.00%	30.00%	100.00%	5.00%	30.73%
Manager 3	6.00%	10.00%	10.00%	5.00%	100.00%	48.57%
Portfolio	7.86%	9.65%				100.00%

manager 2, and $48.57 million with manager 3. We produce a risk budget by converting these allocations into value-at-risk measures. Purely for expediency, I demonstrate the construction of a risk budget under the simplifying assumption that returns are normally distributed. I include a technical appendix at the end of this chapter which relaxes this assumption and shows how to perform the requisite calculations based on the assumption of lognormality.

At a confidence level of 5 percent, manager 1's value at risk equals $6.03 million. This manager could fulfill this assignment by investing the full $20.70 million allocation or by investing a smaller amount and using leverage to bring the value at risk to $6.03 million. The objective is to manage the position so that it has no more than a 5 percent probability of losing more than $6.03 million over a one-year horizon, irrespective of the amount of capital committed.

Table 21.2 shows the value at risk associated with each of the manager allocations as well as for the total portfolio, assuming a 5 percent confidence level.

Note that the sum of the individual value-at-risk measures is more than twice as large as the portfolio value at risk ($16.23 million versus $8.02 million). The reason for this discrepancy is that the assets are less than perfectly correlated with each other and therefore introduce diversification to the portfolio. Also, note that the portfolio has the smallest

TABLE 21.2 Risk Budget

	Efficient Allocations	Value at Risk ($million, 5%)
Manager 1	20.70%	6.03
Manager 2	30.73%	5.12
Manager 3	48.57%	5.08
Portfolio	100.00%	8.02

exposure to manager 1 and the largest exposure to manager 3, yet manager 1 has a higher value at risk than manager 3. This comparison underscores the point that position size is not always a good indication of risk exposure.

If we implement this risk budget by leveraging smaller monetary allocations, it is important that these leveraged positions preserve the expected returns, standard deviations, and correlations associated with the original portfolio allocations, in order to preserve its optimality. If this is done, a risk budget's economic equivalence with monetary allocations will prevail for any confidence level used to measure value at risk.

RISK ATTRIBUTION

Although a risk budget accurately describes the exposure to loss of the various portfolio components, it does not necessarily provide insight about the sources of the total portfolio's exposure to loss. In order to understand how a portfolio's components contribute to its total value at risk, we must measure the sensitivity of a portfolio's value at risk to a small change in the portfolio's exposure to each component. We call this process risk attribution.

Let us once again consider a portfolio that employs three investment managers. In order to attribute the portfolio's value at risk, we must calculate the partial derivative of the portfolio's value at risk with respect to each of the managers' allocations. Once again, I demonstrate this procedure under the assumption that returns are normally distributed, so that the mathematics are reasonably accessible.

We begin by writing the partial derivative of a portfolio's value at risk with respect to manager allocation as the sum of two partial derivatives, which, for manager 1, is given by equation (21.1).

$$\frac{\partial VaR}{\partial w_1} = \frac{\partial \mu_p}{\partial w_1} + \frac{\partial Z\sigma_p}{\partial w_1} \tag{21.1}$$

where w_1 = exposure to manager 1
μ_p = the portfolio's expected return
σ_p = expected portfolio standard deviation

Next, we define portfolio expected return and standard deviation as a function of the portfolio's exposure to the component managers.

$$\mu_p = w_1\mu_1 + w_2\mu_2 + w_3\mu_3 \tag{21.2}$$

where μ_1, μ_2, and μ_3 = expected returns of managers 1, 2, and 3

$$\sigma_p = (w_1^2\sigma_1^2 + w_2^2\sigma_2^2 + w_3^2\sigma_3^2 + 2w_1w_2\rho_{12}\sigma_1\sigma_2$$
$$+ 2w_1w_3\rho_{13}\sigma_1\sigma_3 + 2w_2w_3\rho_{23}\sigma_2\sigma_3)^{1/2} \quad (21.3)$$

where σ_1, σ_2, and σ_3 = standard deviations of managers 1, 2, and 3
ρ = correlation between managers

The derivative of portfolio expected return with respect to exposure to manager 1 is straightforward.

$$\frac{\partial \mu_p}{\partial w_1} = \mu_1 \quad (21.4)$$

The derivative of $Z\sigma_p$ with respect to exposure to manager 1 is slightly more complicated. We need to invoke the chain rule, by which we first take the partial derivative of $Z\sigma_p$ with respect to portfolio variance and then multiply it by the partial derivative of portfolio variance with respect to exposure to manager 1.

$$\frac{\partial Z\sigma_p}{\partial w_1} = \frac{\partial Z\sigma_p}{\partial \sigma_p^2} \times \frac{\partial Z\sigma_p^2}{\partial w_1} \quad (21.5)$$

which equals

$$\frac{\partial Z\sigma_p}{\partial w_1} = -\left(\frac{1}{2}\right)Z\left(\sigma_p^2\right)^{-1/2} \times \left(2w_1\sigma_1^2 + 2w_2\rho_{12}\sigma_1\sigma_2 + 2w_3\rho_{13}\sigma_1\sigma_3\right) \quad (21.6)$$

or, more specifically,

$$\frac{\partial Z\sigma_p}{\partial w_1} = -\left(\frac{1}{2}\right)Z(w_1^2\sigma_1^2 + w_2^2\sigma_2^2 + w_3^2\sigma_3^2 + 2w_1w_2\rho_{12}\sigma_1\sigma_2$$
$$+ 2w_1w_3\rho_{13}\sigma_1\sigma_3 + 2w_2w_3\rho_{23}\sigma_2\sigma_3)^{-1/2} \quad (21.7)$$
$$\times (2w_1\sigma_1^2 + 2w_2\rho_{12}\sigma_1\sigma_2 + 2w_3\rho_{13}\sigma_1\sigma_3)$$

Table 21.3 shows the risk attribution of the portfolio's total value at risk.

Here is how we interpret these sensitivities. If we were to increase the allocation to manager 1 by 1.00 percent, from 20.70 percent to 21.70 per-

TABLE 21.3 Risk Budget

	Efficient Allocations	Value at Risk ($million, 5%)	Value-at-Risk Sensitivity
Manager 1	20.70%	6.03	0.1801
Manager 2	30.73%	5.12	0.0837
Manager 3	48.57%	5.08	0.0355
Portfolio	100.00%	8.02	

cent, total portfolio value at risk would rise from $8.02 million to about $8.20 million.

The ranking of the portfolio's value at risk sensitivities will not necessarily match the ranking of the portfolio's percentage exposures or the ranking of the individual components' values at risk. Note, for example, that manager 1 has the smallest percentage allocation, yet the greatest impact on the portfolio's value at risk. Also, note that although manager 2's value at risk is about the same as manager 3's, an additional $1 allocation to manager 2 increases portfolio value at risk by $0.0837, whereas the same increase in allocation to manager 3 raises portfolio value at risk by less than half as much, $0.0355. The reason for this inconsistency is that even though manager 2 has about the same individual value at risk, this is more than offset by manager 2's higher correlation with the portfolio.

This risk attribution conveys a very important message. If we wish to limit the potential loss of our portfolio, we should focus not on its largest component, nor its most volatile component, nor even the component with the greatest value at risk, but instead on the component to which the portfolio's value at risk is most sensitive.

SUMMARY

1. A risk budget is the conversion of optimal portfolio allocations into value-at-risk measures.
2. Investors who develop a risk budget independently of mean-variance optimization will almost certainly produce an inefficient one.
3. Investors who choose a portfolio by minimizing value at risk implicitly care only about a single outcome. They are indifferent to the extent to which a portfolio might generate a cushion with respect to value at risk, and they are no more averse to losses far greater than value at risk than they are to a loss equal to value at risk.
4. Portfolio choice should be based on the entire probability distributions of the portfolios along the efficient frontier. This approach considers

the pleasure or disutility associated with all possible outcomes, including both gains and losses.

5. Risk attribution measures the sensitivity of a portfolio's value at risk to small changes in asset exposures, which reveals the sources of portfolio value at risk.

APPENDIX: RISK BUDGETING AND ATTRIBUTION WITH LOGNORMAL RETURNS[5]

The following equations show how to calculate value at risk and the sensitivity of portfolio value at risk to its component positions, under the assumption that the portfolio's returns are lognormally distributed. For simplicity, I assume the portfolio contains three components.

In order to calculate value at risk, we first convert the portfolio's discrete expected return and standard deviation into their continuous counterparts.

$$\mu_C = \ln(1 + \mu_D) - \frac{\sigma_C^2}{2} \tag{21.8}$$

$$\sigma_C = \sqrt{\ln\left(\frac{\sigma_D^2}{(1+\mu_D)^2} + 1\right)} \tag{21.9}$$

where μ_C = continuous expected return
μ_D = discrete expected return
σ_C = standard deviation of continuous returns
σ_D = standard deviation of discrete returns

Next we calculate the percentage loss associated with the chosen standardized variable in continuous units and convert it to value at risk.

$$L_C = \mu_C - Z\sigma_C$$

$$VaR = -(e^{L_C} - 1) \times V \tag{21.10}$$

where L_C = percentage loss in continuous units
e = base of natural logarithm (2.71828)

In order to measure the sensitivity of portfolio value at risk to its component positions, we express the continuous portfolio expected return and variance as functions of asset weights w_1, w_2, and w_3:

$$
\begin{aligned}
\mu_C = {}& \ln(1 + w_1\mu_{D1} + w_2\mu_{D2} + w_3\mu_{D3}) \\
& - 1/2\ln[1 + (w_1^2\sigma_{D1}^2 + w_2^2\sigma_{D2}^2 + w_3^2\sigma_{D3}^2 + 2w_1w_2\rho_{12}\sigma_{D1}\sigma_{D2} \\
& + 2w_1w_3\rho_{13}\sigma_{D1}\sigma_{D3} + 2w_2w_3\rho_{23}\sigma_{D2}\sigma_{D3})/ \\
& (1 + w_1\mu_{D1} + w_2\mu_{D2} + w_3\mu_{D3})^2]
\end{aligned}
\tag{21.11}
$$

where $\ln$ = natural logarithm

$$
\begin{aligned}
\sigma_C^2 = {}& \ln[1 + (w_1^2\sigma_{D1}^2 + w_2^2\sigma_{D2}^2 + w_3^2\sigma_{D3}^2 + 2w_1w_2\rho_{12}\sigma_{D1}\sigma_{D2} \\
& + 2w_1w_3\rho_{13}\sigma_{D1}\sigma_{D3} + 2w_2w_3\rho_{23}\sigma_{D2}\sigma_{D3})/ \\
& (1 + w_1\mu_{D1} + w_2\mu_{D2} + w_3\mu_{D3})^2]
\end{aligned}
\tag{21.12}
$$

Next we calculate the derivative of continuous portfolio variance with respect to each component position, which, for the first component, is given by equation (21.13).

$$
\begin{aligned}
\frac{\partial\sigma_C^2}{\partial w_1} = {}& 1/(\sigma_D^2/(1+\mu_D)^2 + 1) \times (1 + w_1\mu_{D1} + w_2\mu_{D2} + w_3\mu_{D3})^2 \\
& \times (2w_1\sigma_{D1}^2 + 2w_2\rho_{12}\sigma_{D1}\sigma_{D2} + 2w_3\rho_{13}\sigma_{D1}\sigma_{D3})/ \\
& (1 + w_1\mu_{D1} + w_2\mu_{D2} + w_3\mu_{D3})^4 - (2\mu_{D1}(1 + w_1\mu_{D1} + w_2\mu_{D2} \\
& + w_3\mu_{D3})\sigma_{D1}^2)/(1 + w_1\mu_{D1} + w_2\mu_{D2} + w_3\mu_{D3})^4
\end{aligned}
\tag{21.13}
$$

Then we calculate the derivative of continuous portfolio expected return with respect to each component position, which, for the first component, is given by equation (21.14).

$$
\frac{\partial\mu_C}{\partial w_1} = \mu_{D1}/(1 + w_1\mu_{D1} + w_2\mu_{D2} + w_3\mu_{D3}) - 1/2\left(\frac{\partial\sigma_C^2}{\partial w_1}\right)
\tag{21.14}
$$

We then let σ_C^2 equal $f(w_1)$ so that

$$
\frac{\partial\sigma_C^2}{\partial w_1} = \frac{\partial f(w_1)}{\partial w_1}
\tag{21.15}
$$

Therefore, by application of the chain rule, the derivative of continuous standard deviation with respect to the first portfolio component equals

$$\frac{\partial \sigma_C^2}{\partial w_1} = 1/2 \frac{\partial f(w_1)}{\partial w_1} \left[f(w_1)^{-1/2} \right] \qquad (21.16)$$

For the penultimate step, we express the derivative of the continuous percentage loss associated with the chosen standardized variable as the sum of the derivatives of continuous portfolio expected return and continuous portfolio standard deviation:

$$\frac{\partial L_C}{\partial w_1} = \frac{\partial \mu_C}{\partial w_1} + Z \frac{\partial \sigma_C}{\partial w_1} \qquad (21.17)$$

Finally, we convert the derivative of percentage loss measured in continuous units into the derivative of value at risk measured in discrete units.

$$\frac{\partial VaR}{\partial w_1} = -\frac{\partial L_C}{\partial w_1} \times \left(e^{L_C} \right) \qquad (21.18)$$

These calculations assume that portfolio returns are lognormally distributed. However, this assumption is not literally true if we assume the portfolio's component returns are lognormally distributed. In most cases the former assumption, although technically false, yields a reasonably accurate approximation. In cases in which the portfolio includes short positions or cases in which its returns are measured relative to a benchmark, the assumption of portfolio lognormality may introduce serious biases to value at risk and sensitivity estimates. In these situations, it is better to estimate value at risk based on an aggregation of the distributions of the individual components.[6]

CHAPTER 22

Hedging

This chapter describes how to control risk through the use of financial futures and forward contracts. I begin with a discussion of the valuation of futures and forward contracts. Then I describe how they can be used to change the asset mix of a portfolio without disrupting the underlying assets. Next, I show how to hedge away the systematic risk and extract the alpha from an actively managed portfolio of short and long positions. I also describe how to remove the currency risk of an internationally diversified portfolio, and I demonstrate why full hedging is not necessarily optimal, even if we disregard hedging costs. Finally, I show how to evaluate the trade-off between the cost of hedging and risk reduction.[1]

VALUATION OF FINANCIAL FUTURES AND FORWARD CONTRACTS

A financial futures contract obligates a seller to pay the value of the futures contract to the buyer at a specified date. Financial futures contracts, which are marked to market daily, have uniform terms with respect to quantity, expiration date, and underlying asset. Forward contracts, by contrast, are negotiated privately; their terms are thus specific to the transaction.

The fair value of a futures or forward contract is based on the notion of arbitrage. Suppose that a stock index is valued at $450, the three-month riskless interest rate is 1.50 percent, and the stock index's expected dividend yield for the next three months equals 1.00 percent. The price of a futures contract on the stock index that expires three months from now should equal $452.25. At this price, we are indifferent between purchasing the stock index on margin or purchasing a futures contract on the index.

Assume the value of a unit of a stock index fund equals 500 times the price of the index and that we purchase a unit with borrowed funds. Now suppose, after three months, the stock index's price rises to $460, at which time we sell our unit. We receive $232,250—the price for which we sell our unit ($230,000) plus dividends equal to $2,250. At the same time, we must pay $228,375—the principal of our loan ($225,000) plus interest of $3,375, for a net gain of $3,875.

If we instead purchase a futures contract on the stock index priced at $452.25 and sell it at expiration when its price equals $460, we earn the same profit—$3,875. The value of a stock index futures contract equals the contract price times 500. We thus purchase the contract for $226,125 and sell it for $230,000.

What happens if the stock index declines to $440 after three months? In this case, the strategy of purchasing the stock index on margin loses $6,125. We experience a capital loss of $5,000, receive dividend income of $2,250, and incur an interest expense of $3,375. If we purchase a futures contract for $226,125 and sell it for $220,000, we experience the same loss of $6,125.

Table 22.1 illustrates the equivalence of a futures contract and a leveraged exposure to the underlying asset. In general, the value of a futures or forward contract equals the price of the underlying asset plus the cost of carry, which for financial assets is defined as the interest cost associated with purchasing the asset on margin less any income the asset generates during the term of the contract.

Arbitrageurs monitor the prices of futures contracts and their underlying assets and engage in arbitrage transactions whenever opportunities exist. This activity prevents futures prices from moving significantly away from their fair values. The range of values around fair value is determined by the ease with which arbitrageurs can profit from a misvalued futures

TABLE 22.1 Equivalence of Futures Contract and Leveraged Exposure

	Stock Index Leveraged	Stock Index Futures Contract
Purchase price	225,000	226,125
	(450 × 500)	(452.25 × 500)
Interest cost	3,375	0
	(0.015 × 225,000)	
Dividend income	2,250	0
	(0.01 × 225,000)	
Sale price	230,000	230,000
	(460 × 500)	(460 × 500)
Profit/loss	3,875	3,875
Sale price	220,000	220,000
	(440 × 500)	(440 × 500)
Profit/loss	–6,125	–6,125

contract. The more expensive or uncertain it is to transact in the underlying asset, the farther away from fair value the futures price is likely to drift before arbitrageurs enter the market.

ASSET ALLOCATION WITH FUTURES CONTRACTS

Suppose we have a $100 million portfolio, 60 percent of which is allocated to a stock index fund and 40 percent of which is allocated to a 20-year treasury bond with a coupon yield of 8 percent. Also, suppose we wish to reduce its stock exposure to 40 percent and increase its bond exposure to 60 percent. One approach would be to sell the underlying stock index securities and invest the proceeds in treasury bonds. Alternatively, we can sell stock index futures contracts and buy treasury bond futures contracts as an overlay to our portfolio.

Because the value of the stock index contract equals 500 times its price, we determine the number of contracts to sell as follows. We divide the value of the position we wish to trade ($20 million) by the quantity 500 times the stock index price. At a stock index price of $450, we should sell 89 futures contracts [20,000,000/(500 x 450)].[2] Suppose a 20-year treasury bond with an 8 percent coupon is currently priced at $110.50. The value of a treasury bond contract equals 1,000 times its price. We should therefore purchase 181 contracts in order to increase our bond exposure proportionately [20,000,000/(1,000 x 110.5)].

Now consider a situation in which we have a $100 million stock index fund, and we wish to convert 20 percent of it to treasury bills. As was true in the previous example, we need to sell 89 stock index futures contracts in order to reduce our stock exposure, but we need not purchase any treasury bill futures contracts. Recall from the discussion about valuation that a futures contract is priced so that it is equivalent to purchasing the underlying asset on margin. The price of the contract equals the price of the underlying asset plus the implicit interest cost less the foregone dividend income. Therefore, by selling a futures contract against the underlying asset, we in effect create a treasury bill exposure.

To see this equivalence, again suppose that the stock index is valued at $450, that its dividend yield over the next three months equals 1.00 percent, and that the three-month riskless yield equals 1.50 percent. As shown earlier, a futures contract on the stock index will be priced at $452.25.

Now suppose, as we did earlier, that the stock index price three months from now rises to $460, at which time the futures contract expires. The $20 million exposure to the stock index yields dividend income equal to $200,000 and a capital gain of $444,444.44. At the same time, the 89 futures contracts that were sold produce a capital loss of $344,875, for a net gain of $299,569.44, which is almost equivalent to a 1.5 percent yield. Had we been able to sell fractional contracts, this arbitrage would have generated precisely $300,000.

If the price of the stock index falls to $440 three months hence, the $20 million exposure to the stock index fund generates a capital loss of $444,444.44 and dividend income of $200,000. The short futures position produces a capital gain of $545,235, for a net gain of $300,680.56, which again equals a yield of about 1.5 percent.

Whether the stock index rises or falls, a long position in the index together with an offsetting short exposure to the stock index futures contracts yields the riskless return, as long as the futures contracts are priced fairly. If they are priced below their fair value, this strategy will generate a return below the treasury bill yield. If they are overpriced relative to their fair value, this strategy will generate a premium over the treasury bill yield.

Now consider a situation in which we wish to change the allocation of a portfolio that consists of an actively managed equity component and an actively managed bond component. We do not wish to vitiate the value we expect to add through active management. We wish only to reallocate the assets so as to reduce our portfolio's exposure to the systematic risk of its equity component and to increase its exposure to the systematic risk of its bond component.

We measure the systematic risk of our equity portfolio by regressing its returns on the returns of the market. The slope of the regression line is called beta, and it represents the sensitivity of our fund's return to the market's return. For example, if our fund's beta equals 1.2, and the market returns 10 percent, we should expect our fund to return 12 percent. The extent to which its return is above or below 12 percent can be attributed to the active management of the fund.[3]

We compute the number of stock index contracts to sell in order to account for our equity portfolio's systematic risk, as shown in equation (22.1).

$$N = \frac{A}{500 \times S} \times \beta \qquad (22.1)$$

where N = number of contracts to trade
A = amount to be reallocated
S = index price
β = beta of equity component

If our equity component has a beta of 1.2 and we wish to reduce our portfolio's systematic equity risk 20 percent, we should sell 107 stock index futures contracts. Although the value of these contracts is greater than

$24 million, this transaction acts to lower our portfolio's systematic equity risk by only 20 percent while retaining its full exposure to security selection skill.

If we wish to increase our portfolio's bond exposure by 20 percent, we must determine the number of treasury bond futures contracts that matches the systematic risk of our portfolio's bond component.

A bond's systematic risk is measured by its sensitivity to changes in the level of interest rates. This measure is called duration, and it equals the average time to receipt of a bond's cash flows weighted by its present values. If a bond's duration equals 10 and interest rates decline by one percentage point, the price of the bond will increase by 10 percent. Duration differs from term to maturity in two ways. First, term to maturity measures the time to receipt of the final principal repayment, whereas duration measures the average time remaining to receipt of all the cash flows, including coupon payments and interim principal repayments. Second, duration is weighted by the present values of the cash flows.[4]

If we wish to increase our portfolio's systematic bond risk by an amount equal to 20 percent of its value, we need to adjust the number of treasury bond futures contracts that we acquire, as shown in equation (22.2).

$$N = \frac{A}{S} \times \frac{D_P}{D_T}$$ (22.2)

where N = number of contracts
A = amount to be reallocated
S = 1,000 times underlying treasury bond price
D_P = duration of portfolio bond component
D_T = duration of treasury bond that underlies futures contract

Suppose the duration of the treasury bond that underlies the futures contract equals 12, while the duration of our bond component equals 10. If, as assumed earlier, the value of a 20-year treasury bond with an 8 percent coupon yield equals $110,500, we should purchase 151 contracts.[5] Although this transaction increases our bond exposure by only $16.61 million, it has the effect of creating a $20 million additional exposure to a bond with a duration equal to 10.

SHORT/LONG STRATEGIES

Suppose we wish to focus on stock selection and immunize our portfolio from broad market movements. That is, we wish to purchase stocks that we believe will outperform the market and to sell short stocks that we believe will underperform the market. If our long position and our short position have the same beta, we can eliminate systematic risk by purchasing and selling equal amounts. If, however, our long and short positions have different betas, then we must adjust our portfolio's long and short exposures to account for the difference in their betas if we want to eliminate systematic risk.

Suppose, for example, that our long position has a beta equal to 1.0 while the beta of our short position equals 0.9. There are various ways we can eliminate systematic risk. For example, we can limit our long position to 90 percent of our short position. This approach, however, places more emphasis on our ability to identify stocks with negative alphas than to identify stocks with positive alphas. As an alternative, we can establish equal long and short exposures to the individual stocks and sell stock index futures contracts to offset 10 percent of our long position. This approach reduces the systematic risk of our long position to that of our short position, while maintaining equal exposure to the stock-specific risk of our long and short positions.

If we believe that our stock selection skill is limited to identifying stocks that we expect to outperform the market, we can neutralize our market exposure by selling stock index futures contracts in an amount based upon the beta of our long position. If we feel more comfortable identifying stocks that we expect to underperform the market, we can eliminate our fund's market exposure by purchasing stock index contracts in an amount based on the beta of our short position.

HEDGING CURRENCY EXPOSURE

The notion of beta can also be applied to hedging currency exposure. Suppose we allocate a fraction of our portfolio to foreign investments. How much of the embedded currency risk of these investments should we hedge? One approach is to sell currency forward or futures contracts in an amount equal to the currency exposure of our investments. Typically, however, this approach will not minimize the currency risk of our portfolio. We are more likely to reduce currency risk if we condition the amount we hedge on the beta of our portfolio with respect to the relevant currency.

Suppose that 30 percent of our portfolio is allocated to the Japanese stock market. Assume that our portfolio has a standard deviation of 12 percent, that the yen has a standard deviation of 10 percent, that our portfolio is 15 percent correlated with the yen, and that, independent of any change in the value of the yen, our portfolio has an expected return of 10 percent. We can think of this independent return as our portfolio's alpha with respect to movements in the yen. In order to minimize the volatility of our portfolio's return associated with changes in the dollar/yen exchange rate, we should sell a forward contract on the yen in amount equal to 18 percent of our portfolio's value; which is to say, we should hedge 60 percent of our portfolio's yen exposure.

The reason that we should hedge only 60 percent of our currency exposure in order to minimize risk is that our portfolio's beta with respect to the yen is 18 percent, and 18 percent of our 30 percent yen exposure equals 60 percent.

A portfolio's beta with respect to the yen equals its correlation with the yen times its standard deviation divided by the yen's standard deviation, as equation (22.3) shows:

$$\beta = \rho \frac{\sigma_p}{\sigma_{FX}} \tag{22.3}$$

where β = portfolio beta with respect to currency
ρ = correlation between portfolio and currency
σ_p = portfolio standard deviation
σ_{FX} = currency standard deviation

In order to determine the effectiveness of this currency hedging strategy, let us assume the yen and the yen forward contract will either increase or decrease by 10 percent. If it increases 10 percent and we do not hedge any of the portfolio's currency exposure, we should expect the portfolio to return 11.8 percent—the sum of the 10 percent expected return that is independent of the yen's return plus 0.18 times the yen's return. By the same reasoning, we should expect the portfolio to return 8.2 percent should the yen decline by 10 percent.

Now suppose we hedge all of the portfolio's exposure to the yen; that is, we sell a forward contract on the yen equal to 30 percent of the portfolio's value. If the yen increases by 10 percent, we should expect the portfolio to return 8.8 percent—the sum of the underlying portfolio's return plus the return of the short forward position (–3.0 percent). If the yen falls by 10 percent, we add the 3 percent return from the short forward position to the return of the underlying portfolio; our expected return is now 11.2 percent.

If, instead, we sell short a forward contract on the yen in an amount equal to 18 percent of our portfolio, which equals 60 percent of our yen exposure, we should expect to eliminate fully the portfolio risk that arises from uncertainty in the yen exchange rate. If the yen rises 10 percent, the forward position loses 1.8 percent for a net return of 10.0 percent. If the yen falls 10 percent, we gain 1.8 percent on the short forward position, which, when added to the underlying portfolio's return, again equals 10 percent. Table 22.2 summarizes these results.

We can also verify that a beta-derived currency hedge ratio minimizes portfolio risk by computing the standard deviation of a portfolio combined with a short position in a currency forward contract, as shown in equation (22.4):

$$\sigma_{p+f} = (\sigma_p^2 + w^2\sigma_f^2 + 2w\rho\sigma_p\sigma_f)^{1/2} \qquad (22.4)$$

where σ_{p+f} = standard deviation of combination of portfolio and forward contract
σ_p = standard deviation of underlying portfolio
σ_f = standard deviation of currency forward contract
w = weighting of currency forward contract
ρ = correlation of underlying portfolio and currency forward contract

By substituting the assumptions given earlier into equation (22.4), we find that the standard deviation of the fully hedged strategy equals 11.92 percent, versus 11.86 percent for the beta-derived hedging strategy.

TABLE 22.2 Effectiveness of Alternative Currency Hedging Strategies
Portfolio Beta with Respect to Yen: 18%
Portfolio Alpha with Respect to Yen: 10%
Portfolio Exposure to Yen: 30%

Alpha +	Beta ×	Yen Return +	Forward Exposure ×	Yen Return =	Portfolio Return
Unhedged					
10.00%	18.00%	10.00%	0.00%	10.00%	11.80%
10.00%	18.00%	−10.00%	0.00%	−10.00%	8.20%
Fully hedged					
10.00%	18.00%	10.00%	−30.00%	10.00%	8.80%
10.00%	18.00%	−10.00%	−30.00%	−10.00%	11.20%
Optimally hedged					
10.00%	18.00%	10.00%	−18.00%	10.00%	10.00%
10.00%	18.00%	−10.00%	−18.00%	−10.00%	10.00%

RISK REDUCTION VERSUS COST OF HEDGING

In the currency hedging example, I assumed that we wish to minimize portfolio risk as a function of currency exposure, regardless of the expected cost of hedging. It is more likely that we would seek to balance risk reduction with the cost of hedging.

The cost of hedging currency risk has several components. There are transaction costs as well as management and administrative fees. In addition, the currency futures or forward contract will sell at a discount to the spot exchange rate when domestic interest rates are lower than foreign interest rates. If the spot exchange rate does not decline to the current forward rate, we will incur a loss on our short forward position. The opposite may also be true; we might experience a gain if we sell a currency forward contract at a premium, and the spot rate fails to appreciate to the forward rate prevailing at the time we sell the contract.

In any event, to the extent we have reason to believe that a currency forward contract's expected return is different from zero, we should reflect this view in our estimate of the cost of hedging. If we anticipate a positive return, we should raise our estimate of the hedging cost by this amount. If we expect a negative return, we should lower our cost estimate.

Once we estimate the cost of hedging, we need to determine how many units of cost we are willing to incur at the margin in order to lower our portfolio's variance by one unit. We can infer this trade-off from our choice of the underlying portfolio. It is the slope of a line that is tangent to the efficient frontier at the location of our portfolio's expected return and risk, assuming risk is measured in units of variance.

The exposure to a currency forward contract that optimally balances our aversion to risk with our reluctance to incur costs is given by equation (22.5), assuming our portfolio is exposed to only one foreign currency.[6] This equation is derived by taking the partial derivative of expected utility with respect to exposure to the currency forward contract and setting this value equal to 0.

$$w = \frac{C_H}{2\lambda\sigma_f^2} - \rho\frac{\sigma_p}{\sigma_f} \tag{22.5}$$

where w = optimal exposure to currency forward contract as a fraction of portfolio value

   C_H = expected cost of hedging, including expected return of forward contract

   λ = trade-off between risk reduction and cost

   σ_f = standard deviation of currency forward contract

   σ_p = standard deviation of underlying portfolio

   ρ = correlation of currency forward contract and underlying portfolio

Suppose, for example, we estimate hedging costs to equal 0.25 percent and we determine we are willing to incur two units of incremental cost to reduce our portfolio's variance by one unit. Based on our earlier assumptions about correlation and standard deviations, we should sell a forward contract on the yen equal to 11.75 percent of our portfolio's value, which corresponds to 39.17 percent of its exposure to the yen. Although this hedging strategy does not minimize the risk due to currency exposure, it optimally balances our willingness to incur cost in order to lower risk.[7]

I have attempted to present some of the basic principles of hedging with financial futures and forward contracts. I have ignored much of the administrative detail associated with the application of these principles. Those who are interested in these important details should consult other sources.

CHAPTER **23**

Option Valuation and Replication

OPTION VALUATION

Although the media and uninformed members of Congress typically portray options as a means for intemperate speculation, in fact, the overwhelming preponderance of options transactions contributes substantially to the amenity of society. Options afford producers and service providers a mechanism for hedging their risks, which allows them to offer their products at lower prices than they would otherwise require. This invaluable benefit to society was not lost on the Nobel Prize selection committee. In October 1997, the committee awarded the Nobel Memorial Prize in Economic Science to Robert Merton and Myron Scholes for their work in option valuation. Sadly, Fischer Black passed away in the previous year. Although the Nobel Prize is not bestowed posthumously, the selection committee departed from tradition by explicitly citing Black's contribution to option valuation.

A financial option gives the owner the right to buy (in the case of a call option) or to sell (in the case of a put option) an asset at a specified price. This right, in the case of an American option, can be exercised at any time over a specified period. A European option can be exercised only at a specified date.

Because a call option does not obligate its owner to purchase the underlying stock, its value at expiration will equal either the stock price less the exercise price if this value is positive, or zero if this value is negative, as shown in Table 23.1.

A put option grants its owner the right but not the obligation to sell the underlying stock; thus it will be valuable at expiration only if the exercise price exceeds the stock price. Again, if we assume a $55 exercise price, Table 23.2 below shows the value of a put option at expiration.

The realized return of the underlying asset determines the option's exact value at expiration, as shown in Tables 23.1 and 23.2. Expectations

TABLE 23.1 Call Option Valuation at Expiration

Stock Price at Expiration	Stock Price Minus Exercise Price	Call Option Value at Expiration
45	−10	0
50	−5	0
55	0	0
60	5	5
65	10	10

TABLE 23.2 Put Option Valuation at Expiration

Stock Price at Expiration	Stock Price Minus Exercise Price	Put Option Value at Expiration
45	−10	10
50	−5	5
55	0	0
60	5	0
65	10	0

about this return, however, have no bearing on the option's value prior to expiration.

The determination of an option's value prior to expiration persisted for many years as one of the great challenges of financial economics. Finally, in 1973, Fischer Black and Myron Scholes, along with Robert E. Merton, solved the option pricing puzzle.

The celebrated Black-Scholes formula, which gives the price of a European option that pays no dividend, is given in equation (23.1).

$$C = S \times N(d) - Xe^{-rT} \times N\left(d - \sigma\sqrt{T}\right) \qquad (23.1)$$

where S = price of underlying asset
X = strike price
T = time remaining until expiration
r = instantaneous riskless rate of interest

$$d = \left[\frac{\ln(S/X) + (r + \sigma^2/2)T}{\sigma\sqrt{T}}\right]$$

ln( ) = natural logarithm

σ = standard deviation (volatility) of underlying asset returns

N( ) = cumulative normal distribution

Notice that this formula includes no assumptions or expectations about the return of the underlying asset. The irrelevance of the underlying asset's expected return was the critical innovation of Black and Scholes. They demonstrated that only five factors determine the value of an option:

1. Price of the underlying asset
2. Exercise price
3. Interest rate
4. Time remaining to expiration
5. Volatility of the underlying asset's return[1]

They recognized that both the expected terminal value of a stock and the expected terminal value of an option on that stock are related to the stock's expected return. The option's expected return is related to the stock's expected return through its relative volatility with respect to the stock. Black and Scholes also realized that one could create a hedged position by purchasing a stock and selling call options in a particular ratio, which would cause the impact of the stock's expected return on its price to offset exactly its impact on the option's price.

A hedged position refers to a combination of assets with offsetting returns under all possible states of the world. Because the returns are offsetting, a hedged position has no risk and should therefore yield the riskless return.

Consider, for example, a $100.00 stock today that could either increase 30 percent or decline 10 percent over the course of one year. If one were to purchase one share of the stock and at the same time sell short one and one-third options with a strike price of $100.00, this combination would always produce an ending value of $90.00. If the stock rises to $130.00, the option is worth $30.00 (130.00 – 100.00). A short position of one and one-third options, therefore, will generate a loss of $40.00 (30.00 × –1.3333) for an ending value on the combined position equal to $90.00. If, instead, the stock falls to $90.00, the option will expire worthless, and the ending value of the combined position will again equal $90.00.

Because the ending value of the hedged position is known today and is riskless, its present value equals its ending value discounted by the riskless rate of return. Suppose the riskless return is 4.00 percent. Under this assumption, the present value of the hedged position one year ahead equals $86.5385 (90.00/1.04). There is now sufficient information to calculate the present value of the option by setting the components of the hedged position equal to $86.5385 and solving for the option's present value.

$$100.00 - (1+\tfrac{1}{3}) \times \text{option value} = 86.5385$$

$$\text{option value} = \frac{100.00 - 86.5385}{1 + \tfrac{1}{3}}$$

$$\text{option value} = 10.0962$$

Notice that this calculation of the option's value does not require any input for the stock's expected return. Again, the irrelevance of expected return arises from the fact that with a hedged position the expectation about the stock's uncertain return cancels out.

This example illustrates the key innovation of the Black-Scholes formula: that the riskless return and not the stock's expected return determines the value of an option. You may argue that this example is unrealistic because it deals with a very unusual stock, one that has only two possible outcomes. However, Black and Scholes, with help from Robert Merton, discovered that when this assumption is relaxed and the stock takes on many values through time, the same fundamental principle about the riskless nature of a hedged position applies.

Black and Scholes used this insight of a replicating portfolio to derive the value of an option under the assumption that stock prices change continuously through time. First, they set up a partial differential equation without any terms that depend on investor risk preferences. It simultaneously incorporates two relationships. It relates the change in the value of an option to the change in the value of the underlying stock and the passage of time, and it relates the change in the value of a hedged portfolio and the passage of time to the riskless return. The solution to this equation gives the value of an option, as was demonstrated in equation (23.1).

OPTION REPLICATION

Despite the wide availability of exchange-traded options, the demand for optionlike payoffs vastly exceeds the supply. A large market in privately negotiated options and in option-replication strategies has thus emerged. These strategies are often used to hedge privately negotiated options by those who write them. More often, though, investors replicate options to create optionlike payoffs on assets or portfolios for which exchange-traded options are not available or for terms different from the terms of exchange-traded options. This section demonstrates how to generate an optionlike payoff by shifting a fund between two assets.

Suppose an employee is granted $1,000,000 of company stock with the provision that she cannot sell this stock for one year from the date it is granted. Let's also assume that the company's stock, Dotcom Inc., is actively traded but there are no options on it. Finally, let's assume that, with the exception of the shares granted to her, she is free to buy and sell shares of Dotcom. How can she protect the value of her grant should Dotcom's price decline over the course of the year, and still retain upside potential should its price rise? A put option to sell Dotcom at its current price or some fraction of its current price would provide downside protection while preserving upside potential, but there are no options on Dotcom's stock.

OPTION REPLICATION USING THE BINOMIAL MODEL

She can replicate the payoff of an option by shifting funds between a riskless asset, such as a one-year treasury bill, and Dotcom stock. Suppose, for example, she wishes to ensure that she will be able to sell her Dotcom stock for at least 95 percent of its current value. Let us begin with the simplifying assumption that Dotcom's stock will either increase 35 percent or decrease 15 percent one year hence, and that these outcomes are equally probable. Let us also assume that the yield on the one-year treasury bill is 5 percent. The only possible values for $1,000,000 of Dotcom stock one year from now are $1,350,000 (Dotcom rises 35 percent) or $850,000 (Dotcom falls 15 percent), as Figure 23.1 shows.

We can easily determine the value of an option to sell her Dotcom shares for $950,000 one year hence. The option will be worth nothing if their value rises to $1,350,000. If their value falls to $850,000, however, the option will be worth $100,000, the difference between the $950,000 the shares can be sold for under the terms of the option contract and the current value of the shares. These contingent values are shown in parenthe-

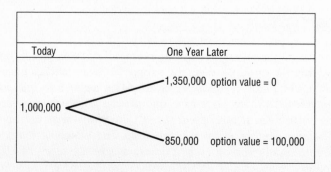

FIGURE 23.1   Binomial model

ses in Figure 23.1. Given the obvious values for this option to sell Dotcom shares for $950,000 one year from now, we can construct two equations that, when solved simultaneously, reveal how we can hedge the option by combining exposure to the Dotcom shares and the treasury bill.

$$1,350,000 \times \text{Dotcom} + 1.05 \times \text{Tbill} = 0$$

$$850,000 \times \text{Dotcom} + 1.05 \times \text{Tbill} = 100,000$$

Here Dotcom represents percentage exposure to Dotcom stock, while Tbill represents dollar exposure to treasury bills. By solving these equations simultaneously, we find that Dotcom equals $-\frac{1}{5}$ and Tbill equals 257,142.86. This indicates that one can hedge an option to sell $950,000 of Dotcom stock by selling the stock short in an amount equal to $200,000.00 and investing $257,142.86 in a treasury bill that yields 5.00 percent. Furthermore, the fair value of this option today must equal the sum of the short position in Dotcom stock and the long position in the treasury bill, which equals $57,142.86.

To validate the equivalence between this hedging strategy and an option to sell Dotcom stock for $950,000 one year forward, let us consider the payoff to an investor who writes such an option and then hedges it as I've just described, assuming the investor charges the fair value of $57,142.86 as the premium. If Dotcom shares rise 35 percent, the option will expire worthless. At the same time, the short position in Dotcom stock will produce a loss of $70,000.00, while the long position in treasury bills will yield a gain of $12,857.14, for a net loss to the hedging strategy of $57,142.86. This loss exactly offsets the premium received for writing the option.

If Dotcom shares fall 15 percent, the option will be worth $100,000. Thus the net loss for writing the option will equal $42,857.14. The short position in Dotcom stock, however, will yield a profit of $30,000.00, which when combined with the yield of the treasury bill of $12,857.14 sums to $42,857.14. This exactly offsets the net loss from writing the option. Table 23.3 summarizes these results.

From the payoffs described in this example, it is easy to see that the investor writing the option can earn a riskless profit by charging a premium in excess of $57,142.86. These results, however, depend on the simplifying assumption that Dotcom stock can only increase 35 percent or decrease by 15 percent in the course of a year, and that both outcomes are equally likely. This assumption is, of course, false. The price of Dotcom shares changes continually throughout the day, every business day. The basic methodology described above can, however, be expanded to accommodate real-world conditions. Expanding the binomial tree in Figure 23.1 to in-

TABLE 23.3   Option Payoffs

Dotcom rises 35 percent	
Put value	0
Premium received	57,142.86
Net return from writing option	57,142.86
Dotcom payoff (–200,000 × 0.35)	–70,000.00
Treasury bill payoff (257,142.86 × 0.05)	12,857.14
Net return from hedging strategy	–57,142.86
Dotcom falls 15 percent	
Put value	100,000.00
Premium received	57,142.86
Net return from writing option	–42,857.14
Dotcom payoff (–200,000 × –0.15)	30,000.00
Treasury bill payoff (257,142.86 × 0.05)	12,857.14
Net return from hedging strategy	42,857.14

clude small changes in the value of Dotcom shares over many short time intervals, based on a realistic estimate of its volatility, would allow us to derive a more precise estimate of the option's fair value today and as the year unfolds. In order to replicate this option, we would need to revise the exposure to Dotcom stock and the treasury bill continually as the share price changes and as time passes.

OPTION REPLICATION USING THE CONTINUOUS-TIME BLACK-SCHOLES MODEL

As the discrete time intervals in the binomial tree become smaller, approaching zero, the results of the binomial model resemble the results that would be obtained by using the continuous-time Black-Scholes model.

Based on the insights of the Black-Scholes model, we can determine the value of an option to sell $1,000,000 of Dotcom stock for no less than $950,000 one year from now by using the following formula for a put option.[2]

$$P = Xe^{-rT} \times N\left[-\left(d - \sigma\sqrt{T}\right)\right] - S \times N(d) \qquad (23.2)$$

where P = value of put option
         X = strike price
         e = equal base of natural logarithm (2.71828)

T = time remaining until expiration

r = instantaneous riskless rate of interest

$$d = \left[\frac{\ln(S/X) + (r + \sigma^2/2)T}{\sigma\sqrt{T}} \right]$$

$\ln(\ )$ = natural logarithm

σ = standard deviation (volatility) of return of Dotcom stock

S = value of Dotcom stock

$N(\ )$ = cumulative normal distribution

Let us assume that Dotcom, a relatively young company, wishes to maximize its growth potential over the foreseeable future and therefore does not pay dividends. Let us also assume the volatility of Dotcom's return equals 25.00 percent and, as before, the discrete riskless interest rate is 5.00 percent. With these assumptions we can demonstrate how to apply the continuous option pricing formula to replicate a put option to sell Dotcom stock for at least 95 percent of its current value. The necessary inputs are displayed below.

S = 1,000,000

X = 950,000

T = 1.00

r = $\ln(1.05)$ = 4.879 percent

σ = 25.00 percent

By substituting these values into the above formula, we discover that d equals 0.525334 and the option's fair value equals \$54,565.83 or about 5.46 percent of its current value. We calculate the option's delta by applying the cumulative normal distribution function to d. Delta represents the amount the option value changes given a one point change in the value of the stock. It equals 0.7003. We replicate this option by selling short Dotcom shares in an amount equal to 1 minus the put's delta (1.00 − 0.7003 = 0.2997) times the exposure to Dotcom, and investing the same amount plus the value of the put in treasury bills. These exposures are shown in Table 23.4.

The exposures derived from this formula represent the starting positions to replicate the option. As the price of Dotcom stock changes, and as time passes, we must repeat the exercise to determine the new exposures. As long as Dotcom's price does not change so abruptly that we cannot execute the requisite trades, and transaction costs are not prohibitive, this dynamic hedging strategy should effectively generate the same payoff as a put option to sell Dotcom stock for no less than \$950,000 one year from now.

TABLE 23.4   Initial Replication Positions

Exposure to Dotcom stock from employer	$1,000,000.00
Short position in Dotcom stock	−299,700.00
Long position in treasury bills	354,265.83

It is important to note that we must add in the implicit cost of the put option when computing the total loss. For example, if Dotcom's share price declines 5.00 percent one year from now, this strategy would lose $104,565.83 (1,000,000 − 950,000 − 54,565.83), which represents 10.46 percent of the initial value of the Dotcom stock.

SUMMARY

The key innovation of the Black-Scholes formula is that the expected return of the underlying asset is irrelevant to the value of the option. This irrelevance arises because investors can construct hedged positions of the asset and the option such that the underlying asset's expected return offsets itself, thus rendering the hedged position riskless.

Not only does this feature allow investors to value options using the riskless return; they can also implement dynamic trading strategies between risky and riskless assets that produce the same payoffs as investment in options.

CHAPTER 24

Commodity Futures Contracts

Investors seek to diversify their portfolios by investing in less traditional assets such as foreign securities, real estate and venture capital, and some investors consider commodities to be an excellent diversifier. Historically, commodities have had a relatively low correlation with traditional asset classes and have offered an effective hedge against inflation.

This chapter reviews the market and describes the sources of value for nonfinancial commodity futures contracts. These contracts fall into four broad categories—grains and oil seeds, livestock and meat, food and fiber, and metals and petroleum.

COMMODITY FUTURES MARKETS

A commodity futures contract obligates the seller to deliver a particular quantity and grade of a commodity to the buyer at a predetermined date and location, for a price agreed upon at the time of the transaction. The terms of the contract are standardized. Only the price of the contract changes with the passage of time. This standardization distinguishes futures contracts from forward contracts, the terms of which must be negotiated privately between the buyer and the seller for each contract. Unlike forward contracts, futures contracts also require margin deposits and are marked to market daily.

Although a commodity futures contract calls for delivery of the relevant commodity at the time of settlement, most futures contracts are liquidated by executing an offsetting transaction prior to the settlement date. If a trader is long July 10, 1993 cotton contracts, he simply enters an order to sell July 10, 1993 cotton contracts in order to close his position. If he were short the contracts, he would liquidate his position by entering an order to buy July 10, 1993 cotton contracts.

If a trader with a long position in commodity futures contracts neglects to liquidate his position by executing an offsetting transaction, he takes delivery of the physical commodity (unless the contract calls for cash settlement). Delivery does not mean that a trader might arrive home one evening from a stressful day at the office to find live hogs, collectively weighing in at 400,000 pounds, roaming around his finely manicured suburban lawn. Each contract designates a location with suitable facilities for delivery. The trader might, however, be required to pay storage and insurance costs while he seeks a buyer for his hogs.

Many commodity futures contracts are entered into by suppliers and consumers of the commodity who desire to hedge their existing exposure. Consequently, some contracts are liquidated by a transaction called an exchange of futures for physicals. For example, a wheat farmer who has yet to harvest his crop may have sold wheat futures contracts to protect himself from a potential decline in the price of wheat. In the meantime, a miller may have purchased wheat futures contracts as a hedge against a price increase prior to the time he is ready to buy the wheat. These parties might agree to exchange wheat for their futures contracts, assuming the wheat can be harvested and delivered before the settlement date of the contract.

Some commodity futures contracts specify cash settlement. For these contracts, the gain or loss that results when the futures price converges to the spot price at the settlement date is simply transferred to the appropriate party.

Commodity futures contracts are traded by institutions called futures commission merchants. A futures commission merchant (FCM) essentially performs the same function as a brokerage house. It maintains trading accounts for its customers, executes trades at the exchanges, and collects margin deposits from its customers.

There are numerous exchanges in the United States and around the world on which commodity futures contracts are traded. They include the Chicago Board of Trade, the Chicago Mercantile Exchange, and the New York Mercantile Exchange. Exchanges, which are also referred to as contract markets, set margin requirements for each contract.

When a trader purchases a futures contract, he is not required to pay the value of the contract to the FCM at that time. Instead, he must deposit initial margin in the form of a treasury bill or a bank letter of credit. The initial margin is, in effect, a performance bond, and the amount required varies from contract to contract, typically as a function of the volatility of the underlying commodity. The amount also depends on whether the trader is hedging an existing exposure to the underlying commodity or simply speculating in the commodity. The initial margin requirement is usually greater for speculators than it is for hedgers.

Once a trader establishes a position in a futures contract, he is also required to pay daily variation margin to cover trading losses as they occur. Suppose, for example, that a trader is long 10 contracts that, as of the previous close, were valued at $50,000 each. Now suppose that at the close of today's trading these contracts settle at a price of $49,500. The total position falls in value by $5,000. The trader must therefore transfer $5,000 from his account to the account of the FCM to cover this loss. If the contracts rise in value to $51,000 the next day, the FCM must transfer $15,000 to the trader's account to meet the required variation margin. Thus the gains and losses of futures contracts are settled on a daily basis, even though the position remains open.

Each exchange is affiliated with a clearinghouse that performs two functions. First, it provides a mechanism by which exchange members clear their positions. Second, it ensures the financial integrity of the exchange by monitoring the creditworthiness of exchange members and by maintaining capital funds as protection against the potential insolvency of any of the members.

Trades are cleared through the following mechanism. The members of the exchange report all their trades to the associated clearinghouse. Once the clearinghouse accepts these trades, it replaces the exchange members as the buyers and the sellers of the contracts. It matches all the trades and computes the members' net gains and losses. The clearinghouse then collects the appropriate payments from the members with net losses and disburses them to the members with net gains.

The federal regulatory agency that oversees trading in commodity futures contracts is called the Commodity Futures Trading Commission (CFTC). It was established in 1974 and derives its authority from the Commodity Exchange Act. The CFTC fulfills a role that is analogous to the function of the Securities and Exchange Commission. Essentially, it is responsible for promoting fair and efficient pricing, trading integrity, and financial soundness.

REPORTING ON COMMODITY TRADING

Let's look at an example of the type of information about commodity futures contracts that is reported in the financial press. The December 17, 1992, edition of the *Wall Street Journal* reported the information given in Table 24.1 for futures contracts on soybean meal. CBT refers to the Chicago Board of Trade, the exchange where futures contracts on soybean meal are traded. Each contract represents 100 tons of soybean meal, and the quoted prices are the dollars per ton for the contracts.

On December 16, 1992, the contract for May 1993 delivery opened at $184 per ton for a total price of $18,400, which was also its high for the day. It traded as low as $183.10 and settled for the day at $183.70, which was $0.70 below the prior day's closing price. The lifetime high for the

TABLE 24.1 Trading Activity for Futures Contracts on Soybean Meal

	Open	High	Low	Settle	Change	Lifetime High	Lifetime Low	Open Interest
Soybean Meal (CBT) 100 tons: $ per ton								
Dec	188.30	188.30	187.40	188.20	-0.50	209.00	176.50	3,013
Jan-93	185.70	185.70	184.50	185.60	-0.20	209.00	177.40	21,934
Mar	184.70	184.50	183.40	184.00	-0.60	210.00	178.30	23,230
May	184.00	184.00	183.10	183.70	-0.70	210.00	179.40	12,172
July	185.10	185.20	184.30	184.80	-0.70	208.00	181.30	9,840
Aug	185.70	186.00	185.20	185.50	-0.40	193.50	182.20	1,751
Sept	186.50	186.70	186.20	186.40	-0.50	193.50	183.10	1,217
Oct	188.00	188.00	187.50	188.00	-0.70	194.50	185.50	416
Dec	189.00	189.00	189.00	189.00	-1.00	191.50	187.20	207

Est vol 16,000: vol Tues 14,719; open int 73,780; 1,175

Source: *Wall Street Journal*, December 17, 1992

May 1993 contract was $210, and its lifetime low was $179.40. As of the close of trading on December 16, 1992, 12,172 contracts remained open. This figure refers to either the long positions or the short positions, not to the sum of the long and short positions, because each long position is also a short position.

The estimated volume on Wednesday, December 16, 1992, was 16,000 contracts, compared with 14,719 contracts on the previous Tuesday. The open interest for all the soybean meal contracts traded on the Chicago Board of Trade totaled 73,780 contracts, a reduction of 1,175 contracts from the previous day.

Note the prices of the various contracts. The prices of the December 1992 through May 1993 contracts decrease with the time remaining to settlement. Beginning with the July 1993 contract, however, the prices of the contracts start to increase with further increases in the time remaining to settlement. The next section reviews the valuation of commodity futures contracts and explains why prices vary as a function of the time remaining to the settlement date.

VALUING COMMODITY FUTURES CONTRACTS

The fair value of a commodity futures contract is based on the principle of arbitrage. Suppose we purchase 100 troy ounces of gold at $350 per ounce and finance this purchase by borrowing $35,000 at a total cost of $500 for three months. Suppose, at the end of three months, the price of a troy ounce of gold appreciates to $365, at which time we sell the 100 ounces and repay the loan. Our total profit from these transactions equals $1,000 ($36,500 − $35,000 − $500).

Now suppose that, instead of purchasing 100 ounces of gold on margin, we purchase a futures contract for 100 ounces of gold for settlement in three months. The fair value of this contract equals the price that yields a $1,000 profit if we hold this futures contract until the settlement date, when it will be worth $36,500. A purchase price of $35,500 yields a profit of $1,000 under this scenario.[1]

If the futures contract sells for less than $35,500—say, $35,200—we could sell 100 ounces of gold short and lend the proceeds of $35,000, earning interest income of $500. At the same time, we could purchase the futures contract at a price of $35,200 and hold it until the settlement date. By then we will have earned a profit of $1,300 on the futures transaction, experienced a loss of $1,500 on the short sale, and earned interest income of $500, for a net profit of $300 without any capital outlay or risk exposure.

If the futures contract sells for $36,000, we could sell the futures contract and borrow $35,000 to purchase 100 ounces of gold. By the settlement date, we will have earned a $1,500 profit on our long position in the gold, suffered a loss of $500 on our short futures position, and incurred an interest expense of $500, for a net profit of $500, again without any capital outlay or exposure to risk.

Arbitrageurs monitor the prices of futures contracts and their underlying commodities and engage in arbitrage transactions whenever the opportunity arises. This activity prevents futures prices from deviating significantly from their fair values.

The pricing model used to determine the fair value of a commodity futures contract is called the cost-of-carry model. According to this model, the fair value of a commodity futures contract equals the spot price of the underlying commodity plus the cost of carrying the commodity, which in the previous example is the financing cost. If we assume that the cost of carrying the commodity is comprised entirely of the financing cost, the cost-of-carry model supposes that the profit or loss on a long futures position equals the profit or loss from acquiring the underlying commodity on margin. Table 24.2 summarizes this relationship.

Thus far we have assumed that the cost of carry is comprised only of the financing cost of acquiring the commodity on margin. Although the financing cost accounts for the preponderance of the cost of carry for precious metals, a significant component of the cost of carrying other commodities consists of storage and transportation costs; for commodities for which the risk of spoilage or damage is a consideration, insurance costs can be significant. If we take all these costs into account, the fair value of a commodity futures contract equals the spot price of the underlying commodity plus the financing, insurance, storage, and transportation costs.

Because the collective costs of carrying a commodity are positive, we might expect the price of a futures contract to exceed the spot price of the underlying commodity. Moreover, as the settlement date approaches, we might expect the difference between the price of the underlying commodity and the price of the futures contract to diminish, because the cost of carry-

TABLE 24.2 Equivalence of Futures Position and Leveraged Acquisition

	Underlying Commodity	Futures Contract
Beginning price	350	355
Financing cost	5	0
Spot price appreciates to:	365	365
Net profit	10	10
Spot price depreciates to:	340	340
Net loss	−15	−15

ing the commodity diminishes with the passage of time. The difference between the spot price and the futures price is called the basis. If the futures price exceeds the spot price, the relationship is referred to as contango.

Table 24.1 reveals that the prices of some of the longer-dated contracts are lower than the prices of some of the shorter-dated contracts. For example, the May 1993 contract settled at $183.70 per ton compared with $185.60 for the January 1993 contract. What's more, the spot price for soybean meal as of the close of trading on December 16, 1992, was $189 per ton based on the average of the bid-ask spread reported in the *Wall Street Journal* the next day.[2] This relationship seems to imply that the cost of carrying soybean meal is negative, a rather unlikely proposition.

When the spot price of the commodity exceeds the price of the futures contract, the futures contract is said to be in backwardation. Based on the arbitrage concept described earlier, backwardation would appear to offer a free lunch.

In theory, an owner of soybean meal could sell his supply at $18,900 per 100 tons, lend the proceeds of this sale at the available five-month interest rate of 1.4 percent, and thereby earn interest of $264.60. At the same time, he could purchase a May 1993 futures contract on soybean meal for $18,370. These transactions would guarantee a riskless profit of $794.60 per 100 tons of soybean meal relative to holding the current supply of soybean meal.[3]

To validate this result, suppose the price of soybean meal appreciates to $195 per ton. The futures position yields a gain of $1,130.00 per contract, which, together with the interest proceeds of $264.60, results in a total gain of $1,394.60. This gain exceeds by $794.60 the foregone profit of $600 per 100 tons of soybean meal the owner would have realized had he kept his supply of soybean meal.

If, instead, the price of soybean meal declines to $185 per ton, the futures position produces a gain of $130 per contract, which is increased by interest proceeds of $264.60 per 100 tons. Had he kept his supply of soybean meal, the owner would have lost $400 per 100 tons. Thus his net advantage again equals $794.60.

To the extent the owners of soybean meal choose not to engage in these transactions, they agree to forego $794.60 of profit per 100 tons of soybean meal. In theory, the price of the futures contract should equal $19,164.60—the sum of $18,900 (the spot price of 100 tons of soybean meal), and the financing cost of $264.60. But the market price is only $18,370—that is, $794.60 less than the theoretical value.

How can we explain this discrepancy? The owners of soybean meal are willing to forego the gain of $794.60 in exchange for the convenience of having soybean meal readily accessible, because during certain times of the year (prior to a harvest, for example) soybean meal is scarce.

Because they need soybean meal to meet their customers' demands or for their own consumption, they are unwilling to part with it, even for a profit. We can think of this foregone profit as the premium the owners pay for accessibility. Arbitrageurs are unable to engage in transactions to correct the theoretical mispricing of the futures contracts, because they are unable to borrow the commodity from the owners. The foregone profit as a percentage of the spot price is called a convenience yield.

In order to determine the fair value of a commodity futures contract, we must reduce the cost of carry, expressed as a percentage of the spot price, by the convenience yield.

$$F = Se^{[(r-y)n/365]} \tag{24.1}$$

where F = the fair value of a commodity futures contract
$\quad S$ = the spot price of the underlying commodity
$\quad e$ = the base of the natural logarithm (2.71828)
$\quad r$ = the annualized rate of total cost of carry including financing cost, insurance cost, storage cost, and transportation cost
$\quad y$ = the annualized convenience yield
$\quad n$ = the number of days remaining until settlement date

INVESTING IN COMMODITY FUTURES CONTRACTS

A commodity futures contract by itself is a highly leveraged investment. Purchasing a futures contract on a commodity is equivalent to acquiring the underlying commodity on margin. We can eliminate the inherent leverage of a futures position by collateralizing the position—that is, by investing an equivalent amount of funds in riskless securities. The lending implicit in a treasury bill investment offsets the borrowing implicit in a futures contract investment.

The return on a collateralized futures portfolio consists of three components: the return on the underlying treasury bill position; the return on the underlying commodity; and the roll yield, which is defined as the return from liquidating an existing futures position and establishing a new position in a contract with a more distant settlement date, controlling for the change in the spot price.

Should investors consider collateralized commodity futures positions as a potential investment?[4] The commodity component of the return on a collateralized futures portfolio offers superb diversification with respect to stocks and bonds. However, the long-run return from the underlying commodities may not be particularly appealing, because improvements in technology over time could increase the supply of commodities such as agricultural products and reduce the demand for commodities such as energy and industrial metals.

The roll yield component of the return on a commodity futures portfolio may offer an opportunity for investors to extract a premium by overweighting commodity futures contracts that are in backwardation (those that have positive roll yields) and underweighting commodity futures contracts that have negative roll yields.

As with most investment opportunities, commodity futures contracts present trade-offs with respect to expected return and risk. Each investor should assess these within the context of his particular needs and attitude toward risk.

CHAPTER 25

Currencies

This chapter reviews some of the key concepts and strategies of currency management and the more common instruments that are used to trade currencies.

EXCHANGE RATES

To begin, it might be useful to review some of the terminology. One of the most basic notions is the exchange rate. The spot exchange rate is the rate at which one currency can be exchanged for another currency, typically for settlement in two days.

The international convention, with notable exceptions such as the Australian dollar, the British pound, and the euro, is to quote exchange rates with the U.S. dollar as the base currency.

Suppose the spot rate to exchange dollars for euros is 0.9500. This means traders are willing to exchange 0.9500 dollars for one euro to be settled in two business days. The reciprocal of this, the euro-equivalent exchange rate, equals 1.0526, which means traders are willing to exchange 1.0526 euros for one dollar. Suppose the spot rate to exchange dollars for pounds as of the same time equals 1.8000. We can infer the cross rate between the euro and the pound by dividing 0.9500 by 1.8000, which equals 0.5278. Therefore, traders are willing to exchange 0.5278 pounds for one euro. The reciprocal of this value, 1.8947, gives the rate at which traders are willing to exchange euros for pounds.

The forward exchange rate is the rate agreed to today at which a currency can be exchanged for another currency at a more distant future date. The value of the forward rate is determined by the relationship among the spot exchange rate and the interest rates in the two countries. This relationship is known as covered interest arbitrage.

Suppose the one-year riskless rate of interest is 5 percent in the United States and 10 percent in the U.K., and the dollar-equivalent spot exchange rate is 1.80. The forward exchange rate must equal the rate that would preclude an arbitrageur from borrowing in the United States at 5 percent and lending in the U.K. at 10 percent without incurring risk. An arbitrageur would hedge away risk by selling the pound forward one year in an amount equal to the amount that must be repaid in one year.

Suppose, for example, the arbitrageur borrows 1 million dollars in the United States at 5 percent and converts this sum to 555,556 pounds in the U.K. at 10 percent. Simultaneously, she sells 600,000 pounds one year forward at a rate of 1.75, which is equivalent to the 1,050,000 dollars required to repay the 1 million dollar loan at 5 percent interest. These transactions would result in a profit of 18,889 dollars should the pound decline to 1.70 dollars one year from now, and 21,111 dollars should it increase to 1.90 dollars one year from now, as Table 25.1 shows.

Regardless of whether the pound rises or falls, the arbitrageur profits from these transactions, given a forward exchange rate of 1.75. If the forward rate were 1.69, the arbitrageur could still profit—by reversing the above transactions.

From these examples, it appears that there is some forward rate between 1.69 and 1.75 at which an arbitrageur would neither profit nor lose by borrowing in one country, lending in another and hedging away the currency risk. This rate is found by multiplying the current spot rate by the quantity 1 plus the U.S. interest rate divided by 1 plus the U.K. interest rate. In our example, this rate equals 1.7182.

$$1.80 \times \left(\frac{1.05}{1.10} \right) = 1.7182$$

Essentially, the cost of hedging away the currency risk of a country with a high interest rate exactly offsets the advantage of lending at the higher interest rate. Table 25.2 shows that a forward rate equal to 1.7182

TABLE 25.1 Arbitrage Payoffs at Pound-Dollar Spot Rate of 1.80 and Forward Rate of 1.75

	Pound Declines to 1.70	Pound Increases to 1.90
Interest cost	$50,000	$50,000
Proceeds from loan	94,444	105,556
Profit/loss on principal	−55,556	55,556
Profit/loss on hedge	30,000	−90,000
Net Profit/loss	18,889	21,111

TABLE 25.2 Arbitrage Payoffs at Pound-Dollar Spot Rate of 1.80 and Forward Rate of 1.7182

	Pound Declines to 1.70	Pound Increases to 1.90
Interest cost	$50,000	$50,000
Proceeds from loan	94,444	105,556
Profit/loss on principal	55,556	55,556
Profit/loss on hedge	11,111	–111,111
Net Profit/loss	0	0

will preclude arbitrage profits or losses regardless of subsequent changes in the spot rate.

One might argue that, given a significant interest rate differential, it may make sense to borrow in the low interest rate country and lend in the high interest rate country, without hedging away the currency exposure. If future spot rates fluctuate randomly around the current spot rate, then such a strategy might make sense over the long run or across several pairs of high and low interest rate countries. We would then be gaining a certain interest rate advantage with an expected but uncertain currency loss of zero (assuming the current spot rate represents the central tendency of future spot rates).

This leads us to a second variation of interest arbitrage—uncovered interest arbitrage. If, on balance, speculators do not pursue such unhedged strategies, we might infer that they expect the currencies of the high interest rate countries to fall relative to the currencies of the low interest rate countries. Moreover, the level to which they must fall so that there is no expected profit or loss is precisely the current forward rate. The forward rate is said to be an "unbiased estimate" of the future spot rate.

This is the theory of uncovered interest arbitrage. It does not suggest that the forward rate is a particularly accurate forecast of the future spot rate; it merely holds that it does not systematically over- or underforecast subsequent changes in the spot rate.

TRADING CURRENCIES

Currencies are traded on exchanges and by private negotiation. The preponderance of volume in currencies is transacted in the interbank market through the use of forward contracts. A forward contract is a privately negotiated contract between two parties, obligating the seller to pay the value of the contract to the buyer at a specified date. If one party wishes to nullify a contract prior to expiration, he or she must enter into another forward contract to offset the exposure of the first contract.

It is conventional for dealers to quote forward contracts in terms of a forward rate's discount or premium to the spot rate. This is because the spot rate may change significantly during the few minutes it takes a trader to call several dealers to obtain the best quote, whereas the discount or premium component of the forward rate is more stable.

Futures contracts serve as an alternative to forward contracts for some of the major currencies. These contracts also obligate the seller to pay the value of the contract to the buyer at a specified date, but they differ from forward contracts in that they have uniform terms regarding price, quantity and expiration. There is thus an active secondary market in which traders can buy and sell futures contracts. This secondary market makes it easier to nullify or reverse an earlier trade. Futures contracts are disadvantaged relative to forward contracts, however, because it is more difficult to customize a position using futures contracts. Furthermore, futures contracts require initial margin as well as variation margin to cover daily price fluctuations, whereas forward contracts do not require margin deposits from creditworthy traders.

When we use forward or futures contracts to offset a currency exposure, we may reduce risk but we also sacrifice any potential to profit from a favorable currency price change. To overcome this regret factor, we can hedge our currency risk and still preserve the opportunity to benefit from a favorable price shift by using currency options.

Exchange-traded options are available for a number of currencies, and exchange-traded options are also available on currency futures contracts. Options on currencies derive their value from the spot exchange rate, whereas options on currency future contracts derive their value from the price of the underlying futures contracts. In addition to exchange-traded currency options, there is a vast over-the-counter market that accommodates the demand for options on non-exchange-traded currencies and customized options.

The valuation of a currency option is analogous to the valuation of a dividend-paying asset. The foreign interest rate is treated as a dividend yield. An American currency option may trade at a higher price than a European currency option with equivalent terms, because it may be advantageous to exercise the option early.[1]

We can also manage currency exposure through the use of currency swaps. This term is applied to several types of transactions. One type of swap refers to an arrangement in which a party agrees to purchase or sell a currency on one date and reverse the transaction at a specified future date. The swap rate, which is the difference between the exchange rate used in the two trades, is agreed upon in advance.

Another variation of a currency swap is an exchange of liabilities between parties in different countries. For example, a U.S. company might need to borrow funds in Germany but may not wish to incur the risk that the dollar could decline during the term of the loan. The U.S. company can seek a German counterpart that needs funds in the U.S. and exchange these liabilities at the prevailing exchange rate. Under a swap arrangement, if one of the parties defaults, the other is automatically released from its obligation. Essentially, a currency swap is tantamount to a series of forward contracts that hedge the interest payments as well as the principal repayment. This hedging is accomplished with a single transaction, however.[2]

TO HEDGE OR NOT TO HEDGE

Empirical evidence for the most part indicates that diversification into foreign assets improves the risk-return trade-off of a securities portfolio. This evidence is sometimes misconstrued to imply that exposure to currencies necessarily lowers portfolio risk. This fallacy rests on the assumption that currencies have low correlations with other portfolio assets and therefore provide diversification benefits. The problem with this reasoning is it ignores the fact that currency exposure introduces uncertainty as well as diversification.

To see the total impact of currency exposure on portfolio risk, consider a portfolio with a 10 percent standard deviation that is exposed to a currency with a 12 percent standard deviation. Let us explore three situations. In the first case, the portfolio returns are uncorrelated with the currency's returns. In the second case, their returns are 50 percent correlated. In the third, they are 75 percent correlated. Table 25.3 shows the amount of currency to sell short as a fraction of the portfolio's value in order to minimize risk, and the extent to which this hedging reduces portfolio risk.[3]

These results are specific to the example described here. It is generally

TABLE 25.3 Minimum Risk Hedge Ratio as a Function of Correlation

	Correlation*		
	0%	50%	75%
Portfolio standard deviation	10.00%	10.00%	10.00%
Currency standard deviation	12.00%	12.00%	12.00%
Minimum risk hedge ratio	0.00%	41.67%	62.50%
Hedged portfolio standard deviation	10.00%	8.66%	6.61%

*Between unhedged portfolio and currency

the case, however, that a portfolio in which the embedded currency exposure is hedged away will be less risky than an unhedged portfolio. Furthermore, there is usually some degree of hedging less than full hedging that optimally balances a currency's diversification properties with the uncertainty it introduces to the portfolio, such that we can reduce portfolio risk even further. Finally, the decision of whether or not to hedge a portfolio's currency risk should reflect a realistic assessment of the costs of hedging this risk.

CURRENCY ANOMALIES

Researchers in both the academic and practitioner communities have discovered empirical regularities of currency returns. Evidence suggests that the forward rate does not behave in accordance with the theory of uncovered interest arbitrage described earlier. (The evidence does not violate covered interest arbitrage, however.) Contrary to theory, the implicit forecast of the forward rate systematically exaggerates subsequent changes in the spot rate. The obvious implication of this evidence is that traders willing to incur risk can profit, on average, by purchasing forward contracts on currencies of high interest rate countries (those that sell at a forward discount) and by selling forward contracts on currencies of low interest rate countries (those that sell at a forward premium).[4]

A second empirical regularity of currencies is that their returns tend to be positively serially correlated. This tendency is independent of the forward rate bias in that the effect persists whether currency returns are derived from spot rates or from forward rates. Positive serial correlation, which we can state more prosaically as trending, suggests that investors can profit from trading rules that call for acquiring currencies as they appreciate and selling currencies as they depreciate.[5] We would be well advised to temper our enthusiasm about these anomalies, however, because the evidence is based on a relatively short history compared with that of other financial assets. It was only in the mid 1970s that currency exchange rates were allowed to float.

WITHIN-HORIZON EXPOSURE TO CURRENCY RISK

We may be reluctant to hedge a portfolio's currency exposure because we believe currency returns wash out over the long run. Although there is little evidence to support this view, even it were true we would still be exposed to significantly more risk throughout a long horizon if we failed to hedge a portfolio's currency exposure.

Figure 25.1 shows the likelihood of a 10 percent or greater loss over a 10-year horizon at the end of the horizon, and at any point since inception throughout the horizon, for an unhedged and an optimally hedged portfolio.[6] This comparison assumes the unhedged portfolio has an expected return of 7.50 percent and a standard deviation of 16.01 percent, while the optimally hedged portfolio has an expected return of 7.41 percent, reflecting the cost of hedging, and a standard deviation of 9.17 percent.

If we were only concerned with the portfolio's performance at the end of the 10-year investment horizon, we might not be particularly impressed by the advantage offered by hedging. It reduces the likelihood of a loss equal to 10 percent or greater, from 6.24 percent to 0.18 percent, and 6.24 percent might not seem like a very large probability to many investors. If, instead, we care about what might happen along the way to the end of the horizon, the advantage of hedging is much more apparent. It reduces the likelihood of a 10 percent loss from 54.00 percent to 13.91 percent, a much more substantial improvement. Thus, even if we believe currency returns wash out over the long run, we still might benefit substantially by hedging our currency risk if what happens along the way matters to us.

SUMMARY

1. Markets for trading currencies and their derivatives are well-established and highly liquid.
2. Covered interest arbitrage explains the relationship between forward discounts and premiums and interest rate differentials. It holds that arbitrageurs cannot earn riskless profits by borrowing in low

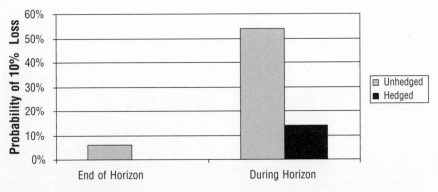

FIGURE 25.1 Risk reduction from hedging (10-year horizon)

interest rate countries and lending in high interest rate countries, because the cost of hedging the currency risk offsets the interest rate advantage.

3. Uncovered interest arbitrage holds that the forward rate is an unbiased estimate of the future spot rate, but this relationship has not been borne out empirically. Forward rates, on balance, have overestimated subsequent changes in spot rates.

4. Currency exposure influences a portfolio's risk in two ways. It introduces diversification, and it introduces volatility. The optimal ratio of currency exposure to hedge depends on the net effect of these influences, along with the cost of hedging.

5. Even if exchange rate fluctuations wash out over the long run, exposure to loss within an investment horizon is typically much higher for unhedged portfolios than it is for optimally hedged portfolios.

APPENDIX: CURRENCY HEDGING MATHEMATICS

Currency exposure affects an asset's risk in two ways. It introduces volatility as well as diversification. It is the net effect of these two influences that determines how currency exposure impacts an asset's risk.

Equation (25.1) expresses a foreign asset's variance in terms of the standard deviation of the returns of the local asset and the standard deviation of the embedded currency exposure.

$$\sigma_{FA}^2 = \sigma_L^2 + \sigma_{FX}^2 + 2\rho_{L,FX}\sigma_L\sigma_{FX} \qquad (25.1)$$

where σ_{FA} = foreign asset standard deviation
σ_L = local component standard deviation
σ_{FX} = currency component standard deviation
$\rho_{L,FX}$ = correlation between local component return and currency component return

Equation (25.2) incorporates exposure to a currency forward contract to show the variance of a hedged foreign asset in which the amount hedged is variable.

$$\sigma_H^2 = \sigma_L^2 + \sigma_C^2 + w^2\sigma_f^2 + 2\rho_{L,FX}\sigma_L\sigma_{FX} + 2w\rho_{Lf}\sigma_L\sigma_f + 2w\rho_{FX,f}\sigma_{FX}\sigma_f \qquad (25.2)$$

where σ_f = forward contract standard deviation
ρ_{Lf} = correlation between local component return and forward contract return

$\rho_{FX,f}$ = correlation between currency component return and forward
          contract return
w = weighting of forward contract

Equations (25.3) through (25.5) show the variance of a foreign asset under the special case in which 100 percent of the embedded currency exposure is hedged and the currency forward contract tracks the embedded currency exposure perfectly. Perfect tracking implies that the variance of the forward contract and the embedded currency exposure are equal, the correlation between the forward contract returns and the local asset returns equals the correlation between the embedded currency returns and the local asset returns, and the correlation between the forward contract returns and the embedded currency returns equals 1.00. Equation (25.5) reveals that under these conditions the variance of the hedged foreign asset, not surprisingly, equals the variance of the local asset returns.

$$\sigma_H^2 = \sigma_L^2 + \sigma_C^2 + \sigma_f^2 \times -1^2 + 2\rho_{L,FX}\sigma_L\sigma_{FX} + 2\rho_{Lf}\sigma_L\sigma_f \times -1$$
$$+ 2\rho_{FX,f}\sigma_{FX}\sigma_f \times -1 \tag{25.3}$$

Assume: $\sigma_{FX} = \sigma_f$ $\rho_{L,FX} = \rho_{Lf}$ $\rho_{FX,f} = 1$

$$\sigma_H^2 = \sigma_L^2 + \sigma_{FX}^2 + \sigma_f^2 - 2\sigma_{FX}\sigma_f \tag{25.4}$$

$$\sigma_H^2 = \sigma_L^2 \tag{25.5}$$

Investors often cite the diversification benefit of currency exposure as a justification not to hedge it. Typically, these investors have an inflated perception of the extent to which currency exposure diversifies a portfolio, because they focus on the correlation between the local asset returns and the embedded currency returns, which may be very low or even negative. The relevant correlation for gauging the diversification effect of currency exposure, however, is the correlation between the investor's base currency–denominated asset returns and the embedded currency returns. This correlation will be much higher because a large part of a foreign asset's return *is* the currency return. For example, if both the local asset and the currency have a standard deviation equal to 10 percent and they are uncorrelated, the correlation between the base currency–denominated asset returns and the currency returns will equal 71 percent.

Equations (25.6) and (25.7) show how to map the correlation between the local asset returns and the embedded currency returns onto the correlation between the investor's base currency–denominated asset returns and the embedded currency returns.

$$\rho_{FA,CC} = \frac{\rho_{L,FX}\sigma_L + \sigma_{FX}}{\sigma_{FA}} \tag{25.6}$$

$$\rho_{FA,CC} = \frac{\rho_{L,FX}\sigma_L + \sigma_{FX}}{\left(\sigma_L^2 + \sigma_{FX}^2 + 2\rho_{L,FX}\sigma_L\sigma_{FX}\right)^{1/2}} \tag{25.7}$$

where $\rho_{FA,C}$ = correlation between foreign asset return and embedded
     currency return

By taking the partial derivative of variance with respect to exposure to the forward contract and setting this quantity equal to 0, we find the forward contract exposure that minimizes variance. It is equal to –1 times the asset's beta with respect to the forward contract, as shown by equations (25.8) through (25.10).

$$\sigma_H^2 = \sigma_{FA}^2 + \sigma_f^2 + w^2\sigma_f^2 + 2w\rho_{FA,f}\sigma_{FA}\sigma_f \tag{25.8}$$

$$\frac{\partial \sigma_H^2}{\partial w} = 2w\sigma_f^2 + 2\rho_{FA,f}\sigma_{FA}\sigma_f = 0 \tag{25.9}$$

$$w = \frac{-(\rho_{FA,f}\sigma_{FA})}{\sigma_f} = -\beta \tag{25.10}$$

It is not always the case that an investor will choose to minimize variance without regard to the cost of achieving this risk reduction. Instead, the investor will seek to balance risk reduction with its associated cost, by maximizing expected utility as a function of exposure to a forward contract. Equation (25.11) defines expected utility, and equations (25.12) through (25.14) derive the exposure to a forward contract that maximizes expected utility, taking both risk reduction and cost into consideration.

$$E(U) = \mu_{FA} + wC_H - \lambda(\sigma_{FA}^2 + \sigma_f^2 + w^2\sigma_f^2 + 2w\rho_{FA,f}\sigma_{FA}\sigma_f) \tag{25.11}$$

where μ_{FA} = foreign asset expected return
     C_H = forward contract hedging cost
     λ = risk aversion, which is defined as the amount of expected
        return one is willing to sacrifice in exchange for one unit of
        risk reduction.

$$E(U) = \mu_A + wC_H - \lambda \times \sigma_{FA}^2 - \lambda \times w^2 \sigma_f^2 - \lambda \times 2w\rho_{FA,f}\sigma_{FA}\sigma_f \quad (25.12)$$

$$\frac{\partial E(U)}{\partial w} = C_H - 2\lambda w \sigma_f^2 - 2\lambda \rho_{FA,f}\sigma_{FA}\sigma_f = 0 \qquad (25.13)$$

$$w = \frac{C_H}{2\lambda\sigma_f^2} - \rho_{FA,f}\frac{\sigma_{FA}}{\sigma_f} \qquad (25.14)$$

Glossary

alpha   (1) The risk-adjusted return of an asset or portfolio, calculated as the portfolio's excess return net of the riskless rate less beta times the market's excess return net of the riskless rate. (2) The intercept of a regression line.

alternative hypothesis   In hypothesis testing, usually the hypothesis that the results are not due to chance.

American option   An option that can be exercised at expiration or anytime prior to expiration, as opposed to a European option, which can only be exercised at expiration.

analysis of variance   In regression analysis, analysis of the variation in the dependent variable. The source of variation is attributed to variation in the independent variable(s) and error.

appraisal ratio   A measure of portfolio management skill, computed as alpha divided by the standard error.

arbitrageur   An investor or speculator who buys an undervalued asset and sells an overvalued asset of similar risk with the intent of generating relatively riskless profits. Arbitrage trades prevent assets from deviating significantly from their fair values.

autocorrelation   A situation in which a series' observations are not serially independent. First-degree autocorrelation occurs when successive observations are correlated. Second-degree autocorrelation refers to correlation among every other observation. Also called serial dependence.

autoregressive conditional heteroskedasticity (ARCH)   A modeling procedure often used to forecast return volatility, which incorporates nonlinearities in the squared residuals of the dependent variable.

backwardation   A situation in which the spot price of a commodity exceeds the price of the futures contract. The owners of the commodity forego a certain profit for the convenience of having the commodity on hand to meet demand.

basis   The difference between the spot price and the futures price.

bell curve Another name for a normal distribution, so called because its shape resembles the curvature of a bell.

Bernoulli trial A random event which must satisfy three properties: Its result must be characterized by a success or a failure. The probability of a success must be the same for all of the trials. The outcome of each trial must be independent of the outcomes of the other trials.

beta A measure of an asset or portfolio's relative volatility with a reference portfolio. It is estimated as the slope of a regression line relating an asset or portfolio's excess return over the riskless return to a reference portfolio's excess return over the riskless return. Within the context of the Capital Asset Pricing Model, beta, when squared and multiplied by the market's variance, represents an asset or portfolio's systematic risk.

binomial model A representation of a return-generating process, often used to value options in which an asset's value can either increase by a specified amount with a given probability or decrease by a specified amount with 1 minus the probability of the increase in a single period from all immediate prior values. The ending distribution of values from a binomial process converges to a normal or lognormal distribution as the number of periods becomes large.

binomial random variable The fraction of successes from a sequence of Bernoulli trials.

Black-Scholes formula A formula that gives the fair value of an option based on five inputs: the price of the underlying asset, the strike price, the riskless interest rate, the time remaining to expiration, and the volatility of the underlying asset's return. It is the solution to a partial differential equation based on a neutral hedge that combines offsetting exposures to an option and its underlying asset.

block bootstrapping A variation of bootstrapping that randomly selects contiguous observations with replacement, as opposed to individual observations, in order to create additional samples. Block bootstrapping is used to preserve the serial dependence of the data.

bootstrapping A simulation procedure by which new samples are generated from an original data set by randomly selecting observations with replacement from the original data.

call option An option that grants its owner the right but not the obligation to purchase an underlying asset at a previously agreed upon price, at or up to a specified future date (American) or only at a specified future date (European).

Capital Asset Pricing Model (CAPM) A theory of market equilibrium which partitions risk into two sources: that caused by changes in the market portfolio, which cannot be diversified away (systematic risk), and that caused by nonmarket factors, which can be diversified away (unsystematic risk). An asset's systematic risk is equal to its beta squared multiplied by the market portfolio's variance. The CAPM implies that investors should incur only systematic risk because they are not compensated for bearing unsystematic risk.

central limit theorem The principle that the distribution of the sum or average of independent random variables, which are not necessarily individually normally distributed, will approach a normal distribution as the number of variables increases. See also normal distribution, random variable.

certainty equivalent A risky gamble or investment that conveys the same amount of expected utility as the utility associated with a certain outcome.

coefficient matrix In matrix algebra, a matrix that is inverted and multiplied by a vector of constants to yield the solution to a system of linear equations.

Commodity Futures Trading Commission (CFTC) A regulatory agency established in 1974 under the Commodity Exchange Act to promote fair and efficient pricing, trading integrity, and financial soundness.

common logarithm The power to which the number 10 must be raised to yield a particular value. The base 10 is popular because the logarithms of 10, 100, 1,000, and so on equal 1, 2, 3 . . . respectively.

constant absolute risk aversion A description of risk aversion that holds that investors allocate the same absolute amount to risky assets as their wealth changes.

constant rate of return The rate of return that, were it to occur on average annually, would produce the cumulative return that actually occurred.

constant relative risk aversion A description of risk aversion that holds that investors allocate the same percentage amount to risky assets as their wealth changes.

contango A situation in which the price of a commodity futures contract exceeds the price of the commodity.

continuous probability distribution A probability distribution in which there are an infinite number of observations covering all possible values along a continuous scale.

continuous rate of return The rate of return that, if compounded continuously or instantaneously, would generate the corresponding discrete return. It is equal to the natural logarithm of the quantity, 1 plus the discrete return.

continuous value at risk At a given probability, the maximum loss or minimum gain that could occur from inception to any point within a specified investment period, assuming continuous monitoring. It is calculated iteratively using the first passage probability formula.

convexity The extent to which duration changes as yield to maturity changes.

correlation A measure of the association between two variables. It ranges in value from 1 to −1. If one variable's values are higher than its average when another variable's values are higher than its average, for example, the correlation will be positive, somewhere between 0 and 1. Alternatively, if one variable's values are lower than its average return when another variable's values are higher than its average, then the correlation will be negative.

cost-of-carry model A model for valuing commodity futures contracts, in which the contract's fair value equals the spot price of the underlying commodity plus the cost of carrying the commodity. If the cost of carrying the commodity consists entirely of the financing cost, the cost-of-carry model holds that the profit or loss on a long futures position equals the profit or loss from acquiring the underlying commodity on margin.

covariance A measure of the co-movement of two variables. It equals the correlation between the two variables times the first variable's standard deviation times the second variable's standard deviation. Combinations of assets that have low covariances are desirable because they offer greater diversification.

covariance matrix A matrix used in portfolio optimization which contains the variances of the assets to be optimized along the diagonal of the matrix and the covariances of the assets in the off-diagonal elements.

covered interest arbitrage The principle that one cannot borrow in a low interest country, convert to the currency of a high interest rate country, lend in the high interest rate country, hedge the currency risk of the loan, and generate a profit. The absence of arbitrage profits from these transactions ensures that the forward exchange rate will equal the spot exchange rate multiplied by the ratio of 1 plus the domestic interest rate to 1 plus the foreign interest rate.

cross-sectional regression analysis A regression analysis in which the observations are measured over the same time period but differ along another dimension. For example, returns across a sample of securities during a particular month may be regressed on differences in certain attributes of these securities for the same month or an earlier or later month.

cumulative rate of return The rate of return that is equal to the product of the quantities, 1 plus the discrete returns, minus 1; or, equivalently, an asset's ending value divided by its beginning value minus 1, assuming reinvestment of income and controlling for contributions and disbursements.

currency swap (1) An arrangement in which a party agrees to purchase or sell a currency on one date and reverse the transaction at a specified future date. The swap rate, which is the difference between the exchange rates used in the two trades, is agreed upon in advance. (2) An exchange of liabilities between parties in different countries. Under a swap arrangement, if one of the parties defaults, the other is automatically released from its obligation. (3) A series of forward contracts that hedge the interest payments as well as the principal repayment, but which are accomplished with a single transaction.

decreasing absolute risk aversion A description of risk aversion that holds that investors decrease their absolute allocation to risky assets as their wealth increases.

decreasing relative risk aversion A description of risk aversion that holds that investors decrease their percentage allocation to risky assets as their wealth increases.

deep-discount bond A bond that sells at a price significantly below its par value.

degrees of freedom The number of values that are free to vary when computing a statistic. Statistics books describe how to calculate and apply degrees of freedom in order to interpret various statistics.

dependent variable In regression analysis, the variable on the left-hand side of the regression equation, whose variation is explained by variation in the independent variable(s) on the right-hand side of the equation.

diminishing marginal utility The notion that investors derive progressively less satisfaction with each increment to wealth. Investors with diminishing marginal utility are risk averse.

discount factor The reciprocal of 1 plus the spot rate raised to the maturity of a bond. The term structure of interest rates is sometimes represented as the relationship between discount factors and maturity.

discrete probability distribution A probability distribution that shows the percentage of observations falling within specified ranges, which collectively account for all of the observations.

discrete rate of return The income produced by an investment during a specified period plus its change in price during that period, all divided by its price at the beginning of the period. Also called holding-period rate of return.

distribution-free test A test of statistical significance that does not depend on any assumption about the random variable's underlying distribution.

diversifiable risk Risk that is specific to an asset and thus not associated with market risk. In an efficient market, investors should not bear diversifiable risk because it is not rewarded. Also called unsystematic risk.

dollar-weighted rate of return The rate of return that discounts an asset or portfolio's ending value and interim cash flows back to its beginning value. It is equivalent to the internal rate of return. It is inappropriate for performance measurement, because it is influenced by the timing and size of cash flows.

downside risk A measure of the variability of returns below the mean return or below a specified target return. It is relevant in situations in which the distribution of returns is asymmetric and investors care about skewness.

duration The average time to receipt of a bond's cash flows, in which each cash flow's time to receipt is weighted by its present value as a percentage of the total present value of all the cash flows. Also called Macaulay's duration.

Durbin-Watson statistic A test for first-degree autocorrelation in the residuals of a regression analysis. As the Durbin-Watson statistic approaches 2, it is less likely the residuals are autocorrelated.

dynamic trading strategy A prespecified set of trading rules that vary a portfolio's exposure between a risky asset and a riskless asset in response to changes in the value of the portfolio. Dynamic trading rules are often used to replicate option strategies or to exploit nonrandomness in asset returns.

e The base of the natural logarithm and the limit of the function $(1+1/n)^n$. To five decimal places, it equals 2.71828. When e is raised to the power of a continuous return, it is equal to 1 plus the discrete return.

efficient frontier A continuum of portfolios plotted in dimensions of expected return and standard deviation that offer the highest expected return for a given level of risk or the lowest risk for a given expected return.

efficient market hypothesis The notion that prices at which securities trade reflect all relevant information about those securities; therefore, investors should not expect to outperform the market portfolio after adjustment for risk.

efficient surface A representation of portfolios plotted in dimensions of expected return, standard deviation, and tracking error. It is bounded on the upper left by the traditional mean-variance efficient frontier, which comprises efficient portfolios in dimensions of expected return and standard deviation. The right boundary of the efficient surface is the mean–tracking error efficient frontier, comprising portfolios that offer the highest expected return for varying levels of tracking error. The lower boundary of the efficient surface comprises combinations of the minimum-risk asset and the benchmark portfolio.

eigenvalue   In a factor analysis of security returns, the sensitivity of a particular security to an eigenvector.

eigenvector   In a factor analysis of security returns, a linear combination of securities, comprising both long and short positions, which explains a fraction of the covariation in the securities' returns.

error maximization   The notion that portfolio optimization favors assets for which return is overestimated and risk is underestimated. This bias leads to two problems. First, the expected return of the optimized portfolio is overstated, while its risk is understated. Second, assets for which return is underestimated and risk is overestimated are underweighted in the optimized portfolio, while assets with opposite errors are overweighted.

European option   An option that can be exercised only at expiration, as opposed to an American option, which can be exercised at expiration or anytime up to expiration.

E-V maxim   The proposition by Harry Markowitz that investors choose portfolios that offer the highest expected return for a given level of variance.

event study   A study that measure the relationship between an event that affects securities and the performance of those securities. These events are often not contemporaneous in calendar time (stock splits, for example) and must be synchronized in order to evaluate pre- and post-event performance.

excess return   An asset or portfolio's return less the riskless return.

expectations hypothesis   The hypothesis that the current term structure of interest rates is determined by the consensus forecast of future interest rates.

expected return   The average or probability-weighted value of all possible returns. The process of compounding causes the expected return to exceed the median return. Thus there is less than a 50 percent chance of exceeding the expected return.

expected utility   The average or probability-weighted utility or measure of satisfaction associated with all possible wealth or consumption levels.

expected value   The average or probability-weighted value of all possible wealth values. It is equal to the initial value compounded forward at the expected return, which, if based on historical returns, equals the arithmetic average return. See also expected return.

exponential   When converting a continuous return to a discrete return, the value we compute by raising e to the power of the continuous return. For example, 1.10 is the exponential of e raised to the power 0.0953. Thus, 10 percent is the discrete counterpart of the continuous return 9.53 percent.

factor analysis   A statistical procedure used to identify factors by observing common variation in the returns of different securities. These factors are statistical constructs that represent some underlying source of risk; that source may or may not be observable. Maximum likelihood factor analysis identifies linear combinations of securities, comprising both long and short positions, which explain virtually all the covariation in the returns of a sample of securities. These linear functions are called eigenvectors, and the sensitivity of a particular security to an eigenvector is called an eigenvalue.

fat-tailed distribution   A probability distribution in which there are more extreme observations than would be expected under a normal distribution. Fat-tailed distributions are called leptokurtic.

first passage time probability   In investment management, the probability that an investment will depreciate to or below a particular value over a finite investment horizon if it is monitored continuously.

forward contract   A contract that obligates a seller to pay the value of the contract to the buyer at a specified date. Forward contracts are negotiated privately; their terms are thus specific to the transaction.

forward discount   In foreign exchange markets, the percentage discount of the forward exchange rate relative to the spot exchange rate, when the foreign interest rate exceeds the domestic interest rate.

forward exchange rate   A previously agreed upon rate at which currencies are exchanged at a specified future date.

forward premium   In foreign exchange markets, the percentage premium of the forward exchange rate relative to the spot exchange rate, when the domestic interest rate exceeds the foreign interest rate.

forward rate   The interest rate that will apply to an instrument commencing at some future date. It can be derived from the spot rates of interest. For example, the forward rate on a one-year instrument one year hence is determined so that an investor is indifferent between purchasing a two-year instrument today and holding it to maturity or purchasing a one-year instrument today and entering into a forward contract to purchase a one-year instrument one year from now.

frequency distribution   A discrete probability distribution.

futures commission merchant (FCM)   An institution that trades commodity futures contracts. FCMs perform the same function as brokerage houses. They maintain trading accounts for their customers, execute trades at the exchanges, and collect margin deposits from their customers.

futures contract A contract that obligates a seller to pay the value of the contract to the buyer at a specified date. Financial futures contracts, which are marked to market daily, have uniform terms with respect to quantity, expiration date, and underlying asset.

Gaussian distribution A normal distribution.

generalized autoregressive conditional heteroskedasticity (GARCH) A modeling procedure often used to forecast return volatility, which incorporates nonlinearities in the squared residuals of the dependent variable as well as lagged values for the dependent variable.

geometric rate of return The average return that, when compounded forward, converts an initial value to an ending value. It is equal to the product of the quantities, 1 plus the discrete returns, raised to the power 1 over the number of discrete returns, less 1. When based on historical returns, an initial value compounded forward at the geometric rate of return yields the median value. The natural logarithm of the quantity 1 plus the geometric rate of return, equals the continuous return. Also called time-weighted rate of return.

heteroskedasticity In regression analysis, a condition in which the absolute values of the standardized residuals increase as the values for the independent variable increase. The errors involved in predicting the dependent variable will grow larger and larger, the higher the value of the independent variable. Heteroskedasticity is often ameliorated by transforming the independent variables into their logarithmic values.

holding-period rate of return The income produced by an investment during a specified period plus its change in price during that period, all divided by its price at the beginning of the period. Also called discrete rate of return.

homoskedasticity In regression analysis, a condition in which the absolute values of the standardized residuals are distributed randomly around an expected value of zero.

hypothesis test A test to distinguish between a null hypothesis and an alternative hypothesis. In investment management, the null hypothesis is usually that a manager has no skill.

identity matrix A matrix that includes ones along its diagonal and zeros for all the other elements. It is analogous to the number 1 in simple algebra, in that a matrix multiplied by an identity matrix yields itself.

immunization A process by which a portfolio is protected from interest rate shifts by setting its duration equal to the holding period. If interest rates rise, the capital loss will be offset by the gain from reinvesting the cash flows at higher yields. Conversely, if interest rates fall, the reduction in income resulting from reinvestment of cash flows at lower rates is offset by the capital gain. However, capital gains and losses are balanced by reinvestment gains and losses only to the extent that short-term rates and long-term rates move together. If long-term rates increase but short-term rates remain unchanged, the portfolio's income will not increase sufficiently to offset the capital loss.

implied volatility   The volatility of an asset's returns that is implied by the price at which an option on that asset trades.

increasing absolute risk aversion   A description of risk aversion that holds that investors increase their absolute allocation to risky assets as their wealth increases.

increasing relative risk aversion   A description of risk aversion that holds that investors increase their percentage allocation to risky assets as their wealth increases.

independent and identically distributed (iid)   A condition in which successive draws from a population are independent of one another and generated from the same underlying distribution, implying that the parameters of an iid distribution are constant across all draws.

independent variable   In regression analysis, the variables on the right-hand side of the regression equation whose variation explains variation in the dependent variable on the left-hand side of the equation.

indifference curve   A curve tracing combinations of expected return and risk that have equal expected utility.

initial margin   When trading commodity futures contracts, an initial deposit that serves as a performance bond. The amount required varies from contract to contract, typically as a function of the volatility of the underlying commodity. The initial margin requirement is usually greater for speculators than it is for hedgers.

internal rate of return   The rate of return that discounts an asset or portfolio's ending value and interim cash flows back to its beginning value. Also called the dollar-weighted rate of return.

invariance propositions   The principles put forth by Franco Modigliani and Merton Miller that the value of a firm is invariant to its capital structure and dividend policy, because investors can individually engage in arbitrage to offset capital structure, and because dividend payments and share repurchases are substitutes.

inverse matrix   Aanalogous to a reciprocal in simple algebra. A matrix multiplied by its inverse yields an identity matrix. An identity matrix includes ones along its diagonal and zeros for all the other elements. It is analogous to the number 1 in simple algebra, in that a matrix multiplied by an identity matrix yields itself. Multiplying a vector or matrix by the inverse of another matrix is analogous to multiplying a number by the reciprocal of another number, hence the analogy with division.

Jensen measure   An investment performance measure equal to the intercept from a regression of a portfolio's excess returns on a benchmark's excess returns. The Jensen measure is a valid performance criterion when evaluating a portfolio in combination with a benchmark portfolio and other actively managed portfolios.

kurtosis   A measure of a distribution's peakedness. It is computed by raising the deviations from the mean to the fourth power and taking the average of these values. It is usually represented as the ratio of this value to the standard deviation raised to the fourth power. A normal distribution has a kurtosis value equal to 3.

Lagrange multiplier   In optimization, a variable introduced to facilitate a solution when there are constraints. It does not always lend itself to economic interpretation.

law of one price   The economic principle that assets with identical cash flows should be priced the same.

leptokurtic distribution   A distribution with a narrow peak and wide tails. Compared to a normal distribution, a larger proportion of the returns are located near the extremes rather than the mean of the distribution. It is prosaically called a fat-tailed distribution.

linear investment rule   A rule that determines an asset's new allocation in a portfolio by multiplying the percentage change in the asset's market value by a constant and adding the product to its market value prior to the change. These rules are often used to exploit nonrandomness in asset returns.

liquidity premium hypothesis   The hypothesis that investors demand compensation for bearing interest rate risk, which may preclude them from selling a bond at a price near its current price.

liquidity premium   A premium required for the convenience of being able to sell an asset at a price close to its current price.

logarithm   The power to which a base must be raised to yield a particular number. For example, the logarithm of 100 to the base 10 equals 2, because 10^2 equals 100.

logarithmic return   The natural logarithm of 1 plus the discrete rate of return. Also called continuous rate of return.

lognormal distribution A distribution of discrete returns or cumulative values that is positively skewed as a result of compounding. Compared to a normal distribution, which is symmetric, a lognormal distribution has a longer right tail than left tail and an average value that exceeds the median value. A lognormal distribution of discrete returns corresponds to a normal distribution of their continuous counterparts.

log-wealth utility function A concave utility function that assumes utility is equal to the logarithm of wealth. It is one of a family of utility functions that assume investors have constant relative risk aversion. For investors with a log-wealth utility function, as wealth increases, its utility also increases but at a diminishing rate.

Macaulay's duration The average time to receipt of a bond's cash flows, in which each cash flow's time to receipt is weighted by its present value as a percentage of the total present value of all the cash flows. Often referred to simply as duration.

matrix algebra Algebraic operations performed on matrices to solve systems of linear equations.

maximum likelihood estimation An estimation procedure yielding a prediction equation that gives the highest probability of predicting the values that are actually observed. It is often used to fit nonlinear relationships.

mean reversion The tendency of an above-average return to be followed by a below-average return and a below-average return to be followed by an above-average return, resulting in a higher incidence of reversals than would be expected from a random process.

mean-variance optimization A portfolio formation technique that identifies combinations of assets that offer the highest expected return (mean) for a given level of risk (variance).

mean-variance–tracking error optimization A portfolio formation technique that identifies combinations of assets that offer the highest expected return (mean) for a given combination of tracking error and variance, or the lowest variance for a given combination of expected return and tracking error, or the lowest tracking error for a given combination of expected return and variance.

measure of central tendency A statistic used to summarize a set of data. Together with measures of dispersion, it allows one to assess the confidence with which an outcome will exceed or fall short of a particular value. Measures of central tendency include the mean, which is the average value; the median, which is the middle value; and the mode, which is the most common value.

measure of dispersion   A statistic used to summarize the variation in a set of data. Together with measures of central tendency, it allows one to assess the confidence with which an outcome will exceed or fall short of a particular value. Measures of dispersion include mean absolute deviation, standard deviation, and variance.

median   The middle value of a set of data. Based on historical returns, an initial value compounded forward at the geometric average return yields the median value.

method of bisection   A search algorithm used to find implied volatility by repeatedly interpolating between high and low estimates.

mode   The most common value of a set of data.

modified duration   Macaulay's duration divided by the quantity 1 plus the yield to maturity. The percentage change in the price of a bond is found by multiplying the basis-point change in yield to maturity by −1 times the bond's modified duration.

Monte Carlo simulation   A process used to simulate the performance of an investment strategy by randomly selecting returns from an underlying theoretical distribution, such as a normal or lognormal distribution, and subjecting the investment strategy to these randomly selected returns. It is used to assess path-dependent investment strategies.

multicolinearity   In multiple linear regression analysis, codependence among two or more independent variables.

multiple linear regression   A linear regression between a dependent variable and two or more independent variables.

natural logarithm   With respect to a rate of return, the continuous return to which e, 2.71828, must be raised to yield 1 plus the corresponding discrete return. For example, e raised to the power 0.0953 gives 1.10, which equals 1 plus the discrete return of 0.10. Therefore, the natural logarithm of the quantity 1 plus the discrete return yields the corresponding continuous return.

Newton-Raphson method   A search algorithm used to find implied volatility by subtracting an amount equal to the estimated option value minus the option's actual price, divided by the derivative of the option formula with respect to volatility evaluated at our estimate for volatility.

nondiversifiable risk   Risk associated with variation in the return of the market portfolio. It is equal to beta squared times the market's variance. In an efficient market, investors should only bear nondiversifiable risk because, unlike diversifiable risk, it is rewarded. Also called systematic risk.

nonparametric test   A test of statistical significance that depends on ordinal differences rather than parameters.

normal distribution   A continuous probability distribution that often arises from the summation of a large number of random variables. It has the convenient property that its mean, median, and mode are all equal. Also, approximately 68 percent of its area falls within a range of the mean plus and minus one standard deviation, and approximately 95 percent of its area falls within a range of the mean plus and minus two standard deviations.

null hypothesis   In hypothesis testing, usually the hypothesis that the results are due to chance.

optimization   In portfolio formation, a technique for identifying portfolios with the highest expected return for a given level of risk, usually measured as standard deviation or tracking error.

option   A contract that grants its owner the right, but not the obligation, to purchase (call option) or sell (put option) an underlying asset at a pre-established price for a specified period of time.

P value   In hypothesis testing, the probability that the test statistic would occur if the null hypothesis were true.

parametric bootstrapping   A variation of bootstrapping that randomly selects observations with replacement from a theoretical distribution, but it relies on historical data to estimate the mean and standard deviation of the distribution.

platykurtic distribution   A distribution with thin tails and a wider, flatter center. Relative to a normal distribution, a greater fraction of its returns are clustered near the center of the distribution, and a smaller fraction lie in the extremes.

power of the test   In hypothesis testing, the quantity 1 minus the probability of a Type II error.

preference free   An approach to valuation that disregards preferences with respect to risk, and depends instead on the absence of arbitrage.

preferred habitat hypothesis   The hypothesis that groups of investors regularly prefer bonds within particular maturity ranges in order to hedge their liabilities or to comply with regulatory requirements. Also called segmented market hypothesis.

present value   The value today of a future cash flow or sequence of cash flows that is derived by discounting them by a discount factor. See also discount rate.

pure discount bond   A bond that does not pay coupons. Instead, it is initially offered at a discount to its face value, so that its yield is equal to the annualized return resulting from its conversion to face value. The yield on a pure discount bond is referred to as the spot rate of interest.

put option   An option that grants its owner the right, but not the obligation, to sell an underlying asset at a previously agreed upon price at or up to a specified future date (American) or only at a specified future date (European).

random variable   A variable that can take on a variety of uncertain values. For example, an asset's value at a future date is a random variable, as is the value resulting from the toss of a die.

random walk   A stochastic process in which future values of a random variable are unrelated to its current value. Variables that are believed to follow a random walk are said to be independent and identically distributed.

residual   In regression analysis, the difference between a value predicted by the regression line and the observed value for the dependent variable.

risk attribution   A process by which the sensitivity of a portfolio's value at risk to a small change in the portfolio's exposure to each component is measured.

risk aversion   Preference for a certain prospect to an uncertain prospect of equal value.

risk budget   The assignment of value-at-risk measures to various components of a portfolio. These components can be defined in many ways, and measured either in absolute terms or relative to a benchmark.

risk neutrality   Indifference between a certain prospect and an uncertain prospect of equal value.

risk seeking   Preference for an uncertain prospect to a certain prospect of equal value.

roll yield   The return from liquidating an existing futures position and establishing a new position in a contract with a more distant settlement date, controlling for the change in the spot price.

R-squared   In regression analysis, the ratio of the sum of the squares due to regression to the total sum of the squares. It equals the fraction of variation in the dependent variable explained by variation in the independent variable. It ranges in value from 0 to 1. A high value for R-squared indicates a strong relationship between the dependent and independent variables, whereas a low value for R-squared indicates a weak relationship. Also called coefficient of determination.

runs test   A nonparametric test for serial dependence. First compute the average value of a series. Then designate every value that is above the mean as positive and every value that is below the mean as negative. A run is an uninterrupted sequence of positive or negative values. For example, a sequence of four positive values (+ + + +) would constitute a single run, whereas a sequence of four alternating values (+ − + −) would constitute four runs.

segmented market hypothesis   The hypothesis that groups of investors regularly prefer bonds within particular maturity ranges in order to hedge their liabilities or to comply with regulatory requirements. Also called preferred habitat hypothesis.

semivariance   A measure of downside risk equal to the average of the squared deviations of return below the mean.

separation theorem   The principle, put forth by James Tobin, that the investment process can be separated into two distinct steps: (1) the choice of a unique optimal portfolio along the efficient frontier, and (2) the decision to combine this portfolio with a riskless investment.

serial dependence   A situation in which a series' observations are not serially independent. Also called autocorrelation.

Sharpe measure   An asset or portfolio's expected return in excess of the riskless return, all divided by its standard deviation. It is used to compare mutually independent investment alternatives.

simple linear regression   A linear regression between a dependent variable and a single independent variable.

single index model   A regression model that relates a portfolio's returns to the market's returns. It does not require the intercept of the regression equation (alpha) to equal 0 percent. It simply posits a single source of systematic, or common, risk. Stated differently, the residuals from the regression equation are uncorrelated with each other. The important practical implication is that it is not necessary to estimate covariances between securities. Each security's contribution to portfolio risk is captured through its beta coefficient.

skewness   The third central moment of a distribution. It measures the asymmetry of a distribution. A positively skewed distribution has a long right tail, and its mean exceeds its median, which in turn exceeds its mode. The exact opposite properties hold for a negatively skewed distribution. Skewness is measured as the average of the cubed deviations from the mean. However, it is usually represented as the ratio of this value to the standard deviation cubed. A normal distribution has skewness equal to 0.

slope   The beta coefficient in a regression equation.

spline smoothing   A method for estimating a smooth curve to represent the term structure, by assuming the discount factors corresponding to the spot interest rates are a cubic function of time to maturity.

spot exchange rate   The rate at which currencies are exchanged at the present time as opposed to a future date.

spot rate of interest   The yield on a pure discount bond.

standard deviation   A measure of dispersion that is commonly used to measure an asset's risk. It is equal to the square root of the average of the squared deviations from the mean, and it is the square root of the variance. Approximately 68 percent of the observations under a normal distribution fall within the mean plus and minus one standard deviation of the mean.

standardized residual   In regression analysis, the residual divided by the standard error. These values are plotted as a function of the independent variable to observe whether the residuals are random.

standardized variable   The distance from the mean in standard deviation units. It is equal to the difference between the value of interest and the mean, divided by the standard deviation.

strike price   The price for the underlying asset that determines whether or not an option is in the money (has value) at expiration. The underlying asset's price must exceed the strike price for a call option to have value, whereas it must be below the strike price for a put option to have value. Also called exercise price or striking price.

sum of the squares due to error   In regression analysis, the sum of the squared differences between the observed values for the dependent variable and the predicted values for the dependent variable.

sum of the squares due to regression   In regression analysis, the sum of the squared differences between the predicted values for the dependent variable and the average of the observed values for the dependent variable.

systematic risk   Risk associated with variation in the return of the market portfolio. It is equal to beta squared times the market's variance. Also called nondiversifiable risk.

term structure of interest rates   The relationship between interest rates and term to maturity, sometimes referred to as the yield curve.

time diversification   The notion that above-average returns tend to offset below-average returns over long time horizons. It does not follow, however, that time reduces risk. Although the likelihood of a loss decreases with time for investments with positive expected returns, the potential magnitude of a loss increases with time.

time-weighted rate of return   The average return that, when compounded forward, converts an initial value to an ending value. It is equal to the product of the quantities 1 plus the discrete returns, raised to the power 1 over the number of discrete returns, less 1. It is suitable for performance measurement, because it is not influenced by the timing or magnitude of cash flows. Also called geometric rate of return.

total sum of the squares   In regression analysis, the sum of the squared differences between the observed values for the dependent variable and the average of those observations.

tracking error   A measure of dispersion that is commonly used to measure an asset's relative risk. It is equal to the square root of the average of an asset or portfolio's squared deviations from a benchmark's returns.

Treynor measure   A portfolio's return in excess of the riskless return divided by its beta. The Treynor measure is a valid performance criterion when evaluating a portfolio in combination with a benchmark portfolio and other actively managed portfolios.

t-statistic   (1) In regression analysis, the value of the coefficient divided by its standard error. A t-statistic of 1.96 implies that the likelihood of observing the coefficient by chance is only 5 percent. (2) In hypothesis testing with small samples, a test statistic that accounts for sampling error.

Type I error   Rejection of the null hypothesis when it is true.

Type II error   Failure to reject the null hypothesis when it is false; that is, when the alternative hypothesis is true.

unbiased estimate   An estimate that is the mean of the distribution of future values.

uncovered interest arbitrage   The notion that one cannot borrow in a low interest rate country, convert to the currency of a high interest rate country, lend in the high interest rate country, and generate a profit. The gains that occur in some periods from these transactions are offset by losses in other periods, so that the average gain is zero. If uncovered interest arbitrage holds, the expected return of a currency forward contract is 0 percent.

uniform distribution   A probability distribution for which there is an equal probability for all of the possible values of a random variable. For example, the distribution of the values from the toss of a single die has a uniform distribution.

unsystematic risk   Risk that is specific to an asset and thus not associated with market risk. Also called diversifiable risk.

utility function   The relationship between varying levels of wealth or consumption of goods and services and the happiness or satisfaction imparted by the different wealth and consumption levels. A commonly invoked utility function for economic modeling is the log-wealth utility function, which implies that utility increases at a decreasing rate as wealth increases.

value at risk   At a given probability, the maximum loss or minimum gain that could occur at the end of a specified investment period.

variance   A measure of dispersion used to characterize an asset's risk. It is equal to the average of the squared deviations from the mean, and its square root is the standard deviation.

variance ratio   A measure of serial dependence computed by dividing the variance of returns estimated from a longer interval by the variance of returns estimated from a shorter interval and then normalizing this value to 1 by dividing it by the ratio of the longer interval to the shorter interval.

variation margin   Daily payments required to cover trading losses on futures positions.

wealth relative   A value equal to 1 plus a discrete rate of return. The geometric rate of return is computed by taking the product of wealth relatives, raising this product to the power, 1 divided by the number of wealth relatives, and subtracting 1. The continuous return is computed as the natural logarithm of the wealth relative.

yield curve   The relationship between interest rates and term to maturity, sometimes referred to as the term structure of interest rates.

yield to maturity   The internal rate of return that discounts a bond's cash flows, including the coupon payments and the repayment of principal, back to its current price.

zero-coupon bond   A bond that pays no coupons, but instead is issued at a discount to its par value.

Notes

CHAPTER 1   The Nobel Prize

1. Harry Markowitz, "Portfolio Selection," *Journal of Finance* (March 1952).
2. There is an amusing and perhaps apocryphal story about this result and the famous mathematician Carl Friedrich Gauss, who was born in 1777 in Braunschweig, Germany. When Gauss was a child at St. Catherine Elementary School, his teacher, who was named Büttner, asked the students in his class to sum the numbers from 1 to 100. Büttner's intent was to distract the students for a while so that he could tend to other business. To Büttner's surprise and annoyance, however, Gauss, after a few seconds, raised his hand and gave the answer—5,050. Büttner was obviously shocked at how quickly Gauss could add, but Gauss confessed that he had found a short cut. He described how he had begun by adding one plus two plus three but became bored and starting adding backward from 100. He then noticed that one plus 100 equals 101, as does two plus 99 and three plus 98. He immediately realized that if he multiplied 100 by 101 and divided by two, so as not to double count, he would arrive at the answer.
3. James Tobin, "Liquidity Preferences as Behavior Toward Risk," *Review of Economic Studies* (February 1958).
4. William Sharpe, "Capital Asset Prices: A Theory of Market Equilibrium Under Conditions of Uncertainty," *Journal of Finance* (September 1964).
5. Franco Modigliani and Merton Miller, "The Cost of Capital, Corporation Finance, and the Theory of Investment," *American Economic Review* (June 1958).
6. Merton Miller and Franco Modigliani, "Dividend Policy, Growth, and the Valuation of Shares," *Journal of Business* (October 1961).

CHAPTER 2   Uncertainty

1. Such diverse phenomena as noise in electromagnetic systems, the dynamics of star clustering, time intervals between eruptions of Old

Faithful, and the evolution of ecological systems behave in accordance with the predictions of the normal distribution.

2. For more about the lognormal distribution, see Chapters 4, 6, and 16.
3. The value of an option depends on the price of the underlying asset, the exercise price, the time to expiration, the riskless rate of interest, and the standard deviation of the underlying asset. All of these values except the standard deviation are observable; thus, the standard deviation can be inferred from the price at which the option trades. The implied value for the standard deviation is solved for iteratively. For a review of this technique, see Chapter 13.
4. For an excellent discussion of this issue, see Richard Bookstaber and Roger Clarke, "Problems in Evaluating the Performance of Portfolios with Options," *Financial Analysts Journal* (January/February 1985).

CHAPTER 3   Utility

1. Daniel Bernoulli, "Exposition of a New Theory on the Measurement of Risk," *Econometrica*, January 1954 (translation from 1738 version). Daniel Bernoulli is one of several celebrated Bernoulli mathematicians. Daniel's father, Johann, made important contributions to calculus, although much of his work was published by the Marquis de l'Hospital. Johann was also the mentor of the famous prodigy Leonhard Euler. The most renowned Bernoulli was Daniel's uncle and Johann's older brother, Jakob. Jakob Bernoulli is known primarily for his contributions to the theory of probability. Finally, Daniel's cousin, Nicolas Bernoulli, was a distinguished mathematician who proposed the famous St. Petersburg paradox, for which Daniel offered a solution in his classic risk measurement paper.
2. Actually, there is a clever way to dispel the notion that people always prefer more wealth to less wealth. Suppose you and a friend are offered $1,000 collectively. Your friend is allowed to determine the split while you are allowed to determine whether or not to accept the grant. Suppose your friend chooses a split of $999.95 for herself and a nickel for you. Would you accept this grant?
3. See Chapter 4 for more about logarithms.
4. Bernoulli, "Measurement of Risk," 29.
5. For more about the efficient frontier, see Chapter 1.
6. For a basic review of utility theory, see Edwin Elton and Martin Gruber, *Modern Portfolio Theory and Investment Analysis*, third edition (New York: John Wiley & Sons, 1987), 179–203. For a more technical discussion of utility theory, see Chi-fu Huang and Robert H. Litzenberger, *Foundations for Financial Economics* (New York: North-Holland, 1988), 1–37.

CHAPTER 5   Return and Risk

1. For a review of logarithms and continuous returns, see Chapter 4.
2. The arithmetic average is the best estimate of future expected value if it is measured without error. To the extent it is subject to measurement error, however, it will overestimate expected value because compounding causes estimation errors to influence the estimate asymmetrically. Positive errors raise the estimate more than negative errors of the same magnitude reduce it. The best estimate of expected value in the presence of measurement error, therefore, is a blend of the arithmetic average and geometric average in which their weights are a function of the sample size and the forecast horizon. See Eric Jacquier, Alex Kane, and Alan Marcus, "Geometric or Arithmetic Mean: A New Take on an Old Controversy," unpublished manuscript (December 18, 2002).
3. See William Sharpe, "Mutual Fund Performance," *Journal of Business*, January 1966.
4. For more about the Capital Asset Pricing Model, see Chapter 1.
5. See Jack Treynor, "How to Rate Management of Investment Funds," *Harvard Business Review*, January/February 1965.
6. See Michael Jensen, "The Performance of Mutual Funds in the Period 1945–1964," *Journal of Finance*, May 1968.
7. See Chapter 15 for more about hypothesis testing.
8. See Chapter 4 for more about lognormality.
9. See Chapter 6 for more about skewness.
10. See W. Van Harlow, "Asset Allocation in a Downside-Risk Framework," *Financial Analysts Journal*, September/October 1991.

CHAPTER 6   Higher Moments

1. For more about the lognormal distribution, see Chapter 4.
2. For more about value at risk, see Chapter 19.
3. See Chapter 4 for an illustration of the effect of compounding on a return distribution.
4. A put option grants its owner the right but not the obligation to sell the underlying asset at a previously agreed upon price at a specified future date. For more about options, see Chapter 23.
5. U.S. stocks are represented by MSCI USA price index, and U.S. bonds are represented by the J.P. Morgan U.S. government bond index.
6. See Chapter 18 for more about bootstrapping.
7. See Chapter 9 for more about serial dependence.
8. See Chapters 1 and 20 for more about mean-variance optimization.
9. When I refer to skewness in these comments, I mean skewness beyond the skewness caused by compounding.

CHAPTER 7   Duration and Convexity

1. Frederick Macaulay, *Some Theoretical Problems Suggested by the Movements of Interest Rates, Bond Yields and Stock Prices in the United States Since 1865* (New York: National Bureau of Economic Research, 1938).
2. For example, see Martin Leibowitz, "How Financial Theory Evolves in the Real World—Or Not: The Case of Duration and Immunization," *Financial Review*, November 1983.
3. This formula assumes that coupons are paid annually. If coupons are paid more frequently, the yield to maturity should be divided by the number of discounting periods per year.

CHAPTER 8   The Term Structure of Interest Rates

1. See Chapter 25 for more about covered and uncovered interest arbitrage.
2. For more about duration, see Chapter 7.
3. For example, see Stephen Brown and Philip Dybvig, "The Empirical Implications of the Cox, Ingersoll, Ross Theory of the Term Structure of Interest Rates," *Journal of Finance*, July 1986; John Cox, Jonathan Ingersoll and Stephen Ross, "A Reexamination of Traditional Hypotheses About the Term Structure of Interest Rates," *Journal of Finance*, September 1981; H. Gifford Fong and Oldrich Vasicek, "Term Structure Modeling," *Journal of Finance*, July 1982; and Michael Gibbons and Krishna Ramaswamy, "A Test of the Cox, Ingersoll and Ross Model of the Term Structure," *Review of Financial Studies*, Vol. 6 (3), 1993.

CHAPTER 9   Serial Dependence

1. For a derivation of the standardized variable based on overlapping observations, see Andrew Lo and A. Craig MacKinlay, "Stock Market Prices Do Not Follow Random Walks: Evidence from a Simple Specification Test," *Review of Financial Studies*, spring 1988.
2. A procedure to correct for heteroskedasticity is given by Lo and MacKinlay, ibid. Be aware, however, that it contains a typographical error. The numerator of equation 19 should include the term nq in front of the summation sign.
3. See Chapter 10 for more about the relationship between horizon and risk tolerance.

CHAPTER 10   Time Diversification

1. These values refer to discrete returns. The mean of the corresponding continuous returns equals 8.61 percent, while the standard deviation of the continuous returns equals 13.57 percent. We use continuous values to determine the range of returns in continuous units and then convert this range back to discrete units. The formula for converting discrete means and standard deviations into their continuous counterparts is given in Chapter 19.
2. For a review of probability estimation, see Chapter 2.
3. For example, see Paul Samuelson, "Risk and Uncertainty: A Fallacy of Large Numbers," *Scientia*, April/May 1963; and "Lifetime Portfolio Selection by Dynamic Stochastic Programming," *Review of Economics and Statistics*, August 1969; and Zvi Bodie, Alex Kane, and Alan Marcus, *Investments* (Homewood, IL: Irwin, 1989), 222–26.
4. For a review of utility theory, see Chapter 3.
5. Zvi Bodie, "On the Risk of Stocks in the Long Run," *Financial Analysts Journal* (May/June 1995).
6. See Chapter 23 for more about option valuation.
7. For a review of within-horizon exposure to loss, see Mark Kritzman and Don Rich, "The Mismeasurement of Risk," *Financial Analysts Journal*, May/June 2002.
8. The first passage probability is described in Samuel Karlin and Howard Taylor, *A First Course in Stochastic Processes*, 2nd edition (San Diego, CA: Academic Press, 1975).
9. Samuelson addresses this result in Paul Samuelson, "Long Run Risk Tolerance When Equity Returns Are Mean Reverting: Pseudoparadoxes and Vindication of 'Businessman' Risk," in W. Brainard, W. Nordhaus, and H. Watts, eds., *Macroeconomics, Finance and Economic Policy: Essays in Honor of James Tobin* (Cambridge, MA: MIT Press, 1991).
10. This idea is attributed to Zvi Bodie and William Samuelson.

CHAPTER 11   Regressions

1. As part of their output, most regression packages include measures of statistical significance such as an F-value and a t-statistic. The F-value is computed as the ratio of the sum of the squares due to regression (adjusted by the degrees of freedom) to the sum of the squares due to error (also adjusted by the degrees of freedom). Its significance depends on the number of variables and observations. The t-statistic measures the significance of the coefficients of the independent variables. It is computed as the ratio of the coefficient to the standard error of the coefficient. The

F-test and the t-test yield the same information for simple linear regressions, but not necessarily for multiple linear regressions.

2. The standard error measures the dispersion of the residuals around the regression line. It is calculated as the square root of the average squared differences of the observed values from the values predicted by the regression line. To estimate the average of the squared differences, we divide the sum of the squared differences by the number of observations less one.

CHAPTER 12   Factor Methods

1. For a review of this methodology, see Karl G. Joreskog, *Statistical Estimation in Factor Analysis* (Stockholm: Almqvist & Wiksell, 1963).
2. For a discussion of eigenvectors and eigenvalues, see Alpha C. Chiang, *Fundamental Methods of Mathematical Economics* (New York: McGraw-Hill, 1974), 340–45.
3. For a review of Markowitz's approach for estimating portfolio risk, see Chapter 1.

CHAPTER 13   Estimating Volatility: Part 1

1. See Chapter 1 for more about the connection between volatility and portfolio formation.
2. In computing the variance, it is sometimes preferable to divide by the number of observations less one, because we use up one degree of freedom to compute the average of the returns. I have not done that in this example.
3. See Chapter 4 for more about lognormality.
4. Chapter 19 shows how to convert an arithmetic average and standard deviation of discrete returns into their continuous counterparts without resorting to the underlying data.
5. For more about this approach, see Stephen Brown, "Estimating Volatility," in Figlewski, Silber, and Subrahmanyam, eds., *Financial Options: From Theory to Practice* (Homewood, IL: Business One Irwin, 1990).

CHAPTER 14   Estimating Volatility: Part 2

1. For more about regressions, see Chapter 11.
2. Tim Bollerslev, "Generalized Autoregressive Conditional Heteroskedasticity," *Journal of Econometrics* 31 (1986), 307–27.
3. Robert F. Engle, "Autoregressive Conditional Heteroskedasticity with Estimates of Variance of U. K. Inflation," *Econometrica* 50 (1982), 987–1008.

CHAPTER 16   Future Value and the Risk of Loss

1. Holding period returns are also referred to as discrete returns or periodic returns.
2. For a review of this assumption, see Chapter 4.
3. The standardized variable, in effect, rescales the distribution to have a mean of 0 and a standard deviation of 1. For a review of this topic, see Chapter 2.
4. This insight was given to me by Alan Marcus. For more about this issue, see Eric Jacquier, Alan Kane, and Alex Marcus, "Geometric or Arithmetic Mean: A New Take on an Old Controversy," unpublished manuscript (December 18, 2002).
5. The first passage probability is described in Samuel Karlin and Howard Taylor, *A First Course in Stochastic Processes*, 2nd edition, Academic Press, 1975.
6. I discuss this probability in Chapter 10 within the context of the time diversification debate.
7. See Chapter 19 for more about value at risk.
8. For more about within horizon exposure to loss, see Mark Kritzman and Don Rich, "The Mismeasurement of Risk," *Financial Analysts Journal*, May/June 2001.

CHAPTER 17   Event Studies

1. Eugene Fama, Lawrence Fisher, Michael Jensen, and Richard Roll, "The Adjustment of Stock Prices to New Information," *International Economic Review* 10, no. 1 (February 1969), 1–21.
2. See Chapter 1 for the rationale for this adjustment and Chapter 11 for more about regressions.
3. Eugene F. Fama and James D. MacBeth, "Risk, Return and Equilibrium: Empirical Tests," *Journal of Political Economy* 81, no. 3 (May/June 1973), 607–36.
4. Stephen Brown and Jerold Warner, "Measuring Security Price Performance," *Journal of Financial Economics* 8 (September 1980), 205–58.
5. See Chapter 15 for more about hypothesis testing.

CHAPTER 18   Simulation

1. M. Browne, "Coin-Tossing Computers Found to Show Subtle Bias," *New York Times*, January 12, 1993.
2. See Chapter 4 for more about lognormality.
3. See Chapter 6 for more about higher moments.
4. See Chapter 19 for more about value at risk.

5. Gary P. Brinson, L. Randolf Hood, and Gilbert L. Beebower, "Determinants of Portfolio Performance," *Financial Analysts Journal*, July-August 1986.
6. Mark Kritzman and Sebastian Page, "The Hierarchy of Investment Choice: A Normative Perspective," *Journal of Portfolio Management*, summer 2003.

CHAPTER 19 Value at Risk

1. We can compute value at risk for any probability, although 5.00 percent seems to be a common choice.
2. The Basle Committee comprises senior officials from the central banks of the G-10 countries, Belgium, Canada, France, Germany, Italy, Japan, the Netherlands, Sweden, the U.K., and the United States, plus Luxembourg and Switzerland.
3. See Chapter 4 to review the connection between compounding and lognormality.
4. This section is based on a paper by the same title co-authored with George Chow: "Value at Risk for Portfolios with Short Positions," *Journal of Portfolio Management*, summer 2001.
5. We assume the correlation remains 30 percent in continuous units. This assumption is not precise, but the impact of this imprecision is negligible.

CHAPTER 20 Optimization

1. See Chapter 1 for more about covariance.
2. The inverse of a matrix is analogous to a reciprocal in simple algebra. If we multiply a matrix by its inverse, we get an identity matrix. An identity matrix includes ones along its diagonal and zeros for all the other elements. It is analogous to the number 1 in simple algebra, in that a matrix multiplied by an identity matrix yields itself. Multiplying a vector or matrix by the inverse of another matrix is analogous to multiplying a number by the reciprocal of another number, hence the analogy with division.
3. For a review of matrix operations, including multiplication and inversion, see Alpha Chaing, *Fundamental Methods of Mathematical Economics* (New York: McGraw-Hill, 1974), 59–132.
4. William Sharpe, "An Algorithm for Portfolio Improvement," *Advances in Mathematical Programming and Financial Planning*, Vol. 1, (Greenwich, CT: JAI Press Inc., 1987). Sharpe's algorithm can easily be adapted to accommodate transaction costs and allocation constraints.

5. For a thorough of this issue, see Richard Michaud, *Efficient Asset Management*, (Boston, MA: Harvard Business School Press, 1998).
6. George Chow, "Portfolio Selection Based on Return, Risk, and Relative Performance," *Financial Analysts Journal*, March/April 1995.
7. Harry Markowitz, "Portfolio Selection," *Journal of Finance*, March 1952.
8. By out-of-sample I mean the estimates of means, variances, and correlations would have been available as inputs at the time of the optimization.
9. We may also choose to incorporate skewness in our objective function if we care about downside risk and believe continuous returns are skewed. See Chapter 6 for more about skewness.

CHAPTER 21   Risk Budgets

1. See Chapter 2 for more about uncertainty.
2. See Chapter 19 for more about value at risk.
3. See Chapters 1 and 20 for more about mean-variance efficiency.
4. See Chapters 3 and 20 for more about risk aversion and optimization.
5. I thank George Chow and Anne-Sophie Vanroyen for assistance in deriving these equations.
6. See Chapter 19 for more about this problem and its resolution.

CHAPTER 22   Hedging

1. Those who are interested in a more detailed review of these topics should see Stephen Figlewski in collaboration with Kose John and John Merrick, *Hedging with Financial Futures for Institutional Investors: From Theory to Practice* (Cambridge, MA: Ballinger Publishing Company, 1986).
2. This result ignores the fact that financial futures contracts are marked to market daily. As a consequence, gains and losses accrue in an interest-bearing margin account. In order to adjust for this daily mark-to-market feature, we should reduce the hedge position to its present value. This adjustment is called "tailing the hedge."
3. According to the Capital Asset Pricing Model, we should estimate systematic risk by regressing a portfolio's returns in excess of the riskless return on the market's excess returns. To the extent the riskless return is stable, though, this approach will yield a similar estimate.
4. For a more detailed description of duration, see Chapter 7.
5. Treasury bond futures contracts can be settled by delivery of a variety of bonds. Therefore, it is sometimes necessary to adjust the hedge ratio by a delivery factor that equates a deliverable bond to the reference bond.

6. This framework assumes we only sell currency forward contracts. If we were to consider purchasing forward contracts, we would reflect the hedging cost net of a forward contract's expected return as a negative value.

7. See the appendix in Chapter 25 for the derivation of the minimum risk and optimal currency hedge ratios.

CHAPTER 23   Option Valuation and Replication

1. The Black-Scholes formula relies on several simplifying assumptions: (1) The term structure of interest rates up to the option's maturity date is known and constant; (2) the distribution of the underlying terminal stock price is lognormal; (3) the volatility of stock returns is constant; (4) the stock does not pay dividends; (5) there are no transaction costs; (6) it is possible to borrow or lend any fraction of the price of a security at the short-term interest rate; and (7) there are no restrictions on short selling.

2. The law of one price ensures a direct correspondence between the values of a call option and a put option. This correspondence is called put-call parity.

CHAPTER 24   Commodity Futures Contracts

1. In this example and in those that follow, I ignore the effect of margin deposits.

2. *Wall Street Journal*, December 17, 1992.

3. This profit estimate assumes that the only cost of carrying soybean meal is the interest cost.

4. For an excellent discussion of the investment suitability of commodities, see James Scott, "Managing Asset Classes," *Financial Analysts Journal*, January/February 1994.

CHAPTER 25   Currencies

1. For an excellent review of currency options, see Richard Stapleton and Constantine Thanassoulas, "Options on Foreign Currencies," in Figlewski, Silber, and Subrahmanyam, eds., *Financial Options: From Theory to Practice* (Homewood, IL: Business One Irwin, 1990).

2. For a more detailed review of currency swaps and other currency related instruments, see Bruno Solnik, *International Investments*, second edition (New York: Addison-Wesley Publishing Company, 1991), 176–183.

3. The mathematics of currency hedging is reviewed in the appendix.

4. See, for example, Mark Kritzman, "The Optimal Currency Hedging Policy with Biased Forward Rates," *Journal of Portfolio Management*, summer 1993.
5. Evidence of serial dependence and its implications is discussed in Mark Kritzman, "Serial Dependence in Currency Returns: Investment Implications," *Journal of Portfolio Management*, fall 1989.
6. For more about within-horizon exposure to loss, see Chapter 16.

Index